GOOGLE
HACKS™

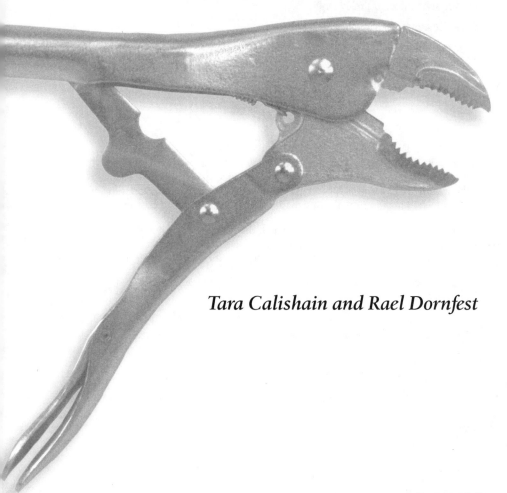

Tara Calishain and Rael Dornfest

O'REILLY®

Beijing · Cambridge · Farnham · Köln · Paris · Sebastopol · Taipei · Tokyo

Google Hacks™
by Tara Calishain and Rael Dornfest

Copyright © 2003 O'Reilly & Associates, Inc. All rights reserved.
Printed in the United States of America.

Published by O'Reilly & Associates, Inc., 1005 Gravenstein Highway North,
Sebastopol, CA 95472.

O'Reilly & Associates books may be purchased for educational, business, or sales promotional use. Online editions are also available for most titles (*safari.oreilly.com*). For
more information, contact our corporate/institutional sales department: (800) 998-9938
or *corporate@oreilly.com*.

Editor:	Rael Dornfest
Production Editor:	Linley Dolby
Cover Designer:	Edie Freedman
Interior Designer:	David Futato

Printing History:

February 2003: First Edition.

ISBN: 0-596-00447-8
[C]

To our Grannies: Olivia and Miriam

Contents

Credits

About the Authors

Tara Calishain is the author or co-author of half-a-dozen books about the Internet. She's the editor of weekly search engine newsletter *ResearchBuzz* (*www.researchbuzz.com*) and a regular columnist for LLRX.com and *SEARCHER* magazine.

Rael Dornfest is a maven at O'Reilly & Associates, Inc., focusing on technologies just beyond the pale. He assesses, experiments, programs, and writes for the O'Reilly Network and O'Reilly publications. Rael has edited, co-authored, and contributed to various O'Reilly books. He is program chair for the O'Reilly Emerging Technology Conference and O'Reilly Mac OS X Conference, chair of the RSS-DEV Working Group, and developer of Meerkat: An Open Wire Service (*meerkat.oreillynet.com*). In his copious free time, Rael develops bits and bobs of freeware and maintains his raelity bytes weblog (*www.raelity.org*).

Contributors

The following people contributed their hacks, writing, and inspiration to this book:

- Tim Allwine is a Senior Software Engineer at O'Reilly & Associates. He develops software for the Market Research group, various spidering tools that collect data from disparate sites, and is involved in the development of web services at O'Reilly.

- AvaQuest (*http://www.avaquest.com/*) is a Massachusetts-based IT services firm that specializes in applying advanced information retrieval, categorization, and text mining technologies to solve real-world problems. GooglePeople and GoogleMovies, created by AvaQuest consultants Nathan Treloar, Sally Kleinfeldt, and Peter Richards, came out of a web mining consulting project the team worked on in the summer of 2002, shortly after the Google Web API was announced.

- Paul Bausch (*http://www.onfocus.com/*) is a freelance web developer and author living in Oregon. He was a co-creator of the weblog software, Blogger, and recently co-wrote a book about weblogs called *We Blog: Publishing Online with Weblogs*. He believes (like Google) that "love" (75,700,000) will conquer "hate" (7,900,000).

- Erik Benson (*http://www.erikbenson.com/*).

- CapeScience.com (*http://www.capescience.com/*) is the development community for Cape Clear Software, a web services company. In addition to providing support for Cape Clear's products, CapeScience makes all sorts of fun web services stuff, including live services, clients to other services, utilities, and other geekware.

- Antoni Chan (*http://www.alltooflat.com/*) is one of the founders of All Too Flat, a bastion of quirky content, pranks, and geeky humor. The Google Mirror is a 2,500 line CGI script that was developed over the period of a year starting in October 2001. When not working on his web site, he enjoys playing music, bowling, and running after a frisbee.

- Tanya Harvey Ciampi (*http://www.multilingual.ch*) grew up in Buckinghamshire, England, and went on to study in Zurich, where she obtained her diploma in translation. She now lives in Ticino, the Italian-speaking region of Switzerland, where she works as an English technical translator (from Italian, German, and French) and proofreader, and teaches translation and Internet search techniques based on her WWW Search Interfaces for Translators. In her free time, she enjoys fishing with her father on the west coast of Ireland, writing poems, and playing celtic music.

- Peter Drayton (*http://www.razorsoft.net/weblog/*)is a program manager in the CLR team at Microsoft. Before joining Microsoft, he was an independent consultant, trainer for DevelopMentor, and author of *C# Essentials* and *C# in a Nutshell* (O'Reilly).

- Andrew Flegg (*http://www.bleb.org/*) works for IBM in the UK having graduated from the University of Warwick a few years ago. He's currently the webmaster of Hursley Lab's intranet site. Most of his work (and fun) at the moment is taken up with Perl, Java, HTML, and CSS. Andrew is particularly keen on clean, reusable code, which always ends up saving time in the long run. He's written several open source projects, as well as a couple of commercial applications for RISC OS (as used in the Iyonix PC: the first desktop computer using an Intel XScale).

In his non-computer time, Andrew is trying to organize a wedding having just got engaged!

- Andrew Goodman (*http://www.page-zero.com*) is cofounder and editor of Traffick.com, an acclaimed guide to search engines and portals. Traffick foresaw trends such as the rise of pay-per-click search engines well before they were adopted by the mainstream. Goodman has published articles in publications such as *Internet Markets*, *The Globe and Mail*, and *Yorkshire Post Magazine*. He is often cited in various business and technology publications, and he often speaks at conferences such as Search Engine Strategies.

- Kevin Hemenway (*http://www.disobey.com/*), better known as Morbus Iff, is the creator of disobey.com, which bills itself as "content for the discontented." Publisher, developer, and writer of more home cooking than you could ever imagine (like the popular open sourced syndicated reader AmphetaDesk, the best-kept gaming secret Gamegrene.com, the popular Ghost Sites and Nonsense Network, the giggle-inducing articles at the O'Reilly Network, a few pieces at Apple's Internet Developer site, etc.), he's an ardent supporter of cloning merely so he can get more work done. He cooks with a Fry Pan of Intellect +2 and lives in Concord, NH.

- Mark Horrell (*http://www.markhorrell.com/*) has worked in search engine optimization since 1996 when he joined Net Resources International, a publisher of industrial engineering web sites, where he conceived and developed the company's Internet marketing strategy. He left in 2002 and is now a freelance web developer based in London, UK, specializing in search engine–friendly design.

- Judy Hourihan (*http://judy.hourihan.com/*).

- Steven Johnson (*http://www.stevenberlinjohnson.com/*) is the author of two books, *Emergence* and *Interface Culture*. He co-created the sites FEED and Plastic.com, and now blogs regularly at *www.stevenberlinjohnson.com*. He writes the monthly "Emerging Technology" column for *Discover Magazine*, and his work has appeared in many publications, including *The New York Times*, *Harper's*, *Wired*, and *The New Yorker*. He lives in Brooklyn, New York.

- Stuart Langridge (*http://www.kryogenix.org/*) gets paid to hack on the Web during the day, and does it for free at nights when he's not arguing about Buffy or Debian GNU/Linux. He's keen on web standards, Python, and strange things you can do with JavaScript, all of which can be seen at his web site and weblog. He's also slightly surprised that the Google Art Creator, which was an amusing little hack done in a day, is the most popular thing he's ever written and got him into a book.

- Beau Lebens (*http://www.dentedreality.com.au*) is a consulting information architect and PHP developer, who is heavily interested in movements such as an increase in online strategy and planning, the REST philosophy, and open source development. Beau has a self-taught background in web technologies and currently works in a clicks 'n' mortar company based out of Perth, Western Australia, and runs his own consultancy at the same time. He firmly believes in making complex systems easy to use and simple to understand, and makes this a primary objective in all of his projects. More information about Beau and what he's up to is available on his web site, the home of his consulting company, Dented Reality, as well as a number of musings and observations on the web industry and technology in general.

- Mark Pilgrim (*http://diveintomark.org/*) is the author of *Dive Into Python*, a free Python book for experienced programmers, and *Dive Into Accessibility*, a free book on web accessibility techniques. He works for MassLight, a Washington DC–based training and web development company, where, unsurprisingly, he does training and web development. But he lives outside Raleigh, North Carolina, because it's warmer.

- Chris Sells (*http://www.sellsbrothers.com/*) is an independent consultant, speaker, and author specializing in distributed applications in .NET and COM. He's written several books and is currently working on *Windows Forms for C# and VB.NET Programmers* and *Mastering Visual Studio .NET*. In his free time, Chris hosts various conferences, directs the Genghis source-available project, plays with Rotor, and in general, makes a pest of himself at Microsoft design reviews.

- Alex Shapiro (*http://www.touchgraph.com/*) is the founder and CTO of TouchGraph LLC. Alex's experience with TouchGraph is paralleled by that of the dotcom survivors described in Newsweek's March 25, 2002 "Welcome Back to Silicon Valley" cover story. When faced with a shrinking technology market, he too decided to take the opportunity to innovate rather than struggling to find generic employment. On January 15, 2001, Alex quit his first job at Sapient, NYC, ahead of the first round of layoffs. Luckily, he was able to find work as an independent consult designing software for a brand valuation firm. His free time was spent polishing off the graph visualization code at the heart of Touch-Graph. In May 2002, Alex passed the brand valuation client to a friend and started working on TouchGraph full time. Since then, things have been very exciting due to the growing popularity and public acclaim for the software. TouchGraph has yet to get first-round funding.

- Kevin Shay (*http://www.staggernation.com/*) is a writer and web programmer who lives in Brooklyn, New York. His Google API scripts, Movable Type plug-ins, and other work can be found at the soon-to-launch staggernation.com.

- Gary Stock (*http://www.googlewhack.com/stock.htm*) coined the term "Google whack" while he had intended to be doing research for UnBlinking (*http://www.unblinking.com/*). When Gary writes for UnBlinking, he might better be focused on his role as CTO of the news clipping and briefing service Nexcerpt (*http://www.nexcerpt.com/*). Gary works at Nexcerpt to get a break from stewardship of unusual flora and fauna on 160 acres of woods and wetland he owns, which in turn, keeps him from spending time with his wife (and Nexcerpt CEO) Julie, whom he married to offset his former all-consuming career as an above-top-secret computer spy, which he first had entered to avoid permanently becoming a jazz arranger and pianist. Seriously.

- Brett Tabke (*http://www.webmasterworld.com*) is the owner/operator of WebmasterWorld.com, the leading news and discussion site for web developers and search engine marketers. Tabke has been involved in computing since the late 70s and is one of the Internet's foremost authorities on search engine optimization.

- Matt Webb (*http://interconnected.org/home/*) is a systems engineer at UpMyStreet.com, specializing in developing UK Government and Public Sector local information sites. Outside of work, he's developed several IM bots (including Googlematic), Dirk (a vast collaborative net of associations), and runs and writes for Upsideclown.com, which publishes short fiction and creative writing and has spawned a book. He is best known for Interconnected, a weblog on society and technology. He lives in London.

Acknowledgments

We would like to thank all those who contributed their ideas and code for Google hacks to this book. Many thanks to Nelson Minar and the rest of the Google Engineering Team, Nate Tyler, and everyone else at Google who provided ideas, suggestions, and answers—not to mention the Google Web API itself. And to Andy Lester, our technical editor, goes much appreciation for his thorough nitpicking.

Tara

Everyone at O'Reilly has been great in helping pull this book together, but I wouldn't have gotten to participate in this book if it hadn't been for Tim All-wine, who first helped me with Perl programs a couple of years ago.

My family, especially my husband, has been great tolerating my distraction as I sat around muttering to myself about variables and subroutines.

Even as this book was being written I needed help understanding what Perl could and couldn't do. Kevin Hemenway was an excellent teacher, patiently explaining, providing examples, and when all else failed, pointing and laughing at my code.

Of course, most of this book wouldn't exist without the release of Google's API. A big thanks to Google for building a playground for us thousands of search engine junkies. And just as big a thanks to the many contributors who so generously allowed their applications to appear in this book.

Finally, a big, big, he-gets-his-own paragraph thanks to Rael Dornfest, who is a great co-author/editor and a lot of fun to work with.

Rael

First and foremost, to Asha and Sam—always my inspiration, joy, and best friends.

My extended family and friends, both local and virtual, who'd begun to wonder if they needed to send in a rescue party.

I'd like to thank Dale Dougherty for bringing me in to work on the Hacks series; working from the other side of the page has been a learning experience and a half. The O'Reilly editors, production, product management, and marketing staff are consummate professionals, hackers, and mensches. They've helped me immeasurably in my fledgling editorial stint. Extra special thanks goes out to my virtual cube-mate, Nat Torkington, and to Laurie Petrycki for showing me the ropes.

Tara, it's been fabulous traveling this road with you and I intend to make sure our paths keep on crossing at interesting intersections.

Karma points to Clay Shirky and Steven Johnson for egging me on to do more with the Google API than late-night fiddling. And, of course, a shout-out goes to the blogosphere population and folks in my Google neighborhood for their inspired prattling on APIs and all other things geekworthy.

Foreword

When we started Google, it was hard to predict how big it would become. That our search engine would someday serve as a catalyst for so many important web developments was a distant dream. We are honored by the growing interest in Google and offer many thanks to those who created this book—the largest and most comprehensive report on Google search technology that has yet to be published.

Search is an amazing field of study, because it offers infinite possibilities for how we might find and make information available to people. We join with the authors in encouraging readers to approach this book with a view toward discovering and creating new ways to search. Google's mission is to organize the world's information and make it universally accessible and useful, and we welcome any contribution you make toward achieving this goal.

Hacking is the creativity that fuels the Web. As software developers ourselves, we applaud this book for its adventurous spirit. We're adventurous, too, and were happy to discover that this book highlights many of the same experiments we conduct on our free time here at Google.

Google is constantly adapting its search algorithms to match the dynamic growth and changing nature of the Web. As you read, please keep in mind that the examples in this book are valid today but, as Google innovates and grows over time, may become obsolete. We encourage you to follow the latest developments and to participate in the ongoing discussions about search as facilitated by books such as this one.

Virtually every engineer at Google has used an O'Reilly publication to help them with their jobs. O'Reilly books are a staple of the Google engineering library, and we hope that *Google Hacks* will be as useful to others as the O'Reilly publications have been to Google.

With the largest collection of web documents in the world, Google is a reflection of the Web. The hacks in this book are not just about Google, they are also about unleashing the vast potential of the Web today and in the years to come. *Google Hacks* is a great resource for search enthusiasts, and we hope you enjoy it as much as we did.

Thanks,

—The Google Engineering Team
December 11, 2002
Mountain View, California

Preface

Search engines for large collections of data preceded the World Wide Web by decades. There were those massive library catalogs, hand-typed with painstaking precision on index cards and eventually, to varying degrees, automated. There were the large data collections of professional information companies such as Dialog and LexisNexis. Then there are the still-extant private, expensive medical, real estate, and legal search services.

Those data collections were not always easy to search, but with a little finesse and a lot of patience, it was always possible to search them thoroughly. Information was grouped according to established ontologies, data preformatted according to particular guidelines.

Then came the Web.

Information on the Web—as anyone knows who's ever looked at half-a-dozen web pages knows—is not all formatted the same way. Nor is it necessarily particularly accurate. Nor up to date. Nor spellchecked. Nonetheless, search engines cropped up, trying to make sense of the rapidly-increasing index of information online. Eventually, special syntaxes were added for searching common parts of the average web page (such as title or URL). Search engines evolved rapidly, trying to encompass all the nuances of the billions of documents online, and they still continue to evolve today.

Google™ threw its hat into the ring in 1998. The second incarnation of a search engine service known as BackRub, the name "Google" was a play on the word "googol," a one followed by a hundred zeros. From the beginning, Google was different from the other major search engines online—AltaVista, Excite, HotBot, and others.

Was it the technology? Partially. The relevance of Google's search results was outstanding and worthy of comment. But more than that, Google's focus and more human face made it stand out online.

With its friendly presentation and its constantly expanding set of options, it's no surprise that Google continues to get lots of fans. There are weblogs devoted to it. Search engine newsletters, such as ResearchBuzz, spend a lot of time covering Google. Legions of devoted fans spend lots of time uncovering undocumented features, creating games (like Google whacking) and even coining new words (like "Googling," the practice of checking out a prospective date or hire via Google's search engine.)

In April 2002, Google reached out to its fan base by offering the Google API. The Google API gives developers a legal way to access the Google search results with automated queries (any other way of accessing Google's search results with automated software is against Google's Terms of Service.)

Why Google Hacks?

"Hacks" are generally considered to be "quick-n-dirty" solutions to programming problems or interesting techniques for getting a task done. But what does this kind of hacking have to do with Google?

Considering the size of the Google index, there are many times when you might want to do a particular kind of search and you get too many results for the search to be useful. Or you may want to do a search that the current Google interface does not support.

The idea of *Google Hacks* is not to give you some exhaustive manual of how every command in the Google syntax works, but rather to show you some tricks for making the best use of a search and show applications of the Google API that perform searches that you can't perform using the regular Google interface. In other words, hacks.

Dozens of programs and interfaces have sprung up from the Google API. Both games and serious applications using Google's database of web pages are available from everybody from the serious programmer to the devoted fan (like me).

How This Book Is Organized

The combination of Google's API and over 3 billion pages of constantly shifting data can do strange things to your imagination and give you lots of new perspectives on how best to search. This book goes beyond the instruction page to the idea of "hacks"—tips, tricks, and techniques you can use to make your Google searching experience more fruitful, more fun, or (in a couple of cases) just more weird. This book is divided into several chapters:

Chapter 1, *Searching Google*

This chapter describes the fundamentals of how Google's search properties work, with some tips for making the most of Google's syntaxes and specialty search offerings. Beyond the list of "this syntax means that," we'll take a look at how to eke every last bit of searching power out of each syntax—and how to mix syntaxes for some truly monster searches.

Chapter 2, *Google Special Services and Collections*

Google goes beyond web searching into several different arenas, including images, USENET, and news. Did you know that these collections have their own syntaxes? As you'll learn in this section, Google's equally adroit at helping you holiday shop or search for current events.

Chapter 3, *Third-Party Google Services*

Not all the hacks are ones that you want to install on your desktop or web server. In this section, we'll take a look at third-party services that integrate the Google API with other applications or act as handy web tools—or even check Google by email!

Chapter 4, *Non-API Google Applications*

Google's API doesn't search all Google properties, but sometimes it'd be real handy to take that search for phone numbers or news stories and save it to a file. This collection of scrapers shows you how.

Chapter 5, *Introducing the Google Web API*

We'll take a look under the hood at Google's API, considering several different languages and how Google works with each one. Hint: if you've always wanted to learn Perl but never knew what to "do with it," this is your section.

Chapter 6, *Google Web API Applications*

Once you've got an understanding of the Google API, you'll start thinking of all kinds of ways you can use it. Take inspiration from this collection of useful applications that use the Google API.

Chapter 7, *Google Pranks and Games*

All work and no play makes for a dull web surfer. This collection of pranks and games turns Google into a poet, a mirror, and a master chef. Well, a chef anyway. Or at least someone who throws ingredients together.

Chapter 8, *The Webmaster Side of Google*

If you're a web wrangler, you see Google from two sides—from the searcher side and from the side of someone who wants to get the best search ranking for a web site. In this section, you'll learn about Google's (in)famous PageRank, cleaning up for a Google visit, and how to make sure your pages aren't indexed by Google if you don't want them there.

How to Use This Book

You can read this book from cover to cover if you like, but for the most part, each hack stands on its own. So feel free to browse, flipping around whatever sections interest you most. If you're a Perl "newbie," you might want to try some of the easier hacks and then tackle the more extensive ones as you get more confident.

Conventions Used in This Book

The following is a list of the typographical conventions used in this book:

Italic

> Used to indicate new terms, URLs, filenames, file extensions, directories, commands and options, program names, and to highlight comments in examples. For example, a path in the filesystem will appear as */Developer/Applications*.

`Constant width`

> Used to show code examples, verbatim Google searches, the contents of files, or the output from commands.

`Constant width bold`

> Used in examples and tables to show commands or other text that should be typed literally.

`Constant width italic`

> Used in examples and tables to show text that should be replaced with user-supplied values.

Color

> The second color is used to indicate a cross-reference within the text.

↵

> A carriage return (↵) at the end of a line of code is used to denote an unnatural line break; that is, you should not enter these as two lines of code, but as one continuous line. Multiple lines are used in these cases due to page width constraints.

You should pay special attention to notes set apart from the text with the following icons:

> This is a tip, suggestion, or a general note. It contains useful supplementary information about the topic at hand.

> This is a warning or note of caution.

The thermometer icons, found next to each hack, indicate the relative complexity of the hack:

beginner   moderate   expert

How to Contact Us

We have tested and verified the information in this book to the best of our ability, but you may find that features have changed (or even that we have made mistakes!). As reader of this book, you can help us to improve future editions by sending us your feedback. Please let us know about any errors, inaccuracies, bugs, misleading or confusing statements, and typos that you find anywhere in this book.

Please also let us know what we can do to make this book more useful to you. We take your comments seriously and will try to incorporate reasonable suggestions into future editions. You can write to us at:

O'Reilly & Associates, Inc.
1005 Gravenstein Hwy N.
Sebastopol, CA 95472
(800) 998-9938 (in the U.S. or Canada)
(707) 829-0515 (international/local)
(707) 829-0104 (fax)

To ask technical questions or to comment on the book, send email to:

bookquestions@oreilly.com

The web site for *Google Hacks* lists examples, errata, and plans for future editions. You can find this page at:

http://www.oreilly.com/catalog/googlehks/

For more information about this book and others, see the O'Reilly web site:

http://www.oreilly.com

Gotta Hack? To explore Hacks books online or to contribute a hack for future titles, visit:

http://hacks.oreilly.com

Searching Google
Hacks #1–28

Google's front page is deceptively simple: a search form and a couple of buttons. Yet that basic interface—so alluring in its simplicity—belies the power of the Google engine underneath and the wealth of information at its disposal. And if you use Google's search syntax to its fullest, the Web is your research oyster.

But first you need to understand what the Google index isn't.

What Google Isn't

The Internet is not a library. The library metaphor presupposes so many things—a central source for resource information, a paid staff dutifully indexing new material as it comes in, a well-understood and rigorously adhered-to ontology—that trying to think of the Internet as a library can be misleading.

Let's take a moment to dispel some of these myths right up front.

Google's index is a snapshot of all that there is online. No search engine—not even Google—knows everything. There's simply too much and its all flowing too fast to keep up. Then there's the content Google notices but chooses not to index at all: movies, audio, Flash animations, and innumerable specialty data formats.

Everything on the Web is credible. It's not. There are things on the Internet that are biased, distorted, or just plain wrong—whether intentional or not. Visit the Urban Legends Reference Pages (*http://www.snopes.com/*) for a taste of the kinds of urban legends and other misinformation making the rounds of the Internet.

Content filtering will protect you from offensive material. While Google's optional content filtering is good, it's certainly not perfect. You may well come across an offending item among your search results.

Google's index is a static snapshot of the Web. It simply cannot be so. The index, as with the Web, is always in flux. A perpetual stream of spiders deliver new-found pages, note changes, and inform of pages now gone. And the Google methodology itself changes as its designers and maintainers learn. Don't get into a rut of searching a particular way; to do so is to deprive yourself of the benefit of Google's evolution.

What Google Is

The way most people use an Internet search engine is to drop in a couple of keywords and see what turns up. While in certain domains that can yield some decent results, it's becoming less and less effective as the Internet gets larger and larger.

Google provides some special syntaxes to help guide its engine in understanding what you're looking for. This section of the book takes a detailed look at Google's syntax and how best to use it. Briefly:

Within the page
> Google supports syntaxes that allow you to restrict your search to certain components of a page, such as the title or the URL.

Kinds of pages
> Google allows you to restrict your search to certain kinds of pages, such as sites from the educational (EDU) domain or pages that were indexed within a particular period of time.

Kinds of content
> With Google, you can find a variety of file types; for example, Microsoft Word documents, Excel spreadsheets, and PDF files. You can even find specialty web pages the likes of XML, SHTML, or RSS.

Special collections
> Google has several different search properties, but some of them aren't as removed from the web index as you might think. You may be aware of Google's index of news stories and images, but did you know about Google's university searches? Or how about the special searches that allow you to restrict your searches by topic, to BSD, Linux, Apple, Microsoft, or the U.S. government?

These special syntaxes are not mutually exclusive. On the contrary, it's in the combination that the true magic of Google lies. Search for certain kinds of pages in special collections or different page elements on different types of pages.

If you get one thing out of this book, get this: the possibilities are (almost) endless. This book can teach you techniques, but if you just learn them by rote and then never apply them, they won't do you any good. Experiment. Play. Keep your search requirements in mind and try to bend the resources provided in this book to your needs—build a toolbox of search techniques that works specifically for you.

Google Basics

Generally speaking, there are two types of search engines on the Internet. The first is called the searchable subject index. This kind of search engine searches only the titles and descriptions of sites, and doesn't search individual pages. Yahoo! is a searchable subject index. Then there's the full-text search engine, which uses computerized "spiders" to index millions, sometimes billions, of pages. These pages can be searched by title or content, allowing for much narrower searches than searchable subject index. Google is a full-text search engine.

Whenever you search for more than one keyword at a time, a search engine has a default method of how to handle that keyword. Will the engine search for both keywords or for either keyword? The answer is called a Boolean default; search engines can default to Boolean AND (it'll search for both keywords) or Boolean OR (it'll search for either keyword). Of course, even if a search engine defaults to searching for both keywords (AND) you can usually give it a special command to instruct it to search for either keyword (OR). But the engine has to know what to do if you don't give it instructions.

Basic Boolean

Google's Boolean default is AND; that means if you enter query words without modifiers, Google will search for all of them. If you search for:

    snowblower Honda "Green Bay"

Google will search for all the words. If you want to specify that either word is acceptable, you put an OR between each item:

    snowblower OR snowmobile OR "Green Bay"

If you want to definitely have one term and have one of two or more other terms, you group them with parentheses, like this:

    snowblower (snowmobile OR "Green Bay")

This query searches for the word "snowmobile" or phrase "Green Bay" along with the word "snowblower." A stand-in for OR borrowed from the computer programming realm is the | (pipe) character, as in:

    snowblower (snowmobile | "Green Bay")

If you want to specify that a query item must not appear in your results, use a – (minus sign or dash).

```
snowblower snowmobile -"Green Bay"
```

This will search for pages that contain both the words "snowblower" *and* "snowmobile," but not the phrase "Green Bay."

Simple Searching and Feeling Lucky

The I'm Feeling Lucky™ button is a thing of beauty. Rather than giving you a list of search results from which to choose, you're whisked away to what Google believes is the most relevant page given your search, a.k.a. the top first result in the list. Entering washington post and clicking the I'm Feeling Lucky button will take you directly to *http://www.washingtonpost.com/*. Trying president will land you at *http://www.whitehouse.gov/*.

Just in Case

Some search engines are "case sensitive"; that is, they search for queries based on how the queries are capitalized. A search for "GEORGE WASHINGTON" on such a search engine would not find "George Washington," "george washington," or any other case combination. Google is not case sensitive. If you search for Three, three, or THREE, you're going to get the same results.

Other Considerations

There are a couple of other considerations you need to keep in mind when using Google. First, Google does not accept more than 10 query words, special syntax included. If you try to use more than ten, they'll be summarily ignored. There are, however, workarounds [Hack #5].

Second, Google does not support "stemming," the ability to use an asterisk (or other wildcard) in the place of letters in a query term. For example, moon* in a search engine that supported stemming would find "moonlight," "moonshot," "moonshadow," etc. Google does, however, support an asterisk as a full word wildcard [Hack #13]. Searching for "three * mice" in Google would find "three blind mice," "three blue mice," "three red mice," and so forth.

On the whole, basic search syntax along with forethought in keyword choice will get you pretty far. Add to that Google's rich special syntaxes, described in the next section, and you've one powerful query language at your disposal.

The Special Syntaxes

In addition to the basic AND, OR, and quoted strings, Google offers some rather extensive special syntaxes for honing your searches.

Google being a full-text search engine, it indexes entire web pages instead of just titles and descriptions. Additional commands, called special syntaxes, let Google users search specific parts of web pages or specific types of information. This comes in handy when you're dealing with 2 billion web pages and need every opportunity to narrow your search results. Specifying that your query words must appear only in the title or URL of a returned web page is a great way to have your results get very specific without making your keywords themselves too specific.

 Some of these syntaxes work well in combination. Others fare not quite as well. Still others do not work at all. For detailed discussion on what does and does not mix, see "Mixing Syntaxes" [Hack #8].

intitle:
  intitle: restricts your search to the titles of web pages. The variation, allintitle: finds pages wherein all the words specified make up the title of the web page. It's probably best to avoid the allintitle: variation, because it doesn't mix well with some of the other syntaxes.

    intitle:"george bush"
    allintitle:"money supply" economics

inurl:
  inurl: restricts your search to the URLs of web pages. This syntax tends to work well for finding search and help pages, because they tend to be rather regular in composition. An allinurl: variation finds all the words listed in a URL but doesn't mix well with some other special syntaxes.

    inurl:help
    allinurl:search help

intext:
  intext: searches only body text (i.e., ignores link text, URLs, and titles). There's an allintext: variation, but again, this doesn't play well with others. While its uses are limited, it's perfect for finding query words that might be too common in URLs or link titles.

    intext:"yahoo.com"
    intext:html

inanchor:
  inanchor: searches for text in a page's link anchors. A link anchor is the descriptive text of a link. For example, the link anchor in the HTML code <a href="http://www.oreilly.com>O'Reilly and Associates</a> is "O'Reilly and Associates."

    inanchor:"tom peters"

site:

> site: allows you to narrow your search by either a site or a top-level domain. AltaVista, for example, has two syntaxes for this function (host: and domain:), but Google has only the one.
>
> ```
> site:loc.gov
> site:thomas.loc.gov
> site:edu
> site:nc.us
> ```

link:

> link: returns a list of pages linking to the specified URL. Enter link: www.google.com and you'll be returned a list of pages that link to Google. Don't worry about including the http:// bit; you don't need it, and, indeed, Google appears to ignore it even if you do put it in. link: works just as well with "deep" URLs—*http://www.raelity.org/lang/perl/ blosxom/* for instance—as with top-level URLs such as *raelity.org*.

cache:

> cache: finds a copy of the page that Google indexed even if that page is no longer available at its original URL or has since changed its content completely. This is particularly useful for pages that change often.
>
> If Google returns a result that appears to have little to do with your query, you're almost sure to find what you're looking for in the latest cached version of the page at Google.
>
> ```
> cache:www.yahoo.com
> ```

daterange:

> daterange: limits your search to a particular date or range of dates that a page was indexed. It's important to note that the search is not limited to when a page was created, but when it was indexed by Google. So a page created on February 2 and not indexed by Google until April 11 could be found with daterange: search on April 11. Remember also that Google reindexes pages. Whether the date range changes depends on whether the page content changed. For example, Google indexes a page on June 1. Google reindexes the page on August 13, but the page content hasn't changed. The date for the purpose of searching with daterange: is still June 1.
>
> Note that daterange: works with Julian [Hack #12], not Gregorian dates (the calendar we use every day.) There are Gregorian/Julian converters online, but if you want to search Google without all that nonsense, use the FaganFinder Google interface (*http://www.faganfinder.com/engines/google. shtml*), offering daterange: searching via a Gregorian date pull-down

menu. Some of the hacks deal with `daterange:` searching without headaches, so you'll see this popping up again and again in the book.

```
"George Bush" daterange:2452389-2452389
neurosurgery daterange:2452389-2452389
```

`filetype:`

> `filetype:` searches the suffixes or filename extensions. These are usually, but not necessarily, different file types. I like to make this distinction, because searching for `filetype:htm` and `filetype:html` will give you different result counts, even though they're the same file type. You can even search for different page generators, such as ASP, PHP, CGI, and so forth—presuming the site isn't hiding them behind redirection and proxying. Google indexes several different Microsoft formats, including: PowerPoint (PPT), Excel (XLS), and Word (DOC).

```
homeschooling filetype:pdf
"leading economic indicators" filetype:ppt
```

`related:`

> `related:`, as you might expect, finds pages that are related to the specified page. Not all pages are related to other pages. This is a good way to find categories of pages; a search for `related:google.com` would return a variety of search engines, including HotBot, Yahoo!, and Northern Light.

```
related:www.yahoo.com
related:www.cnn.com
```

`info:`

> `info:` provides a page of links to more information about a specified URL. Information includes a link to the URL's cache, a list of pages that link to that URL, pages that are related to that URL, and pages that contain that URL. Note that this information is dependent on whether Google has indexed that URL or not. If Google hasn't indexed that URL, information will obviously be more limited.

```
info:www.oreilly.com
info:www.nytimes.com/technology
```

`phonebook:`

> `phonebook:`, as you might expect, looks up phone numbers. For a deeper look, see the section "Consulting the Phonebook" [Hack #17].

```
phonebook:John Doe CA
phonebook:(510) 555-1212
```

As with anything else, the more you use Google's special syntaxes, the more natural they'll become to you. And Google is constantly adding more, much to the delight of regular web-combers.

If, however, you want something more structured and visual than a single query line, Google's Advanced Search should be fit the bill.

Advanced Search

The Google Advanced Search goes well beyond the capabilities of the default simple search, providing a powerful fill-in form for date searching, filtering, and more.

Google's default simple search allows you to do quite a bit, but not all. The Google Advanced Search (*http://www.google.com/advanced_search?hl=en*) page provides more options such as date search and filtering, with "fill in the blank" searching options for those who don't take naturally to memorizing special syntaxes.

Most of the options presented on this page are self-explanatory, but we'll take a quick look at the kinds of searches that you really can't do with any ease using the simple search's single text-field interface.

Query Word Input

Because Google uses Boolean AND by default, it's sometimes hard to logically build out the nuances of just the query you're aiming for. Using the text boxes at the top of the Advanced Search page, you can specify words that *must* appear, exact phrases, lists of words, at least one of which must appear, and words to be excluded.

Language

Using the Language pull-down menu, you can specify what language all returned pages must be in, from Arabic to Turkish.

Filtering

Google's Advanced Search further gives you the option to filter your results using SafeSearch. SafeSearch filters only explicit sexual content (as opposed to some filtering systems that filter pornography, hate material, gambling information, etc.). Please remember that machine filtering isn't 100% perfect.

File Format

The file format option lets you include or exclude several different Microsoft file formats, including Word and Excel. There are a couple of Adobe formats (most notably PDF) and Rich Text Format as options here too. This is where the Advanced Search is at its most limited; there are literally dozens of file formats that Google can search for, and this set of options represents only a small subset.

Date

Date allows you to specify search results updated in the last three months, six months, or year. This date search is much more limited than the daterange: syntax [Hack #11], which can give you results as narrow as one day, but Google stands behind the results generated using the date option on the Advanced Search, while not officially supporting the use of the daterange search.

The rest of the page provides individual search forms for other Google properties, including news search, page-specific search, and links to some of Google's topic-specific searches. The news search and other topic specific searches work independently of the main advanced search form at the top of the page.

The advanced search page is handy when you need to use its unique features or you need some help putting a complicated query together. Its "fill in the blank" interface will come in handy for the beginning searcher or someone who wants to get an advanced search exactly right. That said, bear in mind it is limiting in other ways; it's difficult to use mixed syntaxes or build a single syntax search using OR. For example, there's no way to search for (site:edu OR site:org) using the Advanced Search.

Of course, there's another way you can alter the search results that Google gives you, and it doesn't involve the basic search input or the advanced search page. It's the preferences page.

HACK #1 Setting Preferences

Customize the way you search Google.

Google's preferences provide a nice, easy way to set your searching preferences from this moment forward.

Language

You can set your Interface Language, affecting the language in which tips and messages are displayed. Language choices range from Afrikaans to Welsh, with plenty of odd options including Bork Bork Bork! (the Swedish Chef), Elmer Fudd, and Pig Latin thrown in for fun. Not to be confused with Interface Language, Search Language restricts what languages should be considered when searching Google's page index. The default being any language, you could be interested only in web pages written in Chinese and Japanese, or French, German, and Spanish—the combination is up to you. Figure 1-1 shows the page through which you can set your language preferences.

Figure 1-1. Language Tools page

Filtering

Google's SafeSearch filtering affords you a method of avoiding search results that may offend your sensibilities. The default is no filtering. Moderate filtering rules out explicit images, but not explicit language. Strict filtering filters both on text and images.

Number of Results

Google, by default, displays 10 results per page. For more results, click any of the "Result Page: 1 2 3..." links at the bottom of each result page, or simply click the "Next" link.

You can specify your preferred number of results per page (10, 20, 30, 50, 100) along with whether you want results to open up in the current or a new browser window.

Settings for Researchers

For the purpose of research, it's best to have as many search results as possible on the page. Because it's all text, it doesn't take that much longer to load 100 results than it does 10. If you have a computer with a decent amount of memory, it's also good to have search results open in a new window; it'll keep you from losing your place and leave you a window with all the search results constantly available.

And if you can stand it, leave your filtering turned off, or at least limit the filtering to moderate instead of strict. Machine filtering is not perfect and unfortunately sometimes having filtering on means you might miss something valuable. This is especially true when you're searching for words that might be caught by a filter, like "breast cancer."

Unless you're absolutely sure that you always want to do a search in one language, I'd advise against setting your language preferences on this page. Instead, alter language preferences as needed using the Google Language Tools.

Between the simple search, advanced search, and preferences, you've got all the beginning tools necessary to build just the Google query to suit your particular purposes.

Fair warning: if you have cookies turned off, setting preferences in Google isn't going to do you much good. You'll have to reset them every time you open your browser. If you can't have cookies and you want to use the same preferences every time, consider making a customized search form.

HACK #2 Language Tools

While you shouldn't rely on Google's language tools to do 100% accurate translations of web pages, they can help you in your searches.

In the early days of the Web, it seemed like most web pages were in English. But as more and more countries have come online, materials have become available in a variety of languages—including languages that don't originate with a particular country (such as Esperanto and Klingon).

Google offers several language tools, including one for translation and one for Google's interface. The interface option is much more extensive than the translation option, but the translation has a lot to offer.

Getting to the Language Tools

The language tools are available by clicking "Language Tools" on the front page or by going to *http://www.google.com/language_tools?hl=en*.

The first tool allows you to search for materials from a certain country and/ or in a certain language. This is an excellent way to narrow your searches; searching for French pages from Japan gives you far fewer results than searching for French pages from France. You can narrow the search further by searching for a slang word in another language. For example, search for the English slang word "bonce" on French pages from Japan.

The second tool on this page allows you to translate either a block of text or an entire web page from one language to another. Most of the translations are to and from English.

Machine translation is not nearly as good as human translation, so don't rely on this translation as either the basis of a search or as a completely accurate translation of the page you're looking at. Rely on it instead to give you the "gist" of whatever it translates.

You don't have to come to this page to use the translation tools. When you enter a search, you'll see that some search results that aren't in your language of choice (which you set via Google's preferences) have "[Translate this page]" next to their titles. Click on one of those and you'll be presented with a framed, translated version of the page. The Google frame, at the top, gives you the option of viewing the original version of the page, as well as returning to the results or viewing a copy suitable for printing.

The third tool lets you choose the interface language for Google, from Afrikaans to Welsh. Some of these languages are imaginary (Bork-Bork-Bork and Elmer Fudd) but they do work.

 Be warned that if you set your language preference to Klingon, for example, you'll need to know Klingon to figure out how to set it back. If you're really stuck, delete the Google cookie from your browser and reload the page; this should reset all preferences to the defaults.

How does Google manage to have so many interface languages when they have so few translation languages? Because of the Google in Your Language program, which gathers volunteers from around the world to translate Google's interface. (You can get more information on that program at *http://www.google.com/intl/en/language.html.*)

Finally, the Language Tools page contains a list of region-specific Google home pages—over 30 of them, from Deutschland to Latvija.

Making the Most of Google's Language Tools

While you shouldn't rely on Google's translation tools to give you more than the "gist" of the meaning (machine translation isn't that good) you can use translations to narrow your searches. The first way I described earlier: use unlikely combinations of languages and countries to narrow your results. The second way involves using the translator.

Select a word that matches your topic and use the translator to translate it into another language. (Google's translation tools work very well for single-word translations like this.) Now, search for that word in a country and language that don't match it. For example, you might search for the German word "Landstraße" (highway) on French pages in Canada. Of course, you'll have to be sure to use words that don't have English equivalents or you'll be overwhelmed with results.

HACK #3   Anatomy of a Search Result

Going beyond the obvious in reading Google search results.

You'd think a list of search results would be pretty straightforward, wouldn't you—just a page title and a link, possibly a summary? Not so with Google. Google encompasses so many search properties and has so much data at its disposal that it fills every results page to the rafters. Within a typical search result you can find sponsored links, ads, links to stock quotes, page sizes, spelling suggestions, and more.

By knowing more of the nitty gritty details of what's what in a search result, you'll be able to make some guesses ("Wow, this page that links to my page is very large; perhaps it's a link list") and correct roadblocks ("I can't find my search term on this page; I'll check the version Google has cached"). Furthermore, if you have a good idea what Google provides on its standard search results page, you'll have more of an idea of what's available to you via the Google API.

Let's use the word "flowers" to examine this anatomy. Figure 1-2 shows the result page for flowers.

First, you'll note at the top of the page is a selection of tabs, allowing you to repeat your search across other Google searches, including Google Groups [Hack #30], Google Images [Hack #31], and the Google Directory. Beneath that you'll see a count for the number of results and how long the search took.

Sometimes you'll see results/sites called out on colored backgrounds at the top or right of the results page. These are called "sponsored links" (read: advertisements). Google has a policy of very clearly distinguishing ads and sticking only to text-based advertising rather than throwing flashing banners in your face like many other sites do.

Beneath the sponsored links you'll sometimes see a category list. The category for flowers is Shopping → Flowers → Wire Services. You'll only see a category list if you're searching for very general terms and your search consists of only one word. For example, if you searched for pinwheel flowers, Google wouldn't present the flowers category.

Figure 1-2. Result page for "flowers"

Why are you seeing category results? After all, Google is a full-text search engine, isn't it? It's because Google has taken the information from the Open Directory Project (*http://www.dmoz.org/*) and crossed it with its own popularity rankings to make the Google Directory. When you see categories, you're seeing information from the Google Directory.

The first real result (non-sponsored, that is) of the search for "flowers" is shown in Figure 1-3.

The Original Virtual **Flowers** - VirtualFlowers.Com® - Send Fresh ...
... Only $49.99, Virtual **Flowers** - Now Featuring... ... Thank you for using Virtual **Flowers**
® . VIRTUAL **FLOWERS** & VIRTUAL BOUQUET ARE REGISTERED TRADEMARKS OF JFS INC. ...
www.virtualflowers.com/ - 13k - Cached - Similar pages

Figure 1-3. First (non-sponsored) result for "flowers"

Let's break that down into chunks.

The top line of each result is the page title, hyperlinked to the original page.

The second line offers a brief extract from this site. Sometimes this is a description of the site or a selected sentence or two. Sometimes it's HTML mush. And sometimes it's navigation goo. But Google tends to use description metatags when they're available in place of navigation goo; it's rare that you can't look at a Google search result for even modicum of an idea what the site is all about.

The next line sports several informative bits. First, there's the URL; second, the size of the page (Google will only have the page size available if the page has been cached). There's a link to a cached version of the page if available. Finally, there's a link to find similar pages.

Why Bother?

Why would you bother reading the search result metadata? Why not simply visit the site and see if it has what you want?

If you've got a broadband connection and all the time in the world, you might not want to bother with checking out the search results. But if you have a slower connection and time is at a premium, consider the search result information.

First, check the page summary. Where does your keyword appear? Does it appear in the middle of a list of site names? Does it appear in a way that makes it clear that the context is not what you're looking for?

Check the size of the page if it's available. Is the page very large? Perhaps it's just a link list. Is it just 1 or 2K? It might be too small to find the detailed information you're looking for. If your aim is link lists [Hack #21], keep a look out for pages larger than 20K.

HACK
#4

Specialized Vocabularies: Slang and Terminology

Your choice of words can make a big difference to the search results you get with Google.

When a teenager says something is "phat," that's slang—a specialized vocabulary for a certain section of the world culture. When a copywriter scribbles "stet" on an ad, that's not slang, but it's still specialized vocabulary for a certain section of the world culture—in this case, the advertising industry.

We have distinctive speech patterns that are shaped by our educations, our families, and where we live. Further, we may use another set of words based on our occupation.

Being aware of these specialty words can make all the difference in the world when it comes to searching. Adding specialized words to your search query—whether slang or industry vocabulary—can really change the slant of your search results.

Slang

Slang gives you one more way to break up your search engine results into geographically distinct areas. There's some geographical blurriness when you use slang to narrow your search engine results, but it's amazing how well it works. For example, search Google for football. Now search for football bloke. Totally different results set, isn't it? Now search for football bloke bonce. Now you're into soccer narratives.

Of course, this is not to say that everyone in England automatically uses the word "bloke" any more than everyone in the southern U.S. automatically uses the word "y'all." But adding well-chosen bits of slang (which will take some experimentation) will give a whole different tenor to your search results and may point you in unexpected directions. You can find slang from the following resources:

The Probert Encyclopedia—Slang
http://www.probertencyclopaedia.com/slang.htm

> This site is browseable by first letter or searchable by keyword. (Note that the keyword search covers the entire Probert Encyclopedia—slang results are near the bottom.) Slang is from all over the world. It's often crosslinked, especially drug slang. As with most slang dictionaries, this site will contain materials that might offend.

A Dictionary of Slang
http://www.peevish.co.uk/slang/

> This site focuses on slang heard in the United Kingdom, which means slang from other places as well. It's browseable by letter or via a search engine. Words from outside the UK are marked with their place of origin in brackets. Words are also denoted as having humorous usage, vulgar, derogatory, etc.

Surfing for Slang
http://www.linkopp.com/members/vlaiko/slanglinks.htm

> Of course each area in the world has its own slang. This site has a good meta-list of English and Scandinavian slang resources.

Using Google with Slang

Start out by searching Google for your query without the slang. Check the results and decide where they're falling short. Are they not specific enough? Are they not located in the right geographical area? Are they not covering the right demographic—teenagers, for example?

Introduce one slang word at a time. For example, for a search for football add the word "bonce" and check the results. If they're not narrowed down enough, add the word "bloke." Add one word at a time until you get to the kind of results you want. Using slang is an inexact science, so you'll have to do some experimenting.

Some things to be careful of when using slang in your searches:

- Try many different slang words.
- Don't use slang words that are generally considered offensive except as a last resort. Your results will be skewed.
- Be careful when using teenage slang, which changes constantly.
- Try searching for slang when using Google Groups. Slang crops up often in conversation.
- Minimize your searches for slang when searching for more formal sources like newspaper stories.
- Don't use slang phrases if you can help it; in my experience these change too much to be consistently searchable. Stick to words.

Specialized Vocabularies—Industrial Slang

Specialized vocabularies are those vocabularies used in certain fields. The medical and legal fields are the two I think of most often when I think of specialized vocabularies, though there are many other fields.

When you need to tip your search to the more technical, the more specialized, and the more in-depth, think of a specialized vocabulary. For example, do a Google search for heartburn. Now do a search for heartburn GERD. Now do a search for heartburn GERD "gastric acid". You'll see each of them is very different.

With some fields, finding specialized vocabulary resources will be a snap. But with others it's not that easy. As a jumping-off point, try the Glossarist site at *http://www.glossarist.com*; it's a searchable subject index of about 6,000 different glossaries covering dozens of different topics. There are also several other large online resources covering certain specific vocabularies. These include:

The On-Line Medical Dictionary
http://cancerweb.ncl.ac.uk/omd/

> This dictionary contains vocabulary relating to biochemistry, cell biology, chemistry, medicine, molecular biology, physics, plant biology, radiobiology, science and technology, and currently has over 46,000 listings.

> You may browse the dictionary by letter or search it. Sometimes you can search for a word that you know (bruise) and find another term that might be more common in medical terminology (contusion). You can also browse the dictionary by subject. Bear in mind that this dictionary is in the UK and some spellings may be slightly different for American users (tumour versus tumor, etc.).

MedTerms.com
http://www.medterms.com/

> MedTerms.com has far fewer definitions (around 10,000) but also has extensive articles from MedicineNet. If you're starting from absolute square one with your research and you need some basic information and vocabulary to get started, search MedicineNet for your term (bruise works well) and then move to MedTerms to search for specific words.

Law.com's Legal Dictionary
http://dictionary.law.com/lookup2.asp

> Law.com's legal dictionary is excellent because you can search either words or definitions (you can browse, too.) For example, you can search for the word "inheritance" and get a list of all the entries which contain the word "inheritance" in their definition. Very easy way to get to the words "muniment of title" without knowing the path.

Using Specialized Vocabulary with Google

As with slang, add specialized vocabulary slowly—one word at a time—and anticipate that it will narrow down your search results very quickly. For example, take the word "spudding," often used in association with oil drilling. Searching for spudding by itself finds only about 2500 results on Google. Adding Texas knocks it down to 525 results, and this is still a very general search! Add specialty vocabulary very carefully or you'll narrow down your search results to the point where you can't find what you want.

Getting Around the 10 Word Limit

There are some clever ways around Google's limit of 10 words to a query.

Unless you're fond of long, detailed queries, you might never have noticed that Google has a hard limit of 10 words—that's keywords and special syntaxes combined—summarily ignoring anything beyond. While this has no real effect on casual Google users, search-hounds quickly find this limit rather cramps their style.

Whatever shall you do?

Favor Obscurity

By limiting your query to the more obscure of your keywords or phrase fragments, you'll hone results without squandering precious query words. Let's say you're interested in a phrase from Hamlet: "The lady doth protest too much, methinks." At first blush, you might simply paste the entire phrase into the query field. But that's seven of your 10 allotted words right there, leaving no room for additional query words or search syntax.

The first thing to do is ditch the first couple of words; "The lady" is just too common a phrase. This leaves the five word "doth protest too much, methinks." Neither "methinks" nor "doth" are words you might hear every day, providing a nice Shakespearean anchor for the phrase. That said, one or the other should suffice, leaving the query at an even four words with room to grow:

```
"protest too much methinks"
```

or:

```
"doth protest too much"
```

Either of these will provide you, within the first five results, origins of the phrase and pointers to more information.

Unfortunately, this technique won't do you much good in the case of "Do as I say not as I do," which doesn't provide much in the way of obscurity. Attempt clarification by adding something like quote origin English usage and you're stepping beyond the ten-word limit.

Playing the Wildcard

Help comes in the form of Google's full-word wildcard [Hack #13]. It turns out that Google doesn't count wildcards toward the limit.

So when you have more than 10 words, substitute a wildcard for common words like so:

```
"do as * say not as * do" quote origin English usage
```

Presto! Google runs the search without complaint and you're in for some well-honed results.

> Common words such as "I," "a," "the," and "of" actually do no good in the first place. Called "stop words," they are ignored by Google entirely. To force Google to take a stop word into account, prepend it with a + (plus) character, as in: +the.

Word Order Matters
#6

Rearranging your query can have quite an effect.

Who would have thought it? The order in which you put your keywords in a Google query can be every bit as important as the query words themselves. Rearranging a query can change not only your overall result count but also what results rise to the top. While one might expect this of quote-enclosed phrases—"have you any wool" versus "wool you any have"—it may come as a surprise that it also affects sets of individual query words.

Google does warn you of this right up front: "Keep in mind that the order in which the terms are typed will affect the search results." Yet it provides little in the way of explanation or suggestion as to how best to formulate a query to take full advantage of this fact.

A little experimentation is definitely in order.

Search for the words (but not as a quote-enclosed phrase) hey diddle diddle. Figure 1-4 shows the results.

The top results, as expected, do include the phrase "hey diddle diddle."

Now give diddle hey diddle a whirl. Again, it should come as no surprise that the first result contains the phrase "diddle hey diddle." Figure 1-5 shows the results.

Finally, search for diddle diddle hey (Figure 1-6).

Another set of results, though this time it isn't clear that Google is finding the phrase "diddle diddle hey" first. (It does show up in the third result's snippet.)

Figure 1-4. Result page for "hey diddle diddle"

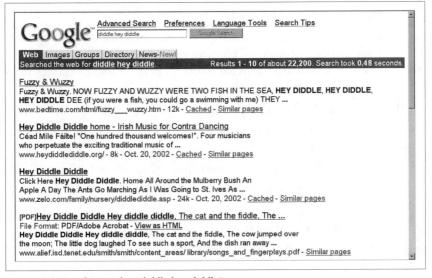

Figure 1-5. Result page for "diddle hey diddle"

What's Going On?

It appears that even if you don't specify a search as a phrase, Google accords any occurrence of the words as a phrase greater weight and more prominence. This is followed by measures of adjacency between the words and then, finally, the weights of the individual words themselves.

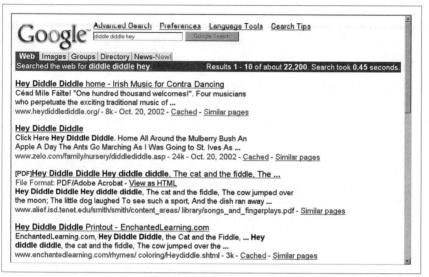

Figure 1-6. Result page for "diddle diddle hey"

Strategies

Searching all query word permutations is a cumbersome thought at best. That said, it can be surprisingly effective in squeezing a few more results from the Google index. If you decide to do so, bear the following strategies in mind:

- Try phrases with and without quotes.

- Make your query as specific as possible, leaving fewer words and thus fewer possible permutations.

- Try the more obvious permutation before the nonsensical—hey diddle diddle before diddle hey diddle.

HACK #7 Repetition Matters

Repetition matters when it comes to keywords weighting your queries.

Using keywords multiple times can have an impact on the types and number of results you get.

Don't believe me? Try searching for internet. At the time of this writing Microsoft was the first result. Now try searching for internet internet. At this writing Yahoo! popped to the top. Experiment with this using other words, putting additional query words in if you want to. You'll see that multiple query words can have an impact on how the search results are ordered and in the number of results returned.

How Does This Work?

Google doesn't talk about this on their web site, so this hack is the result of some conjecture and much experimentation.

First, enter a word one time. Let's use clothes as an example (Figure 1-7). This returns 7,050,000 results, the top being a site called "The Emperor's New Clothes." Let's add another clothes to the query (Figure 1-8). The number of results drops dramatically to 3,490,000, and the first result is for a clothing store. Some different finds move their way up into the top 10 results.

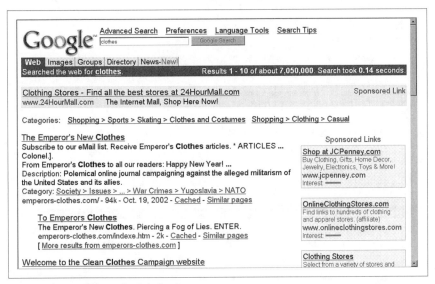

Figure 1-7. Result page for "clothes"

Why stop now? Try clothes clothes clothes (Figure 1-9). The result order and results themselves remain the same.

A Theory

Here's a theory: Google searches for as many matches for each word or phrase you specify, stopping when it can't find any more. So clothes clothes returns pages with two occurrences of the word "clothes." clothes clothes clothes returns the same results, because Google can't do any better than two occurrences of "clothes" in any one page.

So What?

Because Google discards non-matching multiple instances of the same query word, you can use this search as a weighting system for your searches. For

Figure 1-8. Result page for "clothes clothes"

Figure 1-9. Result page for "clothes clothes clothes"

example, say you were interested in pipe systems for the gas industry, but you're more interested in the impact the pipe systems were having on the gas industry (and less so in companies that happen to sell piping systems for the gas industry).

Search for "pipe systems" gas. Now query for "pipe systems" gas gas. You'll notice that the focus of your results changes slightly. Now try "pipe systems" pipe pipe gas gas. Note how the focus slants back the other way.

Based on observations, here are a few guidelines for using multiple iterations of the same query term:

- Multiple iterations of product names or nouns seem to favor shopping sites. This is especially true if the name or noun is plural (e.g., scooters).
- Just because you're not getting different results for the second or third iteration doesn't mean you won't get different results for the fourth or fifth iteration (e.g., successive occurrences of baseball).
- Remember that Google has a limit of 10 words per query, so relegate repetition to only those situations where you can spare the query room.

See Also
- Permuting a Query [Hack #62]

Mixing Syntaxes
HACK #8

What combinations of search syntaxes will and will not fly in your Google search?

There was a time when you couldn't "mix" Google's special syntaxes [in "The Special Syntaxes"]—you were limited to one per query. And while Google released ever more powerful special syntaxes, not being able to combine them for their composite power stunted many a search.

This has since changed. While there remain some syntaxes that you just can't mix, there are plenty to combine in clever and powerful ways. A thoughtful combination can do wonders to narrow a search.

The Antisocial Syntaxes

The antisocial syntaxes are the ones that won't mix and should be used individually for maximum effect. If you try to use them with other syntaxes, you won't get any results.

The syntaxes that request special information—stocks: [Hack #18], rphonebook:, bphonebook:, and phonebook: [Hack #17]—are all antisocial syntaxes. You can't mix them and expect to get a reasonable result.

The other antisocial syntax is the link: syntax. The link: syntax shows you which pages have a link to a specified URL. Wouldn't it be great if you could specify what domains you wanted the pages to be from? Sorry, you can't. The link: syntax does not mix.

For example, say you want to find out what pages link to O'Reilly & Associates, but you don't want to include pages from the *.edu* domain. The query link:www.oreilly.com   -site:edu will not work, because the link: syntax doesn't mix with anything else. Well, that's not quite correct. You will get results, but they'll be for the phrase "link www.oreilly.com" from domains that are not *.edu*.

If you want to search for links and exclude the domain *.edu*, you have a couple of options. First, you can scrape the list of results **[Hack #44]** and sort it in a spreadsheet to remove the *.edu* domain results. If you want to try it through Google, however, there's no command that will absolutely work. This one's a good one to try:

```
inanchor:oreilly -inurl:oreilly -site:edu
```

This search looks for the word O'Reilly in anchor text, the text that's used to define links. It excludes those pages that contain O'Reilly in the search result (e.g., oreilly.com). And, finally, it excludes those pages that come from the *.edu* domain.

But this type of search is nowhere approaching complete. It only finds those links to O'Reilly that include the string oreilly—if someone creates a link like `<a href="http://perl.oreilly.com/">Camel   Book</a>`, it won't be found by the query above. Furthermore, there are other domains that contain the string oreilly, and possibly domains that link to oreilly that contain the string oreilly but aren't oreilly.com. You could alter the string slightly, to omit the oreilly.com site itself, but not other sites containing the string oreilly:

```
inanchor:oreilly -site:oreilly.com -site:edu
```

But you'd still be including many O'Reilly sites that aren't at O'Reilly.com.

So what does mix? Pretty much everything else, but there's a right way and a wrong way to do it.

How Not to Mix Syntaxes

- Don't mix syntaxes that will cancel each other out, such as:

```
site:ucla.edu -inurl:ucla
```

Here you're saying you want all results to come from ucla.edu, but that site results should not have the string "ucla" in the results. Obviously that's not going to result in very much.

- Don't overuse single syntaxes, as in:

```
site:com site:edu
```

While you might think you're asking for results from either *.com* or *.edu* sites, what you're actually saying is that site results should come from both simultaneously. Obviously a single result can come from only one domain. Take the example `perl site:edu site:com`. This search will get you exactly zero results. Why? Because a result page cannot come from a *.edu* domain and a *.com* domain at the same time. If you want results from *.edu* and *.com* domains only, rephrase your search like this:

```
perl (site:edu | site:com)
```

With the pipe character (|), you're specifying that you want results to come either from the *.edu or* the *.com* domain.

- Don't use `allinurl:` or `allintitle:` when mixing syntaxes. It takes a careful hand not to misuse these in a mixed search. Instead, stick to `inurl:` or `intitle:`. If you don't put `allinurl:` in exactly the right place, you'll create odd search results. Let's look at this example:

```
allinurl:perl intitle:programming
```

At first glance it looks like you're searching for the string "perl" in the result URL, and the word "programming" in the title. And you're right, this will work fine. But what happens if you move `allinurl:` to the right of the query?

```
intitle:programming allinurl:perl
```

This won't get any results. Stick to `inurl:` and `intitle:`, which are much more forgiving of where you put them in a query.

- Don't use so many syntaxes that you get too narrow, like:

```
title:agriculture site:ucla.edu inurl:search
```

You might find that it's too narrow to give you any useful results. If you're trying to find something that's so specific that you think you'll need a narrow query, start by building a little bit of the query at a time. Say you want to find plant databases at UCLA. Instead of starting with the query:

```
title:plants site:ucla.edu inurl:database
```

Try something simpler:

```
databases plants site:ucla.edu
```

and then try adding syntaxes to keywords you've already established in your search results:

```
intitle:plants databases site:ucla.edu
```

or:

```
intitle:database plants site:ucla.edu
```

How to Mix Syntaxes

If you're trying to narrow down search results, the `intitle:` and `site:` syntaxes are your best bet.

Titles and sites. For example, say you want to get an idea of what databases are offered by the state of Texas. Run this search:

```
intitle:search intitle:records site:tx.us
```

You'll find 32 very targeted results. And of course, you can narrow down your search even more by adding keywords:

```
birth intitle:search intitle:records
site:tx.us
```

It doesn't seem to matter if you put plain keywords at the beginning or the end of the search query; I put them at the beginning, because they're easier to keep up with.

The `site:` syntax, unlike site syntaxes on other search engines, allows you to get as general as a domain suffix (site:com) or as specific as a domain or subdomain (site:thomas.loc.gov). So if you're looking for records in El Paso, you can use this query:

```
intitle:records site:el-paso.tx.us
```

and you'll get seven results.

Title and URL. Sometimes you'll want to find a certain type of information, but you don't want to narrow by type. Instead, you want to narrow by theme of information—say you want help or a search engine. That's when you need to search in the URL.

The `inurl:` syntax will search for a string in the URL but won't count finding it within a larger URL. So, for example, if you search for `inurl:research`, Google will not find pages from researchbuzz.com, but it would find pages from *www.research-councils.ac.uk.*

Say you want to find information on biology, with an emphasis on learning or assistance. Try:

```
intitle:biology inurl:help
```

This takes you to a manageable 162 results. The whole point is to get a number of results that finds you what you need but isn't so large as to be overwhelming. If you find 162 results overwhelming, you can easily add the `site:` syntax to the search and limit your results to university sites:

```
intitle:biology inurl:help site:edu
```

But beware of using so many special syntaxes, as I mentioned above, that you detail yourself into no results at all.

All the possibilities. It's possible that I could write down every possible syntax-mixing combination and briefly explain how they might be useful, but if I did that, I'd have no room for the rest of the hacks in this book.

Experiment. Experiment a lot. Keep in mind constantly that most of these syntaxes do not stand alone, and you can get more done by combining them than by using them one at a time.

Depending on what kind of research you do, different patterns will emerge over time. You may discover that focusing on only PDF documents (filetype:pdf) finds you the results you need. You may discover that you should concentrate on specific file types in specific domains (filetype:ppt site:tompeters.com). Mix up the syntaxes as many ways as is relevant to your research and see what you get.

Hacking Google URLs
Hacking the URL Google hands you in response to a search.

When you think of hacks you might think of making a cool search form or performing a particularly intricate search. But you can also hack search results by hacking the URL that Google returns after a search. There's at least one thing you can do by hacking the URL that you can do no other way, and there are quick tricks you can do that might save you a trip back to the advanced preferences page otherwise.

Anatomy of a URL

Say you want to search for three blind mice. Your result URL will vary depending on the preferences you've set, but the results URL will look something like this:

```
http://www.google.com/search?num=100&hl=en&q=%22three+blind+mice%22
```

The query itself—&q=%22three+blind+mice%22, %22 being a URL-encoded " (double quote)—is pretty obvious, but let's break down what those extra bits mean.

num=100 refers to the number of search results to a page, 100 in this case. Google accepts any number from 1 to 100. Altering the value of num is a nice shortcut to altering the preferred size of your result set without having to meander over to the Advanced Search page and rerun your search.

Don't see the num= in your query? Simply append it to your query URL using any value between 1 and 100.

 You can add or alter any of the modifiers described here by simply appending them to the URL or changing their values—the part after the = (equals)—to something within the accepted range for the modifier in question.

hl=en means the language interface—the language in which you use Google, reflected in the home page, messages, and buttons—is in English (at least mine is). Google's Language Tools page [Hack #2] provides a list of language choices. Run your mouse over each and notice the change reflected in the URL; the one for Pig Latin looks like this:

```
http://www.google.com/intl/xx-piglatin/
```

The language code is the bit between intl/ and the last /, xx-piglatin in this case. Apply that to the search URL at hand:

```
hl=xx-piglatin
```

What if you put multiple &hl modifiers on a result URL? Google uses whichever one comes last. While it makes for confusing URLs, this means you can always resort to laziness and add an extra modifier at the end rather than editing what's already there.

There are a couple more modifiers that, appended to your URL, may provide some useful modifications of your results:

as_qdr=mx

    Specifies the maximum age of the search results, in months. x is any number between 1 and 12; I find that numbers between 1 and 6 are best.

safe=off

    Means the SafeSearch filter is off. The SafeSearch filter removes search results mostly of a sexually explicit nature. safe=on means the SafeSearch filter is on.

Hacking Google's URL may not seem like the most intuitive way to get results quickly, but it's much faster than reloading the advanced search form and in one case (the "months old" modifier) it's the only way to get at a particular set of results.

Hacking Google Search Forms
Build your own personal, task-specific Google search form.

If you want to do a simple search with Google, you don't need anything but the standard Simple Search form (the Google home page). But if you want to craft specific Google searches you'll be using on a regular basis or providing for others, you can simply put together your own personalized search form.

Start with your garden variety Google search form; something like this will do nicely:

```
<!-- Search Google -->
<form method="get" action="http://www.google.com/search">
<input type="text" name="q" size=31 maxlength=255 value="">
<input type="submit" name="sa" value="Search Google">
</form>
<!-- Search Google -->
```

This is a very simple search form. It takes your query and sends it directly to Google, adding nothing to it. But you can embed some variables to alter your search as needed. You can do this two ways: via hidden variables or by adding more input to your form.

Hidden Variables

As long as you know how to identify a search option in Google, you can add it to your search form via a hidden variable. The fact that it's hidden just means that form users will not be able to alter it. They won't even be able to see it unless they take a look at the source code. Let's take a look at a few examples.

> While it's perfectly legal HTML to put your hidden variables anywhere between the opening and closing <form> tags, it's rather tidy and useful to keep them all together after all the visible form fields.

File type
  As the name suggests, file type specifies filtering your results by a particular file type (e.g., Word DOC, Adobe PDF, PowerPoint PPT, plain text TXT). Add a PowerPoint file type filter, for example, to your search form like so:

```
<input type="hidden" name="as_filetype" value="PPT">
```

Site search

Narrows your search to specific sites. While a suffix like *.com* will work just fine, something more fine-grained like the *example.com* domain is probably better suited:

```
<input type="hidden" name="as_sitesearch" value="example.com">
```

Date searching

Narrows your search to pages indexed within the stated number of months. Acceptable values are between 1 and 12. Restricting our results to items indexed only within the last seven months is just a matter of adding:

```
<input type="hidden" name="as_qdr" value="m7">
```

Number of results

Specifies the number of results you'd like appearing on each page, specified as a value of num between 1 and 100; the following asks for 50 per page:

```
<input type="hidden" name="num" value="50">
```

What would you use this for? If you're regularly looking for an easy way to create a search engine that finds certain file types in a certain place, this works really well. If this is a one-time search, you can always just hack the results URL [Hack #9], tacking the variables and their associated values on to the URL of the results page.

Mixing Hidden File Types: An Example

The site tompeters.com (*http://www.tompeters.com/*) contains several Power-Point (PPT) files. If you want to find just the PowerPoint files on their site, you'd have to figure out how their site search engine works or pester them into adding a file type search option. But you can put together your own search form that finds PowerPoint presentations on the tompeters.com site.

Even though you're creating a handy search form this way, you're still resting on the assumption that Google's indexed most or all of the site you're searching. Until you know otherwise, assume that any search results Google gives you are incomplete.

Your form looks something like:

```
<!-- Search Google for tompeters.com PowerPoints -->
<form method="get" action="http://www.google.com/search">
<input type="text" name="q" size=31 maxlength=255 value="">
<input type="submit" name="sa" value="Search Google">
```

```
<input type="hidden" name="as_filetype" value="ppt">
<input type="hidden" name="as_sitesearch" value="tompeters.com">
<input type="hidden" name="num" value="100">
</form>
<!-- Search Google for tompeters.com PowerPoints -->
```

Using hidden variables is handy when you want to search for one particular thing all the time. But if you want to be flexible in what you're searching for, creating an alternate form is the way to go.

Creating Your Own Google Form

Some variables best stay hidden; however for other options, you can let your form users be much more flexible.

Let's go back to the previous example. You want to let your users search for PowerPoint files, but you also want them to be able to search for Excel files and Microsoft Word files. In addition, you want them to be able to search tompeters.com, the State of California, or the Library of Congress. There are obviously various ways to do this user-interface–wise; this example uses a couple of simple pull-down menus:

```
<!-- Custom Google Search Form-->
<form method="get" action="http://www.google.com/search">
<input type="text" name="q" size=31 maxlength=255 value="">
<br />
Search for file type:
<select name="as_filetype">
<option value="ppt">PowerPoint</option>
<option value="xls">Excel</option>
<option value="doc">Word</option>
</select>
<br />
Search site:
<select name="as_sitesearch"></option>
<option value="tompeters.com">TomPeters.com</option>
<option value="state.ca.us">State of California</option>
<option value="loc.gov">The Library of Congress</option>
</select>
<input type="hidden" name="num" value="100">
<input type="submit" value="Search Google">
</form>
<!-- Custom Google Search Form-->
```

FaganFinder (*http://www.faganfinder.com/engines/google.shtml*) is a wonderful example of a thoroughly customized form.

Date-Range Searching

An undocumented but powerful feature of Google's search and API is the ability to search within a particular date range.

Before delving into the actual use of date-range searching, there are a few things you should understand. The first is this: a date-range search has nothing to do with the creation date of the content and everything to do with the indexing date of the content. If I create a page on March 8, 1999, and Google doesn't get around to indexing it until May 22, 2002, for the purposes of a date-range search, the date in question is May 22, 2002.

The second thing is that Google can index pages several times, and each time it does so the date on it changes. So don't count on a date-range search staying consistent from day to day. The `daterange:` timestamp can change when a page is indexed more than one time. Whether it does change depends on whether the content of the page has changed.

Third, Google doesn't "stand behind" the results of a search done using the date-range syntaxes. So if you get a weird result, you can't complain to them. Google would rather you use the date-range options on their advanced search page, but that page allows you to restrict your options only to the last three months, six months, or year.

The daterange: Syntax

Why would you want to search by `daterange:`? There are several reasons:

- It narrows down your search results to fresher content. Google might find some obscure, out-of-the-way page and index it only once. Two years later this obscure, never-updated page is still turning up in your search results. Limiting your search to a more recent date range will result in only the most current of matches.

- It helps you dodge current events. Say John Doe sets a world record for eating hot dogs and immediately afterward rescues a baby from a burning building. Less than a week after that happens, Google's search results are going to be filled with John Doe. If you're searching for information on (another) John Doe, babies, or burning buildings, you'll scarcely be able to get rid of him.

  However, you can avoid Mr. Doe's exploits by setting the date-range syntax to before the hot dog contest. This also works well for avoiding recent, heavily covered news events such as a crime spree or a forest fire and annual events of at least national importance such as national elections or the Olympics.

- It allows you to compare results over time; for example, if you want to search for occurrences of "Mac OS X" and "Windows XP" over time.

  Of course, a count like this isn't foolproof; indexing dates change over time. But generally it works well enough that you can spot trends.

Using the daterange: syntax is as simple as:

```
daterange:startdate-enddate
```

The catch is that the date must be expressed as a Julian date, a continuous count of days since noon UTC on January 1, 4713 BC. So, for example, July 8, 2002 is Julian date 2452463.5 and May 22, 1968 is 2439998.5. Furthermore, Google isn't fond of decimals in its daterange: queries; use only integers: 2452463 or 2452464 (depending on whether you prefer to round up or down) in the previous example.

> There are plenty of places you can convert Julian dates online. We've found a couple of nice converters at the U.S. Naval Observatory Astronomical Applications Department (*http://aa.usno.navy.mil/data/docs/JulianDate.html*) and Mauro Orlandini's home page (*http://www.tesre.bo.cnr.it/~mauro/JD/*), the latter converting either Julian to Gregorian or vice versa. More may be found via a Google search for julian date (*http://www.google.com/search?hl=en&lr=&ie=ISO-8859-1&q=julian+date*).

You can use the daterange: syntax with most other Google special syntaxes, with the exception of the link: syntax, which doesn't mix [Hack #8] well with other special syntaxes [in "The Special Syntaxes"] and the Google's Special Collections [Chapter 2] (e.g., stocks: and phonebook:).

daterange: does wonders for narrowing your search results. Let's look at a couple of examples. Geri Halliwell left the Spice Girls around May 27, 1998. If you wanted to get a lot of information about the breakup, you could try doing a date search in a ten-day window—Say, May 25 to June 4. That query would look like this:

```
"Geri Halliwell" "Spice Girls" daterange:2450958-2450968
```

At this writing, you'll get about two dozen results, including several news stories about the breakup. If you wanted to find less formal sources, search for Geri or Ginger Spice instead of Geri Halliwell.

That example's a bit on the silly side, but you get the idea. Any event that you can clearly divide into before and after dates—an event, a death, an overwhelming change in circumstances—can be reflected in a date-range search.

You can also use an individual event's date to change the results of a larger search. For example, former ImClone CEO Sam Waksal was arrested on June 12, 2002. You don't have to search for the name Sam Waskal to get a very narrow set of results for June 13, 2002:

```
imclone daterange:2452439-2452439
```

Similarly, if you search for imclone before the date of 2452439, you'll get very different results. And as an interesting exercise, try a search that reflects the arrest, only date it a few days before the actual arrest:

```
imclone investigated daterange:2452000-2452435
```

This is a good way to find information or analysis that predates the actual event, but that provides background that might help explain the event itself. (Unless you use the date-range search, usually this kind of information is buried underneath news of the event itself.)

But what about narrowing your search results based on content creation date?

Searching by Content Creation Date

Searching for materials based on content creation is difficult. There's no standard date format (score one for Julian dates), many people don't date their pages anyway, some pages don't contain date information in their header, and still other content management systems routinely stamp pages with today's date, confusing things still further.

We can offer few suggestions for searching by content creation date. Try adding a string of common date formats to your query. If you wanted something from May 2003, for example, you could try appending:

```
("May * 2003" | "May 2003" | 05/03 | 05/*/03)
```

A query like that uses up most of your ten-query limit, however, so it's best to be judicious—perhaps by cycling through these formats one a time. If any one of these is giving you too many results, try restricting your search to the title tag of the page.

If you're feeling really lucky you can search for a full date, like May 9, 2003. Your decision then is if you want to search for the date in the format above or as one of many variations: 9 May 2003, 9/5/2003, 9 May 03, and so forth. Exact-date searching will severely limit your results and shouldn't be used except as a last-ditch option.

When using date-range searching, you'll have to be flexible in your thinking, more general in your search than you otherwise would be (because the date-range search will narrow your results down a lot), and persistent in your queries because different dates and date ranges will yield very different results. But you'll be rewarded with smaller result sets that are focused on very specific events and topics.

Understanding and Using Julian Dates

Get to know and use Julian Dates.

Date-based searching good! Date-based searching with Julian dates annoying (for a human, anyway)!

The Julian date is the number of days that have passed since January 1, 4713 BC. Unlike Gregorian dates, which begin at midnight, Julian days begin at noon, making them useful for astronomers.

A Julian date is just one number. It's not broken up into month, day, and year. That makes it problematic for humans but handy for computer programming, because to change dates, you simply have to add and subtract from one number, and not worry about month and year changes.

To use Google's date-range syntax in Perl, you'll need a way to convert the computer's local time to Julian. You can use the module Time::JulianDay, which offers a variety of ways to manipulate local time in Julian format. You can get the module and more information at *http://search.cpan.org/search?query=Time%3A%3AJulianDay*.

Hacks that use the Julian date format and date-range searching pop up throughout this book; start by learning more about using the date-range syntax [Hack #11]. Also included are hacks for building recent searches into a customized form [Hack #42], and date-range searches with a client-side application [Hack #60].

Using Full-Word Wildcards

Google's full-word wildcard stands in for any keyword in a query.

Some search engines support a technique called "stemming." Stemming is adding a wildcard character—usually * (asterisk) but sometimes ? (question mark)—to part of your query, requesting the search engine return variants of that query using the wildcard as a placeholder for the rest of the word at hand. For example, moon* would find: moons, moonlight, moonshot, etc.

Google doesn't support stemming.

Instead, Google offers the full-word wildcard. While you can't have a wildcard stand in for part of a word, you can insert a wildcard (Google's wildcard character is *) into a phrase and have the wildcard act as a substitute for one full word. Searching for "three * mice" , therefore, finds: three blind mice, three blue mice, three green mice, etc.

What good is the full-word wildcard? It's certainly not as useful as stemming, but then again, it's not as confusing to the beginner. One * is a stand-in for one word; two * signifies two words, and so on. The full-word wildcard comes in handy in the following situations:

- Avoiding the 10 word limit [Hack #5] on Google queries. You'll most frequently run into these examples when you're trying to find song lyrics or a quote; plugging the phrase "Fourscore and seven years ago, our forefathers brought forth on this continent" into Google will search only as far as the word "on," every word after that will be ignored by Google.

- Checking the frequency of certain phrases and derivatives of phrases, like: intitle:"methinksthe*dothprotesttoo   much" and intitle:"the * of Seville" .

- Filling in the blanks on a fitful memory. Perhaps you remember only a short string of song lyrics; search only using what you remember rather than randomly reconstructed full lines.

Let's take as an example the disco anthem "Good Times" by Chic. Consider the line: "You silly fool, you can't change your fate."

Perhaps you've heard that lyric, but you can't remember if the word "fool" is correct or if it's something else. If you're wrong (if the correct line is, for example, "You silly child, you can't change your fate"), your search will find no results and you'll come away with the sad conclusion that no one on the Internet has bothered to post lyrics to Chic songs.

The solution is to run the query with a wildcard in place of the unknown word, like so:

```
"You silly *, you can't change your fate"
```

You can use this technique for quotes, song lyrics, poetry, and more. You should be mindful, however, to include enough of the quote that you find unique results. Searching for "you * fool" will glean you far too many false hits.

inurl: Versus site:
#14   Use inurl: syntax to search site subdirectories.

The site: special syntax is perfect for those situations in which you want to restrict your search to a certain domain or domain suffix like "example. com," "www.example.org," or "edu": site:edu . But it breaks down when you're trying to search for a site that exists beneath the main or default site (i.e., in a subdirectory like /~sam/album/).

For example, if you're looking for something below the main GeoCities site, you can't use site: to find all the pages in *http://www.geocities.com/Heartland/ Meadows/6485/*; Google will return no results. Enter inurl:, a Google special syntax [in "The Special Syntaxes"] for specifying a string to be found in a resultant URL. That query, then, would work as expected like so:

```
inurl:www.geocities.com/Heartland/Meadows/6485/
```

 While the http:// prefix in a URL is summarily ignored by Google when used with site:, search results come up short when including it in a inurl: query. Be sure to remove prefixes in any inurl: query for the best (read: any) results.

You'll see that using the inurl: query instead of the site: query has two immediate advantages:

- You can use inurl: by itself without using any other query words (which you can't do with site:).
- You can use it to search subdirectories.

How Many Subdomains?

You can also use inurl: in combination with the site: syntax to get information about subdomains. For example, how many subdomains does O'Reilly.com really have? You can't get that information via the query site: oreilly.com, but neither can you get it just from the query inurl:"*. oreilly.com" (because that query will pick up mirrors and other pages containing the string oreilly.com that aren't at the O'Reilly site).

However, this query will work just fine:

```
site:oreilly.com inurl:"*.oreilly" -inurl:"www.oreilly"
```

This query says to Google, "Look on the site O'Reilly.com with page URLs that contain the string '*.oreilly' (remember the full-word wildcard? [Hack #13]) but ignore URLs with the string 'www.oreilly'" (because that's a subdomain you're already very familiar with).

Checking Spelling
#15   Google sometimes takes the liberty of "correcting" what it perceives is a spelling error in your query.

If you've ever used other Internet search engines, you'll have experienced what I call "stupid spellcheck." That's when you enter a proper noun and the search engine suggests a completely ludicrous query ("Elvish Parsley" for "Elvis Presley"). Google's quite a bit smarter than that.

When Google thinks it can spell individual words or complete phrases in your search query better than you can, it'll offer you a suggested "better" search, hyperlinking it directly to a query. For example, if you search for hydrocephelus, Google will suggest that you search instead for hydrocephalus.

Suggestions aside, Google will assume you know of what you speak and return your requested results. Provided, that is, that your query gleaned results.

If your query found no results for the spellings you provided and Google believes it knows better, it will automatically run a new search on its own suggestions. Thus, a search for hydracefallus finding (hopefully) no results will spark a Google-initiated search for hydrocephalus.

Mind you, Google does not arbitrarily come up with its suggestions, but builds them based on its own database of words and phrases found while indexing the Web. If you search for nonsense like garafghafdghasdg, you'll get no results and be offered no suggestions as Figure 1-10 shows.

> This is a lovely side effect and quick and easy way to check the relative frequency of spellings. Query for a particular spelling, making note of the number of results. Then click on Google's suggested spelling and note the number of results. It's surprising how close the counts are sometimes, indicating an oft misspelled word or phrase.

Embrace Misspellings

Don't make the mistake of automatically dismissing the proffered results from a misspelled word, particularly a proper name. I've been a fan of cartoonist Bill Mauldin for years now, but I continually misspell his name as "Bill Maudlin." And judging from a quick Google search I'm not the only one. There is no law saying that every page must be spellchecked before it goes online, so it's often worth taking a look at results despite misspellings.

Figure 1-10. A search that yields no suggestions

As an experiment, try searching for two misspelled words on a related topic, like ventriculostomy hydrocephalis. What kind of information did you get? Could the information you got, if any, be grouped into a particular online "genre"?

At this writing, the search for ventriculostomy hydrocephalis gets only two results. Both of them are for a guestbook at a Developmental (Pediatric) Neurosurgery Unit at Massachusetts General Hospital/Harvard University. The content here is generally from people dealing with various neurosurgical problems. Again, there is no law that says all web materials, especially informal ones like guest book communications, have to be spellchecked.

Use this to your advantage as a researcher. When you're looking for layman accounts of illness and injury, the content you desire might actually be more often misspelled than not. On the other hand, when looking for highly technical information or references from credible sources, filtering out misspelled queries will bring you closer to the information you seek.

Consulting the Dictionary

HACK #16

Google, in addition to its own spellchecking index, provides hooks into Dictionary.com.

Google's own spellchecking [Hack #15] is built upon its own word and phrase database gleaned while indexing web pages. Thus it provides suggestions for lesser known proper names, phrases, common sentence constructs, etc. Google also offers a definition service powered by Dictionary.com (*http://www.dictionary.com/*). Definitions, while coming from a credible source and augmented by various specialty indexes, can be more limited.

Run a search. You'll notice on the results page the phrase "Searched the web for [query words]." If the query words would appear in a dictionary, they will be hyperlinked to a dictionary definition. Identified phrases will be linked as a phrase; for example, the query "jolly roger" will allow you to look up the phrase "jolly roger." On the other hand, the phrase "computer legal" will allow you to look up the separate words "computer" and "legal."

The definition search will sometimes fail on obscure words, very new words, slang, and technical vocabularies (otherwise known as specialized slang). If you search for a word's meaning and Google can't help you, try enlisting the services of a metasearch dictionary, like OneLook (*http://www.onelook.com/*) which indexes over 4 million words in over 700 dictionaries. If that doesn't work, try Google again with one of the following tricks, *queryword* being the word you want to find:

- If you're searching for several words—you're reading a technical manual, for example—search for several of the words at the same time. Sometimes you'll find a glossary this way. For example, maybe you're reading a book about marketing, and you don't know many of the words. If you search for storyboard stet SAU, you'll get only a few search results, and they'll all be glossaries.

- Try searching for your word and the word glossary; say, stet glossary. Be sure to use an unusual word; you may not know what a "spread" is in the context of marketing but searching for spread glossary will get you over 300,000 results for many different kinds of glossaries. See "Google Interface for Translators" [Hack #19] for language translation.

- Try searching for the phrase *queryword* means or the words What does *queryword* mean?.

- If you're searching for a medical or a technical item, narrow your search to educational (*.edu*) sites. If you want a contextual definition for using equine acupuncture and how it might be used to treat laminitis, try "equine acupuncture" laminitis.

- `site:edu` will give you a brief list of results. Furthermore, you'll avoid book lists and online stores; handy if you're seeking information and don't necessarily want to purchase anything. If you're searching for slang, try narrowing your search to sites like Geocities and Tripod, and see what happens. Sometimes young people put fan sites and other informal cultural collections up on free places like Geocities, and using these you can find many examples of slang in context instead of dry lists of definitions. There are an amazing number of glossaries on Geocities; search for `glossary site:geocities.com`, and see for yourself.

Google's connection with Dictionary.com means that simple definition checking is very fast and easy. But even more obscure words can be quickly found if you apply a little creative thinking.

HACK #17 Consulting the Phonebook

Google makes an excellent phonebook, even to the extent of doing reverse lookups.

Google combines residential and business phone number information and its own excellent interface to offer a phonebook lookup that provides listings for businesses and residences in the United States. However, the search offers three different syntaxes, different levels of information provide different results, the syntaxes are finicky, and Google doesn't provide any documentation.

The Three Syntaxes

Google offers three ways to search its phonebook:

phonebook
> Searches the entire Google phonebook

rphonebook
> Searches residential listings only

bphonebook
> Searches business listings only

> The result page for `phonebook:` lookups lists only five results, residential and business combined. The more specific `rphonebook:` and `bphonebook:` searches provide up to 30 results per page. For more chance of finding what you're looking for, use the appropriate targetted lookup.

Using the Syntaxes

Using a standard phonebook requires knowing quite a bit of information about what you're looking for: first name, last name, city, and state. Google's phonebook requires no more than last name and state to get it started. Casting a wide net for all the Smiths in California is as simple as:

    phonebook:smith ca

Try giving 411 a whirl with that request! Figure 1-11 shows the results of the query.

Figure 1-11. phonebook: result page

Notice that, while intuition might tell you there are thousands of Smiths in California, the Google phonebook says there are only 600. Just as Google's regular search engine maxes out at 1000 results, its phonebook maxes out at 600. Fair enough. Try narrowing down your search by adding a first name, city, or both:

    phonebook:john smith los angeles ca

At the time of this writing, the Google phonebook found 3 business and 22 residential listings for John Smith in Los Angeles, California.

Caveats. The phonebook syntaxes are powerful and useful, but they can be difficult to use if you don't remember a few things about how they work.

- The syntaxes are case-sensitive. Searching for phonebook:john doe ca works, while Phonebook:john doe ca (notice the capital P) doesn't.

- Wildcards don't work. Then again, they're not needed; the Google phonebook does all the wildcarding for you. For example, if you want to find shops in New York with "Coffee" in the title, don't bother trying to envision every permutation of "Coffee Shop," "Coffee House," and so on. Just search for bphonebook:coffee new york ny and you'll get a list of any business in New York whose name contains the word "coffee."

- Exclusions don't work. Perhaps you want to find coffee shops that aren't Starbucks. You might think phonebook:coffee -starbucks new york ny would do the trick. After all, you're searching for coffee and not Starbucks, right? Unfortunately not; Google thinks you're looking for both the words "coffee" and "starbucks," yielding just the opposite of what you were hoping for: everything Starbucks in NYC.

- OR doesn't always work. You might start wondering if Google's phonebook accepts OR lookups. You then might experiment, trying to find all the coffee shops in Rhode Island or Hawaii: bphonebook:coffee (ri | hi). Unfortunately that doesn't work; the only listings you'll get are for coffee shops in Hawaii. That's because Google doesn't appear to see the (ri | hi) as a state code, but rather as another element of the search. So if you reversed your search above, and searched for coffee (hi | ri), Google would find listings that contained the string "coffee" and either the strings "hi" or "ri." So you'll find Hi-Tide Coffee (in Massachusetts) and several coffee shops in Rhode Island. It's neater to use OR in the middle of your query, and then specify your state at the end. For example, if you want to find coffee shops that sell either donuts or bagels, this query works fine: bphonebook:coffee (donuts | bagels) ma. That finds stores that contain the word coffee and either the word donuts or the word bagels in Massachusetts. The bottom line: you can use an OR query on the store or resident name, but not on the location.

Reverse phonebook lookup. All three phonebook syntaxes support reverse lookup, though its probably best to use the general phonebook: syntax to avoid not finding what you're looking for due to its residential or business classification.

To do a reverse search, just enter the phone number with area code. Look-ups without area code won't work.

    phonebook:(707) 829-0515

Note that reverse lookups on Google are a hit-and-miss proposition and don't always produce results. If you're not having any luck, you may wish to use a more dedicated phonebook site like WhitePages.com (*http://www. whitepages.com/*).

Finding phonebooks using Google. While Google's phonebook is a good start-ing point, its usefulness is limited. If you're looking for a phone number at a university or other large institution, while you won't find the number in Google, you certainly can find the appropriate phonebook, if it's online.

If you're looking for a university phonebook, try this simple search first: inurl:phone site:*university.edu*, replacing *university.edu* with the domain of the university you're looking for. For example, to find the online phone-book of the University of North Carolina at Chapel Hill, you'd search for:

    inurl:phone site:unc.edu

If that doesn't work, there are several variations you can try, again substitut-ing your preferred university's domain for *unc.edu*:

    title:"phone book" site:*unc.edu*
    (phonebook | "phone book") lookup faculty staff site:*unc.edu*
    inurl:help (phonebook | "phone book") site:*unc.edu*

If you're looking for several university phonebooks, try the same search with the more generic site:edu rather than a specific university's domain. There are also a couple of web sites that list university phonebooks:

- Phonebook Gateway—Server Lookup (*http://www.uiuc.edu/cgi-bin/ph/ lookup*) (over 330 phonebooks)
- Phone Book Servers (*http://www.envmed.rochester.edu/www/ph.html*) (over 400 phonebooks)

Tracking Stocks
HACK #18

A well-crafted Google query will usually net you company information beyond those provided by traditional stock services.

Among the lesser-known pantheon of Google syntaxes is stocks:. Searching for stocks:*symbol*, where *symbol* represents the stock you're looking for, will redirect you to Yahoo! Finance (*http://finance.yahoo.com/*) for details. The Yahoo! page is actually framed by Google; off to the top-left is the Google logo, along with links to Quicken, Fool.com, MSN MoneyCentral, and other financial sites.

Feed Google a bum stock: query and you'll still find yourself at Yahoo! Finance, usually staring at a quote for stock you've never even heard of or a "Stock Not Found" page. Of course, you can use this to your advantage. Enter stocks: followed by the name of a company you're looking for (e.g., stocks:friendly). If the company's name is more than one word, choose the most unique word. Run your query and you'll arrive at the Yahoo! Finance stock lookup page shown in Figure 1-12.

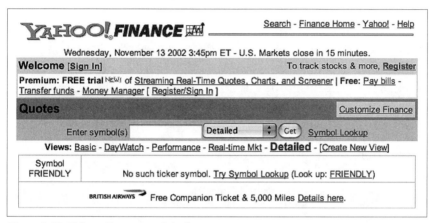

Figure 1-12. Yahoo! Finance stock lookup page

Notice the "Look up: FRIENDLY" link; click it and you'll be offered a list of companies that match "friendly" in some way. From there you can get the stock information you want (assuming the company you wanted is on the list).

Beyond Google for Basic Stock Information

Google isn't particularly set up for basic stock research. You'll have to do your initial groundwork elsewhere, returning to Google armed with a better understanding of what you're looking for. I recommend going straight to Yahoo! Finance (*http://finance.yahoo.com*) to quickly look up stocks by symbol or company name; there you'll find all the basics: quotes, company profiles, charts, and recent news. For more in-depth coverage, I heartily recommend Hoovers (*http://www.hoovers.com*). Some of the information is free. For more depth, you'll have to pay a subscription fee.

More Stock Research with Google

Try searching Google for:

    "Tootsie Roll"

Now add the stock symbol, TR, to your query:

```
"Tootsie Roll" TR
```

Aha! Instantly the search results shift to financial information. Now, add the name of the CEO:

```
"Tootsie Roll" TR "Melvin Gordon"
```

You'll end up with a nice, small, targeted list of results, as shown in Figure 1-13.

Figure 1-13. Using a stock symbol to limit results

Stock symbols are great "fingerprints" for Internet research. They're consistent, they often appear along with the company name, and they're usually enough that they do a nice job of narrowing down your search results to relevant information.

There are also several words and phrases you can use to narrow down your search for company related information. Replacing *company* with the name of the company you're looking for, try these:

- For press releases: "*company* announced", "*company* announces", "*company* reported"

- For financial information: *company* "quarterly report", *company* SEC, *company* financials, *company* "p/e ratio"

- For location information: *company* parking airport location—doesn't always work but sometimes works amazingly well

Google Interface for Translators
Create a customized search form for language translation.

If you do a lot of the same kind of research every day, you might find that a customized search form makes your job easier. If you spend enough time on it, you may find that it's elaborate enough that other people may find it useful as well.

WWW Search Interfaces for Translators (*http://www.multilingual.ch*) offers three different tools for finding material of use to translators. Created by Tanya Harvey Ciampi from Switzerland, the tools are available in AltaVista and Google flavors. A user-defined query term is combined with a set of specific search criteria to narrow down the search to yield highly relevant results.

The first tool, shown in Figure 1-14, finds glossaries. The pull-down menu finds synonyms of the word "glossary" in various parts of a search result (title, URL, or anywhere). For example, imagine having to seek out numerous specialized computer dictionaries before finding one containing a definition of the term "firewall." This glossary search tool spares you the work by setting a clear condition: "Find a glossary that contains my term!"

If you're getting too many results for the glossary word you searched for, try searching for it in the title of the results instead; instead of searching for firewall, try searching for intitle:firewall.

The second tool, shown in Figure 1-15, finds "parallel texts," identical pages in two or more languages, useful for multilingual terminology research.

Finding pages in two or more languages is not easy; one of the few places to do it easily is with Canadian government pages, which are available in French and English. This tool provides several difference search combinations between SL (source language) and TL (target language).

Figure 1-14. WWW Search Interfaces for Translators glossary tool

The first set of searches actually works with AltaVista. It provides several language sets (English-German, English-Spanish, English-French, etc.) and gives you options for searching in each one (SL in URL, link to TL, page in TL country, etc.).

The second set of searches works in Google. Again, there are several language sets and several ways to search them (three different ways to search for the source language in the URL, keyword on the page in the target language, etc.). This tool also lets you in some cases specify the country for the target language (for example, French could be a target language in Canada, France, or Switzerland).

The third tool, shown in Figure 1-16, finds variations on the word "abbreviations" in the title or URL of a search result to find lists of abbreviations.

These search tools are available in several languages and do a lot of work for translators; in fact, they pull out so much information that you might think they'd require the Google API. But they don't; the query is generated on the client side and then passed to Google.

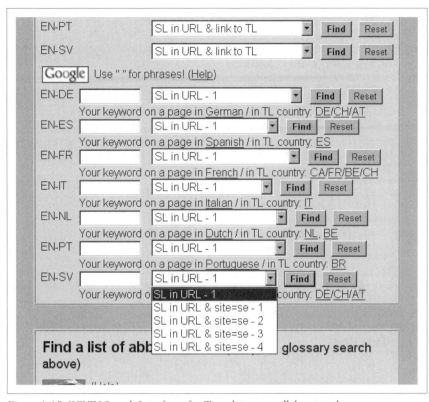

Figure 1-15. WWW Search Interfaces for Translators parallel text tool

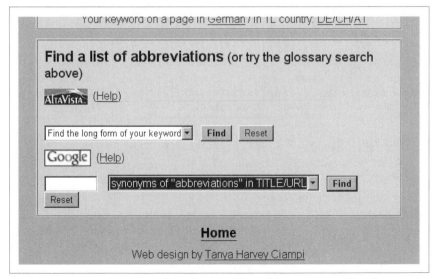

Figure 1-16. WWW Search Interfaces for Translators abbreviation search tool

It's accomplished quite elegantly. First, take a look at the source code for the form and see if you notice anything. Here's a hint: pay attention to the form element names. Notice that this hack integrates search synonyms without having to use the Google API or any kind of CGI. Everything's done via the form.

```
<!-- Initializing the form and opening a Google search
in a new window -->
<form method="GET" target="_blank"
action="http://www.google.com/search">

<!-- Taking the keyword search specified by the user -->
<input type="text" name="q" size="12">
<select name="q" size="1">

<!-- This is the cool stuff. These options provide several
different modifiers designed to catch glossaries
in Google. -->
<option selected value="intitle:dictionary OR intitle:glossary
OR intitle:lexicon OR intitle:definitions">
synonyms of "glossary" in TITLE - 1</option>
<option value="intitle:terminology OR intitle:vocabulary
OR intitle:definition OR intitle:jargon">
synonyms of "glossary" in TITLE - 2</option>
<option value="inurl:dictionary OR inurl:glossary OR inurl:lexicon
OR inurl:definitions">
synonyms of "glossary" in URL - 1</option>
<option value="inurl:terminology OR inurl:vocabulary
OR inurl:definition
OR inurl:jargon">synonyms of "glossary" in URL - 2</option>
<option value="inurl:dict OR inurl:gloss OR inurl:glos
OR inurl:dic">
abbreviations for "glossary" in URL</option>
<option value="dictionary OR glossary OR lexicon
OR definitions">synonyms of "glossary" ANYWHERE</option>
</select>

<!-- Ending the submission form. -->
<input type="submit" value="Find">
<input type="reset" value="Reset" name="B2">
</form>
```

The magic at work here is to be found in the following two lines:

```
<input type="text" name="q" size="12">
<select name="q" size="1">
```

Notice that both the query text field and glossary pop-up menu are named the same thing: name="q". When the form is submitted to Google, the values of both fields are effectively combined and treated as one query. So entering a query of dentistry and selecting synonyms of "glossary" in TITLE - 1 from the pop-up menu result in a combined Google query of:

```
dentistry intitle:dictionary OR intitle:glossary OR intitle:lexicon OR
intitle:definitions
```

This hack uses customized Google forms as an interface for translators, but you could use this idea for just about anything. Do you need to find legal statutes? Financial materials? Information from a particular vertical market? Anything that has its own specialized vocabulary that you can add to a form can be channeled into a hack like this. What kind of interface would you design?

Searching Article Archives
#20
Google serves as a handy searchable archive for back issues of online publications.

Not all sites have their own search engines, and even the ones that do are sometimes difficult to use. Complicated or incomplete search engines are more pain than gain when attempting to search through archives of published articles. If you follow a couple of rules, Google is handy for finding back issues of published resources.

The trick is to use a common phrase to find the information you're looking for. Let's use the New York Times as an example.

Articles from the NYT

Your first intuition when searching for previously published articles from NYTimes.com might be to simply use site:nytimes.com in your Google query. For example, if I wanted to find articles on George Bush, why not use:

```
"george bush" site:nytimes.com
```

This will indeed find you all articles mentioning George Bush published on NYTimes.com. What it won't find is all the articles produced by the New York Times but republished elsewhere.

> While doing research, keep credibility firmly in mind. If you're doing casual research, maybe you don't need to double-check a story to make sure it actually comes from the New York Times, but if you're researching a term paper, double-check the veracity of every article you find that isn't actually on the New York Times site.

What you actually want is a clear identifier, no matter the site of origin, that an article comes from the New York Times. Copyright disclaimers are perfect for the job. A New York Times copyright notice typically reads:

```
Copyright 2001 The New York Times Company
```

Of course, this would only find articles from 2001. A simple workaround is to replace the year with a Google full-word wildcard [Hack #13]:

```
Copyright * The New York Times Company
```

Let's try that George Bush search again, this time using the snippet of copyright disclaimer instead of the site: restriction:

```
"Copyright *  The New York Times Company" "George Bush"
```

At this writing, you get over three times as many results for this search as for the earlier attempt.

Magazine Articles

Copyright disclaimers are also useful for finding magazine articles. For example, Scientific American's typical copyright disclaimer looks like this:

```
Scientific American, Inc. All rights reserved.
```

(The date appears before the disclaimer, so I just dropped it to avoid having to bother with wildcards.)

Using that disclaimer as a quote-delimited phrase along with a search word—hologram, for example—yields the Google query:

```
hologram "Scientific American, Inc. All rights reserved."
```

At this writing, you'll get one result, which seems like a small number for a general query like hologram. When you get fewer results than you'd expect, fall back on using the site: syntax to go back to the originating site itself.

```
hologram site:sciam.com
```

In this example, you'll find several results that you can grab from Google's cache but are no longer available on the Scientific American site.

Most publications that I've come across have some kind of common text string that you can use when searching Google for its archives. Usually it's a copyright disclaimer and most often it's at the bottom of a page. Use Google to search for that string and whatever query words you're interested in, and if that doesn't work, fall back on searching for the query string and domain name.

Finding Directories of Information
Use Google to find directories, link lists, and other collections of information.

Sometimes you're more interested in large information collections than scouring for specific bits and bobs. Using Google, there are a couple of different ways of finding directories, link lists [Hack #44], and other information

---

collections. The first way makes use of Google's full-word wildcards [Hack #13] and the intitle: [in "The Special Syntaxes"] syntax. The second is judicious use of particular keywords.

Title Tags and Wildcards

Pick something you'd like to find collections of information about. We'll use "trees" as our example. The first thing we'll look for is any page with the words "directory" and "trees" in its title. In fact, we'll build in a little buffering for words that might appear between the two using a couple of full-word wildcards [Hack #13] (* characters). The resultant query looks something like this:

    intitle:"directory * * trees"

This query will find "directories of evergreen trees," "South African trees," and of course "directories containing simply trees."

What if you wanted to take things up a notch, taxonomically speaking, and find directories of botanical information? You'd use a combination of intitle: and keywords like so:

    botany intitle:"directory of"

And you'd get over 6,600 results. Changing the tenor of the information might be a matter of restricting results to those coming from academic institutions. Appending an "edu" site specification brings you to:

    botany intitle:"directory of" site:edu

This gets you around 120 results, a mixture of resource directories and, unsurprisingly, directories of university professors.

Mixing these syntaxes works rather well when you're searching for something that might also be an offline print resource. For example:

    cars intitle:"encyclopedia of"

This query pulls in results from Amazon and other sites selling car encyclopedias. Filter out some of the more obvious book finds by tweaking the query slightly:

    cars intitle:"encyclopedia of" -site:amazon.com
    -inurl:book -inurl:products

The query specifies that search results should not come from Amazon.com, should not have the word "book" in the URL, or the word "products," which eliminates a fair amount of online stores. Play with this query by changing the word "cars" to whatever you'd like for some interesting finds.

(Of course there are lots of sites selling books online, but when it comes to injecting "noise" into results when you're trying to find online resources, research-oriented information, Amazon is the biggest offender. If you're actually looking for books, try `+site:amazon.com` instead.)

If mixing syntaxes doesn't do the trick for the resources you want, there are some clever keyword combinations that might just do the trick.

Finding Searchable Subject Indexes with Google

There are a few major searchable subject indexes and myriad minor ones that deal with a particular topic or idea. You can find the smaller subject indexes by customizing a few generic searches. `"what's new" "what's cool" directory`, while gleaning a a few false results, is a great way of finding searchable subject indexes. `directory "gossamer threads" new` is an interesting one. Gossamer Threads is the creator of a popular link directory program. This is a good way to find searchable subject indexes without too many false hits. `directory "what's new" categories cool` doesn't work particularly well, because the word "directory" is not a very reliable search term; but you will pull in some things with this query that you might otherwise miss.

Let's put a few of these into practice:

```
"what's new" "what's cool" directory phylum
"what's new" "what's cool" directory carburetor
"what's new" "what's cool" directory "investigative journalism"
"what's new" directory categories gardening
directory "gossamer threads" new sailboats
directory "what's new" categories cool "basset hounds"
```

The real trick is to use a more general word, but make it unique enough that it applies mostly to your topic and not to many other topics.

Take acupuncture, for instance. Start narrowing it down by topic: what kind of acupuncture? For people or animals? If for people, what kind of conditions are being treated? If for animals, what kind of animals? Maybe you should be searching for `"cat acupuncture"` or maybe you should be searching for `acupuncture arthritis`. If this first round doesn't narrow down search results enough for you, keep going. Are you looking for education or treatment? You can skew results one way or the other by using the `site:` syntax. So maybe you want `"cat acupuncture" site:com` or `arthritis acupuncture site:edu`. Just by taking a few steps to narrow things down, you can get a reasonable number of search results focused around your topic.

HACK
#22   Finding Technical Definitions

Overwhelmed with "geek speak"? Google can help you find the answers.

Specialized vocabularies remain, for the most part, fairly static—words don't suddenly change their meaning all that often. Not so with technical and computer-related jargon. It seems like every 12 seconds someone comes up with a new buzzword or term relating to computers or the Internet, and then 12 minutes later it becomes obsolete or means something completely different—often more than one thing at a time. Maybe it's not that bad. It just feels that way.

Google can help you in two ways; by helping you look up words and by helping you figure out what words you don't know that you need to know.

Technology Terminology

You've just got out of the conference room and so many new words were slung at you your head is buzzing. The problem at this point is that you don't know if you've been hearing slang, hardware/software specific terminology, or general terminology. How do you determine which is which?

As with any new vocabulary, you're going to have to use contextual clues. In what part of the conversation was the term used? Was it used most often in relation to something? Did only one person use the term? It might just be slang [Hack #4]. Is it written down anywhere? Try to get all the information about it that you can. If there is no information about it available—your boss stuck her head in your cubicle and said, "We're thinking of spending $20 million on a project using X. What do you think?"—treat it as general terminology.

Google Glossary

Before you start your search at Google, check and see if Google Labs [Hack #35] is still offering the Google Glossary (*http://labs.google.com/glossary/*). Google Glossary provides definitions of terms both technical and nontechnical. If that didn't turn up anything useful, move on to Google.

Researching Terminology with Google

First things first: for heaven's sake, please don't just plug the abbreviation into the query box! For example, searching for XSLT will net you 900,000 results. While combing through the sites Google turns up may eventually lead you to a definition, there's simply more to life than that. Instead, add "stands +for" to the query if it's an abbreviation or acronym. "XSLT stands +for" returns around 29 results, and the very first is a tutorial glossary. If you're still getting too many results ("XML stands +for" gives you almost 1,000 results) try adding beginners or newbie to the query. "XML stands +for" beginners brings in 35 results, the first being "XML for beginners."

If you're still not getting the results you want, try "What is X?" or "X +is short +for" or X beginners FAQ, where X is the acronym or term. These should be regarded as second-tier methods, because most sites don't tend to use phrases like "What is X?" on their pages, "X is short for" is uncommon language usage, and X might be so new (or so obscure) that it doesn't yet have an FAQ entry. Then again, your mileage may vary and it's worth a shot; there's a lot of terminology out there.

If you have hardware- or software-specific terminology—as opposed to hardware- or software-related—try the word or phrase along with anything you might know about its usage. For example, DynaLoader is software-specific terminology; it's a Perl module. That much known, simply give the two words a spin:

```
DynaLoader Perl
```

If the results you're finding are too advanced, assuming you already know what a DynaLoader is, start playing with the words beginners, newbie, and the like to bring you closer to information for beginners:

```
DynaLoader Perl Beginners
```

If you still can't find the word in Google, there are a few possible causes: perhaps it's slang specific to your area, your coworkers are playing with your mind, you heard it wrong (or there was a typo on the printout you got), or it's very, very new.

Where to Go When It's Not on Google

Despite your best efforts, you're not finding good explanations of the terminology on Google. There are a few other sites that might have what you're looking for.

Whatis (http://whatis.techtarget.com)
> A searchable subject index of computer terminology, from software to telecom. This is especially useful if you're got a hardware- or software-specific word, because the definitions are divided up into categories. You can also browse alphabetically. Annotations are good and are often cross-indexed.

Webopedia (http://www.pcwebopaedia.com/)
> Searchable by keyword or browseable by category. Also has a list of the newest entries on the front page so you can check for new words.

Netlingo (http://www.netlingo.com/framesindex.html)
> This is more Internet-oriented. This site shows up with a frame on the left containing the words, with the definitions on the right. It includes lots of cross-referencing and really old slang.

Tech Encyclopedia (http://www.techweb.com/encyclopedia/)
> Features definitions and information on over 20,000 words. Top 10 terms searched for are listed so you can see if everyone else is as confused as you are. Though entries had before-the-listing and after-the-listing lists of words, I saw only moderate cross-referencing.

Geek terminology proliferates almost as quickly as web pages. Don't worry too much about deliberately keeping up—it's just about impossible. Instead, use Google as a "ready reference" resource for definitions.

See Also

- Specialized Vocabularies: Slang and Terminology [Hack #4]
- Google Labs [Hack #35]

 ## HACK #23 Finding Weblog Commentary
Building queries to search only recent commentary appearing in weblogs.

Time was when you needed to find current commentary, you didn't turn to a full-text search engine like Google. You searched Usenet, combed mailing lists, or searched through current news sites like CNN.com and hoped for the best.

But as search engines have evolved, they've been able to index pages more quickly than once every few weeks. In fact, Google tunes its engine to more readily index sites with a high information churn rate. At the same time, a phenomenon called the weblog (*http://www.oreilly.com/catalog/essblogging/*) has arisen, an online site keeps a running commentary and associated links, updated daily—and indeed, even more often in many cases. Google indexes many of these sites on an accelerated schedule. If you know how to find them, you can build a query that searches just these sites for recent commentary.

Finding weblogs. When weblogs first appeared on the Internet, they were generally updated manually or by using homemade programs. Thus, there were no standard words you could add to a search engine to find them. Now, however, many weblogs are created using either specialized software packages (like Movable Type, *http://www.movabletype.org/*, or Radio Userland, *http://radio.userland.com/*) or as web services (like Blogger, *http://www.blogger.com/*). These programs and services are more easily found online with some clever use of special syntaxes [in "The Special Syntaxes"] or magic words.

For hosted weblogs, the site: syntax makes things easy. Blogger weblogs hosted at blog*spot (*http://www.blogspot.com/*) can be found using site: blogspot.com. Even though Radio Userland is a software program able to post its weblogs to any web server, you can find the majority of Radio User-land weblogs at the Radio Userland community server (*http://radio.weblogs.com/*) using `site:radio.weblogs.com`.

Finding weblogs powered by weblog software and hosted elsewhere is more problematic; Movable Type weblogs, for example, can be found all over the Internet. However, most of them sport a "powered by movable type" link of some sort; searching for the phrase `"powered by movable type"` will, therefore, find many of them.

It comes down to magic words typically found on weblog pages, shout-outs, if you will, to the software or hosting sites. The following is a list of some of these packages and services and the magic words used to find them in Google:

Blogger
> `"powered by blogger"` or `site:blogspot.com`

Blosxom
> `"powered by blosxom"`

Greymatter
> `"powered by greymatter"`

Geeklog
> `"powered by geeklog"`

Manila
> `"a manila site"` or `site:editthispage.com`

Pitas (a service)
> `site:pitas.com`

pMachine
> `"powered by pmachine"`

uJournal (a service)
> `site:ujournal.org`

LiveJournal (a service)
> `site:livejournal.com`

Radio Userland
> `intitle:"radio weblog"` or `site:radio.weblogs.com`

Using These "Magic Words"

Because you can't have more than 10 words in a Google query, there's no way to build a query that includes every conceivable weblog's magic words. It's best to experiment with the various words, and see which weblogs have the materials you're interested in.

First of all, realize that weblogs are usually informal commentary and you'll have to keep an eye out for misspelled words, names, etc. Generally, it's better to search by event than by name, if possible. For example, if you were looking for commentary on a potential strike, the phrase "baseball strike" would be a better search, initially, than a search for the name of the Commissioner of Major League Baseball, Bud Selig.

You can also try to search for a word or phrase relevant to the event. For example, for a baseball strike you could try searching for "baseball strike" "red sox" (or "baseball strike" bosox)—if you're searching for information on a wildfire and wondering if anyone had been arrested for arson, try wildfire arrested and if that doesn't work, wildfire arrested arson . (Why not search for arson to begin with? Because it's not certain that a weblog commentator would use the word "arson." Instead, he might just refer to someone being arrested for setting the fire. "Arrested" in this case is a more certain word than "arson.")

The Google Toolbar
If you use Internet Explorer, Google's got a toolbar for you.

Unlike many search engines, Google never became a "portal"; that is, it did not try to provide all information to all people as well as put ads on every square inch of its web site.

Because of that, it was never important that Google get people to its front page; all its ads are on its pages of search results. So it made sense that Google was able to offer the Google Toolbar™.

The Google Toolbar is an add-on, currently only available for Internet Explorer, that offers all the functionality of the Google site without having to visit the site itself. In fact, the Google Toolbar offers more functionality; it's the only way you can see exactly what a site's PageRank™ is.

PageRank is Google's assessment of just how popular a page is. The higher the PageRank, the higher it'll appear in Google search results.

You can download the Google Toolbar for free at *http://toolbar.google.com/*. You will need Internet Explorer with ActiveX functions enabled to download and install the toolbar.

Once installed, the Google Toolbar actively keeps track of what you're viewing and asks Google (by passing on the URL) for anything it knows about the page, including PageRank and categorization. Some people might be concerned that Google could misuse the information being sent, so Google offers the option of installing the toolbar without the PageRank features, which protects your privacy. If you don't know which you want to do, go ahead and choose the complete download. You can always disable the PageRank and Category tools later using the toolbar options. The installed toolbar is shown in Figure 1-17.

Figure 1-17. The Google Toolbar

Using the toolbar for web search is simple: enter some text in the query box and hit enter. You'll see that you'll get a page of Google results and that some of the tools on the toolbar will light up. You'll be able to retrieve information about the returned page, move up one directory from the current page (in this case, it'd move you to the Google home page) and use the highlight tool to highlight all occurrences of your search term in the document.

The toolbar works just as well when you're surfing using Internet Explorer's URL box. The Page Info button will give you the option of seeing a cached version of the page you're viewing (assuming Google has a cached version in stock) as well as showing backward links to the page, similar pages, and the opportunity to translate the page into English if it isn't already in English. Generally speaking, the more popular a page is, the more likely it is to have backward links and similar pages.

But where are all the other offerings, such as the image search, the catalog search, and the Google Groups search? They're available, but the default install of the Google Toolbar turns them off. Click on the Google logo on the left side of the toolbar and choose Toolbar Options.

You'll see that the options page allows you to add several more search buttons, including the I'm Feeling Lucky button (that'll take you directly to Google's first search result), the image search button, the Google Groups search button, and the Google Directory search button. If you feel like expressing your opinion, you can also activate the voting buttons; when you visit a page, you can click on the happy face or sad face button to express your opinion of the page.

If you're feeling adventurous, use the "Experimental Features" link at the bottom of the screen. This option will let you set up a Combined Search button. The Combined Search button looks like the Search web button already on the toolbar, with a small triangle next to it. Click on the triangle and you'll get a drop-down menu that lets you search several Google properties, including images, Usenet, dictionary, stock quotes, and several of the specialty searches such as Linux, Apple Macintosh, and Microsoft.

> If you don't have Internet Explorer, you can get close with the Mozilla Toolbar [Hack #25] for the Mozilla browser or a newer version of Netscape Navigator (Version 7). If you don't use Mozilla, IE, or a Mozilla-based browser, try the browser-independent Quick Search Toolbar [Hack #26].

 ## HACK #25 The Mozilla Google Toolbar

Googlebar for Mozilla-based browsers emulates many of the features of the official Google Toolbar.

The official Google Toolbar [Hack #24] runs only on Internet Explorer for Windows, making it unavailable to those who use other operating systems or prefer other browsers such as Mozilla, Netscape, and Opera.

While still in its early stage, a team at Mozdev.org (*http://www.mozdev.org/*) has created a third-party toolbar, Googlebar (*http://googlebar.mozdev.org/*), that brings much of the functionality of the Google Toolbar to the Mozilla and Netscape browsers. The only notable missing feature is the PageRank [Hack #95] indicator.

> Make sure you have software installation enabled in your preferences before installing the Googlebar or this won't work.) Go to Preferences → Advanced → Software Installation, and make sure the box is checked.

The latest Googlebar is available for download from *http://googlebar. mozdev.org/installation.html*. Installation is a snap, performed from right inside Mozilla/Netscape itself. Visit the download URL and choose the

"Install Version" link. You'll be prompted to install the software, which will take only a moment. After it's been installed you'll need to restart your browser.

If you've used the "official" Google Toolbar, the first thing you'll notice is that Googlebar looks almost exactly like it.

The default toolbar gives you the options to search all of Google, search a single domain, use the I'm Feeling Lucky feature, or search Google Groups [Hack #30] or the Google Directory [Hack #29]. Filling out the query box and hitting enter will give you search results in the same window; however, filling out the box and using Ctrl-Enter opens the search result in a new Mozilla tab—handy for when you don't want to abandon your current surfing to do a search. You'll also notice when you enter a query term in the box that it appears on the toolbar as a button; click that button to find the term on the web page you're currently viewing.

Besides the major Google searches, you can also invoke several special searches, including Google Images, Google Catalogs, and Google's Uncle-Sam search. There's a separate button for Google's computer-related special searches (including BSD and Linux). You can also get information about a page you're viewing (including a cached version, if available, similar pages, links to the page, and an English translation if necessary.)

Right-clicking on the toolbar gives you the option to perform a Google search on any word or words you may highlight on the current web page. If you click the Googlebar logo on the left of the bar, you'll find links to several Google properties, including Google Images [Hack #31] and the Google Directory [Hack #29]. You'll also have a chance here to set up a keyboard shortcut to take advantage of the Googlebar without your mouse.

At the time of this writing, the Googlebar is in the early stages, but rather stable, nonetheless. If you use Mozilla or Netscape and spend any time at Google properties, it's a must-have.

HACK #26   The Quick Search Toolbar

Why do you have to even launch your browser to search Google? This tool lets you search Google and over 100 other search engines from your Windows status bar.

Why should you have to launch a browser to get access to Google's over 2 billion pages' worth of information? You don't. If you want to go about as far beyond the browser as you can go without actually leaving the computer, check out Dave's Quick Search Deskbar (*http://notesbydave.com/toolbar/doc.htm*), shown in Figure 1-18.

This is a quick little download, all of 322K. You'll need to have Windows 95 or better and IE 5.5 or later to use it. Once you've downloaded and installed it, right-click your mouse on the Windows taskbar at the bottom of your screen and choose Toolbars → Add Quick Search.

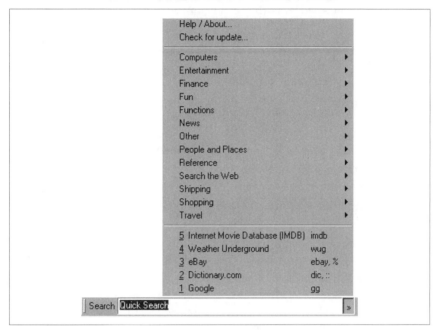

Figure 1-18. Dave's Quick Search Deskbar

Basic Browser Use

The Quick Search tool is a veritable Swiss Army knife of functions, but we'll start with the basics; enter a query in the box and hit the enter key on your keyboard. Your default browser will pop up the Google result page.

The complicated stuff isn't that much more complicated. To go directly to the first hit of a result (using Google's I'm Feeling Lucky feature) add an exclamation point to your search:

    "washington post"!

Make sure the exclamation point is on the outside of a phrase (i.e., isn't contained within the quotes) or it won't work. You can, of course, add the exclamation point to the end of a multiple word query:

    yahoo what's new!

Triggers and Switches

The Quick Search Deskbar is powered by a few triggers and lots of switches. The triggers specify which facet of Google is to be searched, and the switches specify either which facet should be searched or the kind of results that should be returned. And they can be mixed and matched.

The triggers. Triggers are characters placed before your query, altering the domains they search and the sorts of queries they construct.

> Constructs a Google Advanced Search [in "Advanced Search"] based on your entered query information. Remember, though, that Google's advanced search page can't handle overly complex queries. If you try to send a complicated query the likes of > fiscal responsibility -site:com -site:org, it won't be accurately represented in the resulting advanced search page.

> > cholesterol drugs +site:edu

?? Searches the Google Directory [Hack #29].

> ?? "George Bush"

, Searches Google Groups [Hack #30]. You can use the Groups-specific special syntaxes with this trigger.

> , group:sci.med* dermatology</pre

The switches. Switches are characters added on to the end of your query, altering the query in various ways.

/ifl
> Invokes the equivalent of Google's I'm Feeling Lucky button, taking you directly to the highest ranked Google result for your query. A shortcut is to simply postfix your query with a ! (exclamation point).

> > yahoo what's new /ifl yahoo what's new!

/advanced
> Works like the Advanced Search trigger above.

/groups
> Works like the Google Groups trigger above.

/directory
> Works like the Google Directory trigger above.

<code>/images
> Searches Google Images. You can add the Google Images special syntaxes for this search.

> > intitle:cat /images

/news
> Restrict searches to Google News. You can use the Google News spe-
> cial syntaxes with this search.
>
>   intitle:"Tony Blair" /news

/since:*days*
> Searches for pages indexed *days* ago. For example, for web sites about
> Jimmy Carter indexed in the last year, you'd use "Jimmy Carter" /
> since:365. There are some quick shortcuts for this as well: /since:t
> finds things indexed today, /since:y means yesterday, /since:w is the
> last seven days, and /since:m ("m" as in month) is the last 30 days.

/cache
> Returns the cached version of the URL specified or an error, if the page
> is not in Google's cache.
>
>   http://www.oreilly.com /cache

/related
> Finds pages Google thinks are most related to the specified URL. If
> nothing's related, however unlikely, you'll get an error message.
>
>   http://www.researchbuzz.com /related

/link
> Finds pages that link to the specified URL.
>
>   http://www.google.com /link

Location switches
> Allow you to specify that the results you get are from local (or not local,
> if you prefer) versions of Google.

/canada *(Canada)*
/deutschland *(Germany)*
/france *(France)*
/italia *(Italy)*
/uk *(United Kingdom)*
/language:*xx*
> Allow you to change the Google web interface to whatever language you
> prefer, specified as a language code in place of *xx*. For a complete list of
> available languages, visit the Google Language Tools (*http://www.
> google.com/language_tools*) page. For example, to query Google in
> Malay, you'd add /language:ms to your query.
>
>   python /language:ms

Navigating Your Searches

With all these switches, you might imagine that you could do a lot of experimenting with Google searches. And you'd be right!

The Search tool has a built-in way to go over all the different searches you've done by clicking in the search box and repeatedly hitting the down arrow on your keyboard.

And the Rest

I've spent this hack discussing Dave's Quick Search Taskbar Toolbar Deskbar in the context of Google, because that's what this book is all about. But the tool does a lot more than Google. Click on the >> next to the text box. You'll get a list of search tools in several categories, from Computers to Reference to Shopping. Once you're finished seeing how cool this tool is when used with Google, check it out with over a hundred other different search interfaces.

See Also

- The Google Toolbar [Hack #24]
- The Mozilla Google Toolbar [Hack #25]
- Huevos (*http://ranchero.com/software/huevos/*), a standalone search widget for Mac OS X

<h2>H A C K
#27 GAPIS</h2>

A standalone Google search application for Windows.

A lot of the hacks in this book have been either browser-based or somehow integrated into other applications. There haven't been too many standalone applications built to take advantage of Google's search capacity. GAPIS (Google API Searching in an Application) is a small standalone application that performs Google searches on its own (and it can also be set to browser searching).

GAPIS (*http://www.searchenginelab.com/common/products/gapis/*) is available for free download either as an application executable, complete with uninstaller, or as an plain executable file with no uninstaller. GAPIS runs only under Windows 95 or later. Because it uses the Google Web API, you'll need your own Google API developer's key to run your queries.

The GAPIS interface is very simple, providing a basic window for searching and another screen for options.

There's a field to enter your developer's key alongside the query box. A pulldown box allows you to access previous queries. You have two viewing options: regular mode, which provides information about search results that you'd usually see from a Google search, and spreadsheet mode, which provides information in a table format like you'd see in a spreadsheet. Figure 1-19 illustrates the GAPIS interface.

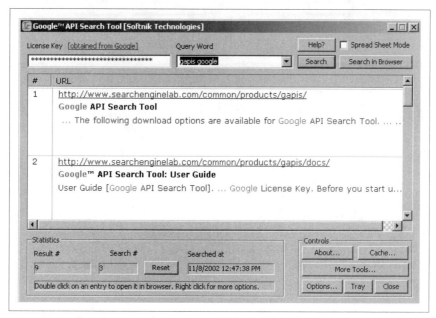

Figure 1-19. The GAPIS interface

Options

The Options screen allows you to set several search parameters, including SafeSearch filtering, filtering similar results, and the maximum number of results returned. (GAPIS will return up to 30 results.) Figure 1-20 shows the Options page.

Searching

Once you run a search, GAPIS will return the list of results on the main page in the format you specify (regular or spreadsheet mode, shown in Figure 1-21).

To open an entry in your web browser, double-click on it. To go directly to a web search in the browser (if you want more than 30 results, for example), click on the Search In Browser button.

If you need to create a set of your favorite searches, with more of an eye toward an overview of the results instead of a deep browsing, GAPIS is a quick and handy tool.

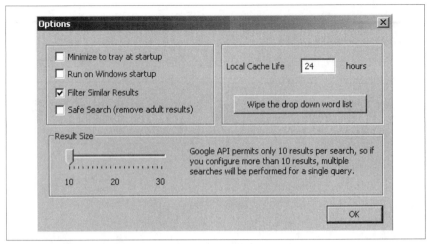

Figure 1-20. The GAPIS Options page

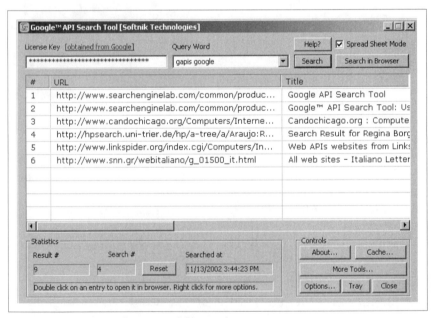

Figure 1-21. GAPIS results in spreadsheet mode

Googling with Bookmarklets
#28

Create interactive bookmarklets to perform Google functions from the comfort of your own browser.

You probably know what bookmarks are. But what are bookmarklets? Bookmarklets are like bookmarks but with an extra bit of JavaScript magic added. This makes them more interactive then regular bookmarks; they can perform small functions like opening a window, grabbing highlighted text from a web page, or submitting a query to a search engine. There are several bookmarklets that allow you to perform useful Google functions right from the comfort of your own browser.

> If you're using Internet Explorer for Windows, you're in gravy: all these bookmarklets will most likely work as advertised. But if you're using a less-appreciated browser (such as Opera) or operating system (such as Mac OS X), pay attention to the bookmarklet requirements and instructions; there may be special magic needed to get a particular bookmark working, or indeed, you may not be able to use the bookmarklet at all.

Before you try any other site, try Google's Browser Buttons (read: bookmarklets). Google Search queries Google for any text you've highlighted on the current web page. Google Scout performs a related: [in "The Special Syntaxes"] search on the current web page.

Google's bookmarklets are designed for the Internet Explorer browser.

Google Translate!
(http://www.microcontentnews.com/resources/translator.htm)
> Puts Google's translation [Hack #2] tools into a bookmarklet, enabling one-button translation of the current web page.

Google Jump
(http://www.angelfire.com/dc/dcbookmarkletlab/Bookmarklets/s cript002.html)
> Prompts you for search terms, performs a Google search, and takes you straight to the top hit thanks to the magic of Google's I'm Feeling Lucky [in "Google Basics"] function.

The Dooyoo Bookmarklets
(http://dooyoo-uk.tripod.com/bookmarklets2.html) collection
> Features several bookmarklets for use with different search engines—two for Google. Similar to Google's Browser Buttons, one finds highlighted text and the other finds related pages.

Joe Maller's Translation Bookmarkets
(http://www.joemaller.com/translation_bookmarklets.shtml)

>   Translate the current page into the specified language via Google or AltaVista.

Bookmarklets for Opera
(http://www.philburns.com/bookmarklets.html)

>   Includes a Google translation bookmarklet, a Google bookmarklet that restricts searches to the current domain, and a bookmarklet that searches Google Groups [Hack #30]. As you might imagine, these bookmarklets were created for use with the Opera browser.

GoogleIt!
(http://www.code9.com/googleit.html)

>   Another bookmarklet that searches Google for any text you highlight on the current web page.

Google Special Services and Collections

Hacks #29–35

Google is famous as a web search engine, but it goes far beyond that. For the last couple of years, Google has been quietly adding components that search a variety of data collections. Here's an overview of what's available.

> Each data collection has its own unique special syntaxes, discussed in detail in specific hacks for specific collections.

Google's Current Offerings

Google's web search (*http://www.google.com/*) covers over 3 billion pages. In addition to HTML pages, Google's web search also indexes PDF, Postscript, Microsoft Word, Microsoft Excel, Microsoft Powerpoint, and Rich Text Format (RTF). Google's web search also offers some syntaxes that find specific information, like stock quotes and phone numbers, but we'll save that for later in the book.

Google Directory **[Hack #29]**

The Google Directory (*http://directory.google.com/*) is a searchable subject index based on The Open Directory Project (*http://www.dmoz.org*). As it indexes sites (not pages), it's much smaller than the web search but better for general searches. Google has applied its popularity algorithm to the listings so that more popular sites rise to the top.

Google Groups **[Hack #30]**

Usenet is a worldwide network of discussion groups. Google Groups (*http://groups.google.com/*) has archived Usenet's discussions back 20 years in some places, providing an archive that offers over 700 million messages.

Google Images [Hack #31]

Google Images (*http://images.google.com/*) offers an archive of over 330 million images culled from sites all over the web. Images range from icon sized to wallpaper sized, with a variety of search engines for homing in on the closest one.

Google News [Hack #32]

Google News (*http://news.google.com/*) is still in beta at the time of this writing. It checks over 4,000 sources for news and updates the database once an hour. Google News is different from most other search engines in that it "clusters" headlines on its front page into similar topics.

Google Catalogs [Hack #33]

Searching print mail-order catalogs probably isn't the first thing that pops into your mind when you think of Google, but you can do it here. Google Catalogs (*http://catalogs.google.com/*) has digitized and made available catalogs in a dozen different categories. If you don't see your favorite catalog here, you can submit it for possible consideration.

Froogle [Hack #34]

Google Catalogs is a great way to do offline shopping, especially if you like to browse with nothing more than a couple of keywords. However, if you're the modern type who insists on doing all your shopping online, you'll want to check out Froogle (*http://froogle.google.com/*). Froogle, a combination of the words "Google" and "frugal," is a searchable shopping index that looks a lot like the Google Directory with a focus on getting you right to an online point of purchase for the item you're interested in. The service was launched in December 2002 and, at the time of this writing, is still in beta.

Google Labs [Hack #35]

There's no telling what you'll find at Google Labs (*http://labs.google.com/*); it's where Google parks their works-in-progress and lets the general public play with 'em. At the time of this writing, you'll find a way to search Google via phone, a glossary search, keyboard navigation, and a search that allows you to create a set of similar words from a few search results.

Google Answers

Google's search engine is all about clever computing, but Google Answers (*http://answers.google.com/*) is all about smart folks. Independent Google Answers answer questions for a price set by the person asking the questions. Sources used are restricted to open web collections, and Google is building a database of the answers. If the service keeps up, this offering will be very large and very cool in a year or so.

Topic-Specific Search

Google's Topic-Specific Search (*http://www.google.com/advanced_search*) provides some narrowed views of its index along various lines and topics, including:

- UncleSam (*http://www.google.com/unclesam*) for U.S. government sites
- Linux (*http://www.google.com/linux*), BSD Unix (*http://www.google.com/bsd*), Apple Macintosh (*http://www.google.com/mac*), and Microsoft (*http://www.google.com/microsoft.html*) computer operating system-specific collections
- Universities (*http://www.google.com/options/universities.html*), from Abilene Christian to York University

Google of the Future—Google Shopping?

Google's a private company, and as such the public isn't privy to their financial status. But it's been said they're profitable now, even though they haven't delved too deeply into that holy grail of online companies: e-commerce.

Considering Google's unique way of doing things, it should come as no surprise that their way of getting into shopping online was just as contrary as their other many innovations. Instead of building a mall or online catalogs as many other search engines have attempted, Google took their search technology and used it to make a excellent search engine of products from offline, paper catalogs. And in some ways, it's much more effective than online catalogs. It's easier to read the paper catalogs, something you're used to doing if you have a physical mailbox. And if you're on a broadband connection, you can flip through them quickly. Google gathered enough of them together that you can find a wide range of products easily.

Though Google offers many specialty searches, I'm focusing on this one to make a point: Google seems to take a sideways approach to search innovation (and that's not meant as pejorative). They might decide to join in when other search engines are offering certain features, but always with their own particular twist on the offering. Seeing how they handled the idea of online shopping with the Google Catalogs collection might give you a glimpse into Google's future.

Google in the 2010s

Speaking of the future, you've already gotten a peek at the sorts of things they're exploring in Google Labs. Google Labs is a playground for Google engineers to experiment with new ideas and new technology. It was also one of the most difficult things to write up in the book, because it's likely that it'll change between now and the time you hold this book in your hands.

But pay attention to what's there. Check out the voice search and see how large a list you can generate with the Google Sets. These ideas might be integrated into search syntaxes or specialty searches later on, and if you can come up with some interesting ways of using them now, you're that much ahead of the search engine game.

Google's already got plenty of search collection offerings, and they're not going to get anything but more extensive! In the meantime, browse through this section for an introduction to what Google has now.

HACK
#29   Google Directory

Google has a searchable subject index in addition to its 2 billion page web search.

Google's web search indexes over 2 billion pages, which means that it isn't suitable for all searches. When you've got a search that you can't narrow down, like if you're looking for information on a person about whom you know nothing, 2 billion pages will get very frustrating very quickly.

But you don't have to limit your searches to the web search. Google also has a searchable subject index, the Google Directory, at *http://directory.google. com*. Instead of indexing the entirety of billions of pages, the directory describes sites instead, indexing about 1.5 million URLs. This makes it a much better search for general topics.

Does Google spend time building a searchable subject index in addition to a full-text index? No. Google bases its directory on the Open Directory Project data at *http://dmoz.org/*. The collection of URLs at the Open Directory Project is gathered and maintained by a group of volunteers, but Google does add some of its own Googlish magic to it.

As you can see, the front of the site is organized into several topics. To find what you're looking for, you can either do a keyword search, or "drill down" through the hierarchies of subjects.

Beside most of the listings, you'll see a green bar. The green bar is an approximate indicator of the site's PageRank in the Google search engine. (Not every listing in the Google Directory has a corresponding PageRank in the Google web index.) Web sites are listed in the default order of Google PageRank, but you also have the option to list them in alphabetical order.

One thing you'll notice about the Google Directory is how the annotations and other information varies between the categories. That's because the information in the directory is maintained by a small army of volunteers (about 20,000) who are each responsible for one or more categories. For the most part, annotation is pretty good. Figure 2-1 shows the Google Directory.

Figure 2-1. The Google Directory

Searching the Google Directory

The Google Directory does not have the various complicated special syntaxes for searching that the web search does. That's because this is a far smaller collection of URLs, ideal for more general searching. However, there are a couple of special syntaxes you should know about.

`intitle:`
Just like the Google web special syntax, `intitle:` restricts the query word search to the title of a page.

`inurl:`
Restricts the query word search to the URL of a page.

When you're searching on Google's web index, your overwhelming concern is probably how to get your list of search results to something manageable. With that in mind, you might start by coming up with the narrowest search possible.

That's a reasonable strategy for the web index, but because you have a narrower pool of sites in the Google Directory, you want to start more general with your Google Directory search.

For example, say you were looking for information on author P. G. Wode-house. A simple search on P. G. Wodehouse in Google's web index will get you over 25,000 results, possibly compelling you to immediately narrow down your search. But doing the same search in the Google Directory returns only 96 results. You might consider that a manageable number of results, or you might want to carefully start narrowing down your result further.

The Directory is also good for searching for events. A Google web search for "Korean War" will find you literally hundreds of thousands of results, while searching the Google Directory will find you just over 1,200. This is a case where you will probably need to narrow down your search. Use general words indicating what kind of information you want—timeline, for example, or archives, or lesson plans. Don't narrow down your search with names or locations—that's not the best way to use the Google Directory.

The Google Directory and the Google API

Unfortunately the Google Directory is not covered by the Google API.

HACK
#30   Google Groups

You can search Usenet newsgroups, both recent and from times past, through Google Groups.

Usenet Groups, text-based discussion groups covering literally hundreds of thousands of topics, have been around since long before the World Wide Web. And now they're available for search and perusal as Google Groups (*http://groups.google.com/*). Its search interface is rather different from the Google web search, as all messages are divided into groups, and the groups themselves are divided into topics called hierarchies.

The Google Groups archive begins in 1981 and covers up to the present day. Over 200 million messages are archived. As you might imagine, that's a pretty big archive, covering literally decades of discussion. Stuck in an ancient computer game? Need help with that sewing machine you bought in 1982? You might be able to find the answers here.

Google Groups also allows you to participate in Usenet discussions, handy because not all ISPs provide access to Usenet these days (and even those that do tend to limit the number of newsgroups they carry). See the Google Groups posting FAQ (*http://groups.google.com/googlegroups/posting_faq.html*) for instructions on how to post to a newsgroup. You'll have to start with locating the group to which you want to post, and that means using the hierarchy.

Ten Seconds of Hierarchy Funk

There are regional and smaller hiearchies, but the main ones are: *alt*, *biz*, *comp*, *humanities*, *misc*, *news*, *rec*, *sci*, *soc*, and *talk*. Most web groups are created through a voting process and are put under the hiearchy that's most applicable to the topic.

Browsing Groups

From the main Google Groups page, you can browse through the list of groups by picking a hiearchy from the front page. You'll see that there are subtopics, sub-subtopics, sub-sub-subtopics, and—well, you get the picture. For example, in the *comp* (computers) hierarchy you'll find the subtopic *comp.sys*, or computer systems. Beneath that lie 75 groups and subtopics, including *comp.sys.mac*, a branch of the hierarchy devoted to the Macintosh computer system. There are 24 Mac subtopics, one of which is *comp.sys.mac.hardware*, which has, in turn, three groups beneath it. Once you've drilled down to the most specific group applicable to your interests, Google Groups presents the postings themselves, sorted in reverse chronological order.

This strategy works fine when you want to read a slow (of very little traffic) or moderated group, but when you want to read a busy, free-for-all group, you may wish to use the Google Groups search engine. The search on the main page works very much like the regular Google search; your only clue that things are different is the Google Groups tab and each result has an associated group and posting date.

The Advanced Groups Search (*http://groups.google.com/advanced_group_search*), however, looks much different. You can restrict your searches to a certain newsgroup or newsgroup topic. For example, you can restrict your search as broadly as the entire *comp* hierarchy (comp* would do it) or as narrowly as a single group like *comp.robotics.misc*. You may restrict messages to subject and author, or restrict messages by message ID.

Of course, any options on the Advanced Groups Search page can be expressed via a little URL hacking [Hack #9].

Possibly the biggest difference between Google Groups and Google web search is the date searching. With Google web search, date searching is notoriously inexact, *date* referring to when a page was added to the index rather than the date the page was created. Each Google Groups message is stamped with the day it was actually posted to the newsgroup. Thus the date searches on Google Groups are accurate and indicative of when content was produced. And, thankfully, they use the more familiar Gregorian dates rather than the Google web search's Julian dates [Hack #11].

Google Groups and Special Syntaxes

You can do some precise searching from the Google Groups advanced search page. And, just as with Google web, you have some special syntaxes [in "The Special Syntaxes" in Chapter 1] at your disposal.

 Google Groups is an archive of conversations. Thus, when you're searching, you'll be more successful if you try looking for conversational and informal language, not the carefully structured language you'll find on Internet sites—well, some Internet sites, anyway.

intitle:
> Searches posting titles for query words.
>> intitle:rocketry

group:
> Restricts your search to a certain group or set of groups (topic). The wildcard * (asterisk) modifies a group: syntax to include everything beneath the specified group or topic. rec.humor* or rec.humor.* (effectively the same) will find results in the group *rec.humor*, as well as *rec.humor.funny*, *rec.humor.jewish*, and so forth.
>> group:rec.humor*
>> group:alt*
>> group:comp.lang.perl.misc

author:
> Specifies the author of a newsgroup post. This can be a full or partial name, even an email address.
>> author:fred
>> author:fred flintstone
>> author:flintstone@bedrock.gov

Mixing syntaxes in Google Groups. Google Groups is much more friendly to syntax mixing [Hack #8] than Google web search. You can mix any syntaxes together in a Google Groups search, as exemplified by the following typical searches:

> intitle:literature group:humanities* author:john
> intitle:hardware group:comp.sys.ibm* pda

Some common search scenarios. There are several ways you can "mine" Google Groups for research information. Remember, though, to view any information you get here with a certain amount of skepticism—all Usenet is is hundreds of thousands of people tossing around links; in that respect, it's just like the Web.

Tech support. Ever used Windows and discovered that there's some program running you've never heard of? Uncomfortable, isn't it? If you're wondering if HIDSERV is something nefarious, Google Groups can tell you. Just search Google Groups for HIDSERV. You'll find that plenty of people had the same question before you did, and it's been answered.

I find that Google Groups is sometimes more useful than manufacturers' web sites. For example, I was trying to install a set of flight devices for a friend—a joystick, throttle, and rudder pedals. The web site for the manufacturer couldn't help me figure out why they weren't working. I described the problem as best I could in a Google Groups search—using the name of the parts and the manufacturer's brand name—and it wasn't easy, but I was able to find an answer.

Sometimes your problem isn't as serious but it's just as annoying; you might be stuck in a computer game. If the game has been out for more than a few months your answer is probably in Google Groups. If you want the answer to an entire game, try the magic word "walkthrough." So if you're looking for a walkthrough for Quake II, try the search "quake ii" walkthrough. (You don't need to restrict your search to newsgroups; walkthrough is a word strongly associated with gamers.)

Finding commentary immediately after an event. With Google Groups, date searching is very precise (unlike date searching Google's web index). So it's an excellent way to get commentary during or immediately after events.

Barbra Streisand and James Brolin were married on July 1, 1998. Searching for "Barbra Streisand" "James Brolin" between June 30, 1998 and July 3, 1998 leads to over 40 results, including reprinted wire articles, links to news stories, and commentary from fans. Searching for "barbra streisand" "james brolin" without a date specification finds more than 1,300 results.

Usenet is also much older than the Web and is ideal for finding information about an event that occured before the Web. Coca-Cola released "New Coke" in April 1985. You can find information about the release on the Web, of course, but finding contemporary commentary would be more difficult. After some playing around with the dates (just because it's been released doesn't mean it's in every store) I found plenty of commentary about "New Coke" in Google Groups by searching for the phrase "new coke" during the

month of May 1985. Information included poll results, taste tests, and specu-
lation on the new formula. Searching later in the summer yields information
on Coke re-releasing old Coke under the name "Classic Coke."

Google Groups and the Google API

At the time of this writing, Google Groups is not supported by the Google
API. If you want to save your searches in a comma-delimited file, however,
you can use the Google Groups scraper [Hack #46].

Google Images

Find a picture of your childhood friend or the national flag of Zimbabwe
amongst the over 390 million indexed Google Images.

Take a break from text-crawling and check out Google Images (*http://
images.google.com/*), an index of over 390 million images available on the
Web. While sorely lacking in special syntaxes [in "The Special Syntaxes" in Chapter 1],
the Advanced Image Search (*http://images.google.com/advanced_image_
search*) does offer some interesting options.

Of course, any options on the Advanced Image Search page
can be expressed via a little URL hacking [Hack #9].

Google's image search starts with a plain keyword search. Images are indexed
under a variety of keywords, some broader than others; be as specific as possible. If you're searching for cats, don't use cat as a keyword unless you don't
mind getting results that include "cat scan." Use words that are more
uniquely cat-related, like feline or kitten. Narrow down your query as
much as possible, using as few words as possible. A query like feline fang,
which would get you over 3,000 results on Google, will get you no results on
Google Image Search; in this case, cat fang works better. (Building queries
for image searching takes a lot of patience and experimentation.)

Search results include a thumbnail, name, size (both pixels and kilobytes),
and the URL where the picture is to be found. Clicking the picture will
present a framed page, Google's thumbnail of the image at the top, and the
page where the image originally appeared at the bottom. Figure 2-2 shows a
Google Images page.

Searching Google Images can be a real crapshoot, because it's difficult to
build multiple-word queries, and single-word queries lead to thousands of

Figure 2-2. A Google Images page

results. You do have more options to narrow your search both through the Advanced Image Search interface and through the Google Image Search special syntaxes.

Google Images Advanced Search Interface

The Google Advanced Image Search (*http://images.google.com/advanced_image_search*) allows you to specify the size (expressed in pixels, not kilobytes) of the returned image. You can also specify the kind of pictures you want to find (Google Images indexes only JPEG and GIF files), image color (black and white, grayscale, or full color), and any domain to which you wish to restrict your search.

Google Image search also uses three levels of filtering: none, moderate, and strict. Moderate filters only explicit images, while strict filters both images and text. While automatic filtering doesn't guarantee that you won't find any offensive content, it will help. However, sometimes filtering works against you. If you're searching for images related to breast cancer, Google's strict filtering will cut down greatly on your potential number of results. Any time you're using a word that might be considered offensive—even in an innocent context—you'll have to consider turning off the filters or risk missing relevant results. One way to get around the filterings is to try alternate words. If you're searching for breast cancer images, try searching for mammograms or Tamoxifen, a drug used to treat breast cancer.

Google Images Special Syntaxes

Google Images offers a few special syntaxes:

`intitle:`
> Finds keywords in the page title. This is an excellent way to narrow down search results.

`filetype:`
> Finds pictures of a particular type. This only works for JPEG and GIF, not BMP, PNG, or any number of other formats Google doesn't index. Note that searching for `filetype:jpg` and `filetype:jpeg` will get you different results, because the filtering is based on file extension, not some deeper understanding of the file type.

`inurl:`
> As with any regular Google search, finds the search term in the URL. The results for this one can be confusing. For example, you may search for `inurl:cat` and get the following URL as part of the search result:
>> `www.example.com/something/somethingelse/something.html`
>
> Hey, where's the cat? Because Google indexes the graphic name as part of the URL, it's probably there. If the page above includes a graphic named *cat.jpg*, that's what Google is finding when you search for `inurl:cat`. It's finding the cat in the name of the picture, not in the URL itself.

`site:`
> As with any other Google web search, restricts your results to a specified host or domain. Don't use this to restrict results to a certain host unless you're really sure what's there. Instead, use it to restrict results to certain domains. For example, search for `football.site:uk` and then search for `football`.
>
> `site:com` is a good example of how dramatic a difference using `site:` can make.

Google Images and the Google API

At the time of this writing, Google Images is not included in the Google API.

HACK
#32   Google News
Reading the latest news across myriad sources using Google News.

We've all been a little spoiled by Google. It seems like whenever they release something, we expect it to be super cool immediately.

Alas, Google News is cool, but it isn't the greatest news tool in my opinion. It's barely in my top three for getting news off the Internet. To be fair to Google, though, News Search is, at this writing, still in beta.

The search form functions like Google web search—all searches are default AND. Search results group like news stories into clusters, providing title, source, date, and a brief summary (the link to the full story is included in the title). The only option beyond that searchers have is to sort their searches by relevance or date; there is no advanced search. The sort option appears on the right of the results page as you search.

Special Syntaxes

Google's News Search supports two special syntaxes.

intitle:
> Finds words in an article headline.
>
>> intitle:miners

site:
> Finds articles from a particular source. Unfortunately, Google News does not offer a list of its over 4,000 sources so you have to guess a little when you're looking around.
>
>> miners site:bbc.co.uk

Making the Most of Google News

The best thing about Google News is its clustering capabilities. On an ordinary news search engine, a breaking news story can overwhelm search results. For example, in late July 2002, a story broke that hormone replacement therapy might increase the risk of cancer. Suddenly using a news search engine to find the phrase "breast cancer" was an exercise in futility, because dozens of stories around the same topic were clogging the results page.

That doesn't happen when you search the Google news engine, because Google groups like stories by topic. You'd find a large cluster of stories about hormone replacement therapy, but they'd be in one place, leaving you to find other news about breast cancer.

Does this always work perfectly? In my experience, no. Some searches cluster easily; they're specialized or tend to spawn limited topics. But other queries—like "George Bush"—spawn lots of results and several different clusters. If you need to search for a famous name or a general topic (like crime, for example) narrow your search results in one of the following ways:

- Add a topic modifier that will significantly narrow your search results, as in: "George Bush" environment, crime arson.

- Limit your search with one of the special syntaxes, for example: intitle:"George Bush".

- Limit your search to a particular site. Be warned that, while this works well for a major breaking news story, you might miss local stories. If you're searching for a major American story, CNN is a good choice (site:cnn.com). If the story you're researching is more international in origin, the BBC works well (site:bbc.co.uk).

If your searches are narrow or relatively obscure, the clustering issue may never come up for you. In that case, you won't get to take advantage of Google's greatest strength and will instead notice its weaknesses: inability to search by date, inability to sort by source, limitations on searching by language or source, etc. In that case, you might want to try an alternative.

Beyond Google for News Search

After a long dry spell, news search engines have popped up all over the Internet. Here are my top four:

FAST News Search (http://www.alltheweb.com/?cat=news)
  Great for both local and international sources. Advanced search lets you narrow your search by language, news source category (business, sports, etc.), and date the material was indexed. Drawback: little press release indexing.

Rocketinfo (http://www.rocketnews.com/)
  Does not use the most extensive sources in the world, but lesser known press release outlets (like PETA) and very technical outlets (OncoLink, BioSpace, Insurance News Net) are to be found here. Rocketinfo's main drawback is its limited search and sort options.

Yahoo! Daily News (http://dailynews.yahoo.com)
  Sports its source list right on the advanced search page. A 30 day index means sometimes you can find things that have slipped off the other engines. Provides free news alerts for registered Yahoo! users. One drawback is that Yahoo! Daily News has few technical sources, which means sometimes stories appear over and over in search results.

Northern Light News Search (http://www.northernlight.com/news.html)
  Has absolutely the best press release coverage I've found and a good selection of international news wires. News search results are organized into topical folders. Free alerts are available. Drawbacks are: only two weeks' worth of sources, and the source list is not particularly large.

Google News and the Google API

The Google API, at this writing, does not support Google News.

Google Catalogs

#33
Comb through your favorite catalogs or peruse a collection of over 4,500 with Google Catalogs.

At the start of the dotcom boom, all the retailers rushed to put their catalogs online. Google's sauntered along, and long after all the hoopla has died down, put up catalogs in a different way. Instead of designing a web site that looks like a catalog, Google simply scanned in pages from catalogs—over 4,500 of them—and made them available via a search engine.

From the front page of Google Catalogs (*http://catalogs.google.com*), you may either do a simple keyword search or browse through a subject index of catalogs. Each catalog listing gives you the option to view the catalog, view previous editions, or link to the catalog's site (if available). If you choose to browse the catalog, you'll be presented with a series of page thumbnails. Catalog pages also offer a search bar at the right of the page that allows you to search just that catalog.

If you're interested in a particular class of item (like electronics or toys or whatever) stick with the topical catalog browsing. If you're searching for a particular item, use the keyword search on the front page. If your search is somewhere in between, use the advanced search page.

The Advanced Catalog Search (*http://catalogs.google.com/advanced_catalog_search*) lets you narrow down your search by categories (from Apparel and Accessories to Toys and Games), specify if you want to search only current catalogs or all past and current catalogs, and specify if you'd prefer to filter results using SafeSearch.

Of course, any options on the Advanced Catalog Search page can be expressed via a little URL hacking [Hack #9].

Search results are very different from other Google properties. They include the catalog name and issue date, a picture of the catalog's front page, the first page where your search term appears (a link to additional results with your search term, if any, appears on the line with the name and date of the catalog), and a close-up of where your search term appears on the page. Generally, the pages in the search results aren't very readable, but that varies depending on the catalog. Click on the page to get a larger version of the entire page.

Special Syntaxes

Google Catalogs search does not have any special syntaxes.

Google Catalogs and the Google API

Google's Catalog search is not, at the time of this writing, supported in the Google API.

HACK #34   Froogle

Shop 'til you drop with Froogle, Google's online shopping index.

Google Catalogs is a great way to do offline shopping, especially if you like to browse with nothing more than a couple of keywords. However, if you're the modern type who insists on doing all shopping online, you'll want to check out Froogle (*http://froogle.google.com/*). Froogle, a combination of the words "Google" and "frugal," is a searchable shopping index that looks a lot like the Google Directory with a focus on getting you right to an online point of purchase for the item you're interested in. The service was launched in December 2002 and, at the time of this writing, is still in beta.

There are two ways of finding items in this directory: browsing and searching. In the same way as browsing and searching, Google can lead to different results, so too will you find different products depending on the road you take in Froogle.

Browsing for Purchases

The Froogle home page lists a set of top-level categories, each with a representative smattering of subcategories. To browse a particular category, just click on the link. You'll find that even after some drilling down to just the subcategory you're after, there are still bound to be a lot of items. For example, there are over 2,500 results on the flower arrangement category.

Listings include a picture when available (as is most often the case), price, the store selling the item, a brief description of the item, and a link leading to all items from that particular vendor in the category at hand. You can narrow things down by choosing to view only items within a particular price range.

Unless you have a lot of time and really like shopping, the browsing option is less than optimal. Searching Froogle works much better, especially when you're in a hurry and have something specific in mind.

Searching for Purchases

Froogle sports a basic keyword search, but to get the most out of your search, you'll probably want the Advanced Froogle Search (*http://froogle. google.com/froogle_advanced_search*).

Some of the Advanced Search will look familiar if you've used the standard Google Advanced Search; you can specify words, phrases, and words that should be excluded. But you can also specify products that are below a specified price or within a particular price range. You can also specify if your keywords should appear within the product name, the product description, or both; this gives you some nice additional fine-grained control. Finally, you can specify the category in which your results should appear—from Apparel & Accessories to Toys & Games.

Personally, I don't like advanced search forms very much, so I prefer using special syntaxes when I can, and Froogle does have some special syntaxes up its sleeve. `intitle:` restricts results to the title of the item, while `intext:` restricts results to the description. You can use these in combination, so `intitle:giraffe intext:figurine` will work as expected. There's also an `OR`, specified by a `|` (the pipe character); for example, to find a glass giraffe or elephant, you'd search for: `glass (intitle:giraffe | intitle:elephant)`.

Adding a Merchant to Froogle

With Google's prominence in the regular search space, it's reasonable to expect that Froogle will quickly become a popular shopping destination. If you sell things online, you might be wondering how much Google charges a vendor to be a part of the Froogle stable.

The short answer is: nothing! Yup, you can be listed in Froogle without paying a dime. There are some limitations, though. Currently, Froogle only accepts English-language web sites and products priced in U.S. dollars.

Merchants who wish to be included on the site are invited to submit a data feed-read: a tab-delimited file generated by your favorite spreadsheet program, in-house content-management system, product database, or the like. For more information on making your products available via Froogle, see *http://froogle.google.com/froogle/merchants.html*.

Froogle and the Google API

At the time of this writing, Froogle does not support the Google API.

#35 Google Labs

Google Labs, as the name suggests, sports Google's experiments, fun little hacks, and inspirational uses of the Google engine and database.

Be sure not to miss Google Labs (*http://labs.google.com/*). The whole point of this part of Google's site is that things will appear, vanish, change, and basically do whatever they want. So it may be different by the time you read this, but it's still worth covering what's here now; you might find one of the tools here useful in sparking ideas.

At the time of this writing, there are four experiments running at the lab:

Google Glossary (http://labs1.google.com/glossary)
A search engine for acronyms and abbreviations. It found TMTOWDI and Ventriculoperitoneal Shunt, but missed on MST3K and google-whack. Entries include a brief definition, a link to an informative page, definition links to Dictionary.com and Merriam-Webster, and related phrases if any.

Google Sets (http://labs1.google.com/sets)
Enter a few terms, and Google will try to come up with an appropriate set of phrases. For example, enter Amazon and Borders, and Google will come up with Borders, Amazon, Barnes Noble, Buy Com, Media Play, Suncoast, Samgoody, etc. It doesn't always work like you'd expect. Enter vegan and vegetarian and you'll get veal, Valentine's Day, Tasmania—it goes a bit far afield. Clicking any item in the group list will launch a regular Google search.

Google Voice Search (http://labs1.google.com/gvs.html)
Dial the number on the page, and you'll be prompted to say a search. Speak your search and then click on the specified link. Every time you say a new search, the result page will refresh with your new query. You must have JavaScript enabled for this to work.

Unfortunately, Google Voice Search doesn't always understand your requests. When I gave it a whirl, it got Eliot Ness right, and George Bush without problem, but Fred became Friend and Ethel Merman became Apple Mountain. It also goes rather quickly. When you use Google Voice Search, don't let the computer voice rush you.

Google Keyboard Shortcuts (http://labs1.google.com/keys/)
If you're using an "alternative" browser like Opera, this might not work. Try it in Mozilla, IE, or Netscape. Google Keyboard Shortcuts is a way to move around search results using only the keyboard. Instead of a cursor, you follow a little cluster of balls on the right side of the screen.

From there you navigate via your keyboard. The I and K keys move up and down, while the J and L keys move left and right.

Google WebQuotes (http://labs.google.com/cgi-bin/webquotes/)
Many times you can learn the most about a web page by what other web pages say about it. Google WebQuotes takes advantage of this fact by providing a preview of what other sites are saying about a particular link before you actually meander over to the site itself.

From the Google WebQuotes home page, specify how many Web-Quotes you'd like for a particular search (the default is three, a number I find works well) and enter a search term. Google WebQuotes shows you the top 10 sites (or, if you suffix the resultant URL with &num=100, the top 100 sites) with as many WebQuotes for each page as you specified. Note, however, that not every page has a WebQuote.

This comes in rather handy when you're doing some general research and want to know immediately whether the search result is relevant. When you're searching for famous people, you can get some useful information on them this way, too—and all without leaving the search results page!

Google Viewer (http://labs.google.com/gviewer.html)

Google Viewer presents Google search results as a slide show. You'll have to use one of the more recent browsers to get it to work; Google recommends Internet Explorer 5 and above or Netscape 6 and above for Mac and PC users, Mozilla for those running a variant of Unix.

To fire up Google Viewer, perform a Google search as you usually would, only from the Google Viewer home page (*http://labs.google.com/gviewer.html*) rather than the main Google home page. The results page looks just like the regular Google results page you know and love. Notice, however, the toolbar across the top of the page. Use the toolbar buttons to go forward, backward, or to the first result, alter the speed of the presentation, or run another search. The slide show itself should start automatically; if it doesn't, click the green triangular play button on the toolbar.

Google will present the first search result along with a live image of the page itself. About five seconds later, the second result will scroll into place, and the third, and so on. If you need a break, stop the slide show by clicking the red square stop button and resume by clicking the green triangular play button.

Unfortunately, there's no scrollbar on the web page, so you'll have to click the image of the displayed page itself and drag your mouse around to move within it.

Unless you hit a really good (or a really limited-result) query, this Google Labs experiment is of limited use. But if Google ever applies the Google Viewer to Google News, look out!

Google Labs and the Google API

At this writing, none of the Google Labs tools have been integrated into the Google API.

Third-Party Google Services
Hacks #36–40

Here's a nice Zen question for you: is Google a search engine or a technology?

Weird question, huh? Isn't Google just a search engine? Doesn't it provide the ability to search several different data collections? Or is it more? Isn't it a technology that other people can apply to their own search purposes?

Thanks to the Google API and good old-fashioned ingenuity, it's easy for third-party developers to take Google's technology and develop them into applications that have nothing to do with Google outside of the application of their technology.

Of Google, but Not Google

In this section, you'll see several examples of third-party services that integrate Google's technology, but—with the exception of codevelopment projects that are announced on Google's site—aren't sanctioned or created by Google. Google probably can't monitor directly the thousands of people who are using their API. Further, unless a program is violating Google's terms of services or the terms of service of the API, Google will probably not take action about an application. So if you see a application that doesn't work as advertised or doesn't work at all, discuss the issue with the developer instead of bringing it up with Google. If the application violates the Google or Google API terms of service, alert Google.

Tinkering with the UI

Developing third-party services—interfaces or programs that integrate Google's search technology—doesn't have to mean big API projects. One of the hacks in this section is a simplifier that takes Google Group URLs and makes them easier to handle. That's not the most complicated application in the world, but it sure makes Google Groups URLs easier to handle if you're a researcher or an archivist.

Of course, you can go even further with the Google API, building services that access Google's search results from within other applications.

Expanding the Options with the Google API

When you have the Google API, you can go way outside a traditional search interface. One of the hacks in this section looks at a Google search you can check by email. Another one shows you how you can integrate Google searching into Flash applications. With the Google API, it's amazing where Google search can go!

Thinking Way Outside the Box

Of course, there are plenty of other people who are developing Google services on a much larger scale. From the basics of getting to Google via a Logitech keyboard (*http://www.google.com/press/pressrel/logitech.html*) to the wow-worthy teaming up with BMW for voice-activated searching in Internet-ready cars (*http://www.google.com/press/highlights.html*), who knows what else Google will come up with in the years to come?

HACK #36 XooMLe: The Google API in Plain Old XML

Getting Google results in XML using the XooMLe wrapper.

When Google released their Web APIs in April 2002, everyone agreed that it was fantastic, but some thought it could have been better. Google's API was to be driven by Simple Object Access Protocol (SOAP), which wasn't exactly what everyone was hoping for.

What's wrong with SOAP? Google made the biggest, best search engine in the world available as a true web service, so it must be a good thing, right? Sure, but a lot of people argued that by using SOAP, they had made it unnecessarily difficult to access Google's service. They argued that using simple HTTP-based technologies would have provided everything they needed, while also making it a much simpler service to use.

The irony of this was not lost on everyone—Google, being so well-known and widely used, in part because of its simplicity, was now being slammed for making their service difficult to access for developers.

The argument was out there: SOAP was bad, Google needed a REST! Representational State Transfer (REST) is a model for web services that makes use of existing protocols and technologies, such as HTTP GET requests, URIs, and XML to provide a transaction-based approach to web services. The argument was that REST provided a much simpler means of achieving the same results, given Google's limited array of functionality.

REST proponents claimed that Google should have made their API available through the simpler approach of requesting a defined URI, including query string–based parameters such as the search term and the output encoding. The response would then be a simple XML document that included results or an error of some sort.

After playing with the Google API, I had enough exposure to at least know my way around the WSDL and other bits and pieces involved in working with Google. I read a lot of the suggestions and proposals for how Google "should have done it" and set about actually doing it. The result was XooMLe (*http://www.dentedreality.com.au/xoomle/*).

The first step was to create a solid architecture for accessing the Google API. I was working with the popular and very powerful scripting language, PHP, so this was made very simple by grabbing a copy of Dietrich Ayala's SOAP access class called NuSOAP. Once I had that in place, it was a simple process of writing a few functions and bits and pieces to call the SOAP class, query Google, then reformat the response to something a bit "lighter."

I chose to implement a system that would accept a request for a single URL (because at this stage I wasn't too familiar with the RESTful way of doing things) containing a number of parameters, depending on which method was being called from Google. The information returned would depend on the type of request, as outlined here:

Google method	Return type
doGoogleSearch	XML document containing structured information about the results and the actual search process
doGoogleSpellingSuggestion	Plain text response containing suggested spelling correction
doGetCachedPage	HTML source for the page requested

All the methods would also optionally return a standardized, XML-encoded error message if something went wrong, which would allow developers to easily determine if their requests were successful.

Providing this interface required only a small amount of processing before returning the information back to the user. In the case of a call to doGoogleSearch, the results were just mapped across to the XML template then returned, doSpellingSuggestion just had to pull out the suggestion and send that back, while doGetCachedPage had to decode the result (from base-64 encoding) then strip off the first 5 lines of HTML, which contained a Google header. This allowed XooMLe to return just what the user requested; a clean, cached copy of a page, a simple spelling suggestion, or a set of results matching a search term. Searching was XooMLe's first hurdle—returning SOAP-encoded results from Google in clean, custom XML tags, minus the "fluff."

I chose to use an XML template rather than hardcoding the structure directly into my code. The template holds the basic structure of a result set returned from Google. It includes things like the amount of time the search took, the title of each result, their URLs, plus other information that Google tracks. This XML template is based directly on the structure outlined in the WSDL and obviously on the actual information returned from Google. It is parsed, and then sections of it are duplicated and modified as required, so that a clean XML document is populated with the results, then sent to the user. If something goes wrong, an error message is encoded in a different XML template and sent back instead.

Once searching was operational, spelling suggestions were quickly added, simply removing the suggestion from its SOAP envelope and returning it as plain text. Moving on to the cached pages proved to require a small amount of manipulation, where the returned information had to be converted back to a plain string (originally a base-64 encoded string from Google) and then the Google header, which is automatically added to the pages in their cache, had to be removed. Once that was complete, the page was streamed back to the user, so that if she printed the results of the request directly to the screen, a cached copy of the web page would be displayed directly.

After posting the results of this burst of development to the DentedReality web site, nothing much happened. No one knew about XooMLe, so no one used it. I happened to be reading Dave Winer's Scripting News, so I fired off an email to him about XooMLe, just suggesting that he might be interested in it. Five minutes later (literally) there was a link to it on Scripting News describing it as a "REST-style interface," and within 12 hours, I had received approximately 700 hits to the site! It didn't stop there; the next morning when I checked my email, I had a message from Paul Prescod with some suggestions for making it more RESTful and improving the general functionality of it as a service.

After exchanging a few emails directly with Prescod, plus receiving a few other suggestions and comments from people on the REST-discuss Yahoo! Group (which I quickly became a member of), I went ahead and made a major revision to XooMLe. This version introduced a number of changes:

- Moved away from a single URI for all methods, introducing /search/, /cache/ and /spell/ so that there was a unique URI for each method.
- Google's limit of 10 results per query was bypassed by making XooMLe loop through search requests, compiling the results, and sending them back in a single XML document.
- Added a cachedVersion element to each result item, which contained a link to retrieve a cached copy of a document via XooMLe.

- If related information was available via Google, an additional link was supplied that would retrieve those pages.
- Added an XLink to the URL, `relatedInformation` and `cachedVersion` elements of each returned result, which could be used to automatically create a link via XML technologies.
- Added the ability to specify an XSLT when performing a search, making it simple to use pure XML technologies to format the output in a human-readable form.

And thus a RESTful web service was born. XooMLe implements the full functionality of the Google API (and actually extends it in a few places), using a much simpler interface and output format. A XooMLe result set can be bookmarked, a spelling suggestion can be very easily obtained via a bookmarklet, results can be parsed in pretty much every programming language using simple, native functions, and cached pages are immediately usable upon retrieval.

XooMLe demonstrates that it was indeed quite feasible for Google to implement their API using the REST architecture, and provides a useful wrapper to the SOAP functionality they have chosen to expose. It is currently being used as an example of "REST done right" by a number of proponents of the model, including some Amazon/Google linked services being developed by one of the REST-discuss members.

On its own, XooMLe may not be particularly useful, but teamed with the imagination and programming prowess of the web services community, it will no doubt help create a new wave of toys, tools, and talking points.

How It Works

Basically, to use XooMLe you just need to "request" a web page, then do something with the result that gets sent back to you. Some people might call this a request-response architecture, whatever—you ask XooMLe for something, it asks Google for the same thing, then formats the results in a certain format and gives it to you, from there on, you can do what you like with it. Long story short—everything you can ask the Google SOAP API, you can ask XooMLe.

Google Method: doGoogleSearch

- XooMLe URI: *http://xoomle.dentedreality.com.au/search/*
- Successful Response Format: Returns an XML-formatted response containing the results of the Google-search that you specified.

- Failure Response: An XML-based error message, including all arguments you sent to XooMLe (here's an example: *http://www.dentedreality.com.au/xoomle/sample_error.xml*). The message will change, depending on what went wrong, as outlined below.

Extra Features

- maxResults: Also supports setting maxResults well above the Google-limit of 10, performing looped queries to gather the results and then sending them all back in one hit.

- cachedVersion: Each result item will include an element called "cachedVersion" which is a URI to retrieve the cached version of that particular result.

- xsl: You may specify a variable called "xsl" in addition to the others in the querystring. The value of this variable will be used as a reference to an external XSLT Stylesheet, and will be used to format the XML output of the document.

- relatedInformation: If it is detected that there is related information available for a particular resultElement, then this element will contain a link to retrieve those related items from XooMLe.

- xlink: There is now an xlink attribute added to the cachedVersion and relatedInformation elements of each result.

Google Method: doSpellingSuggestion

- XooMLe URI: *http://xoomle.dentedreality.com.au/spell/*

- Successful Response Format: Returns a text-only response containing the suggested correction for the phrase that you passed to Google (through XooMLe). You will get HTTP headers and stuff like that as well, but assuming you are accessing XooMLe over HTTP in the first place, the body of the response is just text.

- Failure Response: An XML-based error message, including all arguments you sent to XooMLe. The message will change, depending on what went wrong.

Google Method: doGetCachedPage

- XooMLe URI: *http://xoomle.dentedreality.com.au/cache/*

- Successful Response Format: Returns the complete contents of the cached page requested, WITHOUT THE GOOGLE INFORMATION-HEADER. The header that Google adds, which says it's a cached page, is stripped out BEFORE you are given the page, so don't expect it to be there. You should get nothing but the HTML required to render the page.

- Failure Response: An XML-based error message, including all arguments you sent to XooMLe.

Asking XooMLe Something (Forming Requests). Asking XooMLe something is really easy; you can do it in a normal hyperlink, a bookmark, a Favorite, whatever. A request to XooMLe exists as a URL, which contains some special information. It looks something like this:

```
http://xoomle.dentedreality.com.au/search/
?key=YourGoogleDeveloperKey&q=dented+reality
```

Enough generic examples! If you are talking to XooMLe, the address you need is:

```
http://xoomle.dentedreality.com.au/<method keyword>/
```

Your requests might look something like the previous example, or they might be fully fleshed out like the following:

```
http://xoomle.dentedreality.com.au/search/
?key=YourKey
&q=dented+realty
&maxResults=1
&start=0
&hl=en
&ie=ISO-8859-1
&filter=0
&restrict=countryAU
&safeSearch=1
&lr=en
&ie=latin1
&oe=latin1
&xsl=myxsl.xsl
```

Note that each option is on a different line so they're easier to read; properly formatted they would be in one long string.

All the available parameters are defined in the Google documentation, but just to refresh your memory:

key means your Google Developer Key, go get one if you don't have one already (and remember to URL-encode it when passing it in the query string as well!).

Another thing you might like to know is that XooMLe makes use of some fancy looping to allow you to request more than the allowed 10 results in one request. If you ask XooMLe to get (for example) 300 results, it will perform multiple queries to Google and send back 300 results to you in XML format. Keep in mind that this still uses up your request limit (1,000 queries per day) in blocks of 10 though, so in this case, you'd drop 30 queries in one hit (and it would take a while to return that many results).

Error Messages

If you do something wrong, XooMLe will tell you in a nice little XML package. The errors all look something like this, but they have a different error message and contain that "arguments" array, which includes everything you asked it. Below are all the error messages that you can get, and why you will get them.

Google API key not supplied
> You forgot to provide XooMLe with your Google API key. You need this so that XooMLe can communicate with Google on your behalf. Specify it like this: key=*insert key here* and get one from Google if you don't have one already.

Search string not specified
> You were smart enough to specify that you wanted to do a search (using method=doGoogleSearch) but forgot to tell XooMLe what you were searching for. Fix this by adding something like q=*Your+search+terms* (your search phrase should be URL-encoded and is subject to the same limitations as the Google API).

Invalid Google API key supplied
> There's something wrong with your Google API key (did you URL-encode it like I told you?).

Your search found no results
> This one should be rather obvious.

Phrase not specified
> If you ask for a spelling suggestion (using method=doSpellingSuggestion), you should also tell XooMLe what you are trying to correct, using phrase=stoopid+speling+here. (URL-encode it.)

No suggestion available
> Hey, Google ain't perfect. Sometimes the attempts at spelling just don't even warrant a response (or possibly Google can't decipher your bad spelling).

URL not specified
> You want a cached page from Google? The least you could do is ask for it using url=http://thepagehere.com.

Cached page not available
> Something was wrong with the cached page that Google returned (or it couldn't find it in the database). Not all Google listings have cached pages available.

Couldn't contact Google server
> There was a problem contacting the Google server, so your request could not be processed.

Putting XooMLe to Work: A SOAP::Lite Substitution Module

XooMLe is not only a handy way to get Google results in XML, it's a handy way to replace the required SOAP::Lite module that a lot of ISPs don't support. *XooMLe.pm* is a little Perl module best saved into the same directory as your hacks themselves.

```perl
# XooMLe.pm
# XooMLe is a drop-in replacement for SOAP::Lite designed to use
# the plain old XML to Google SOAP bridge provided by the XooMLe
# service.

package XooMLe;
use strict;
use LWP::Simple; use XML::Simple;

sub new {
  my $self  = {};
  bless($self);
  return $self;
}

sub doGoogleSearch {
  my($self, %args); ($self, @args{qw/ key q start maxResults
  filter restrict safeSearch lr ie oe /}) = @_;
  my $xoomle_url = 'http://xoomle.dentedreality.com.au';

  my $xoomle_service = 'search';
  # Query Google via XooMLe

   my $content = get(
    "$xoomle_url/$xoomle_service/?" .
    join '&', map { "$_=$args{$_}" } keys %args
  );
  # Parse the XML
  my $results = XMLin($content);
  # Normalize

  $results->{GoogleSearchResult}->{resultElements} =
    $results->{GoogleSearchResult}->{resultElements}->{item};

  foreach (@{$results->{GoogleSearchResult}->{'resultElements'}}) {
    $_->{URL} = $_->{URL}->{content};
    ref $_->{snippet} eq 'HASH' and $_->{snippet} = '';
    ref $_->{title} eq 'HASH' and  $_->{title} = '';
  }
  return $results->{GoogleSearchResult};

}
1;
```

Using the XooMLe Module

Here's a little script to show our home-brewed XooMLe module in action. Its no different, really, from any number of hacks in this book. The only minor alterations necessary to make use of XooMLe instead of SOAP::Lite are highlighted in bold.

```perl
#!/usr/bin/perl
# xoomle_google2csv.pl
# Google Web Search Results via XooMLe 3rd party web service
# exported to CSV suitable for import into Excel
# Usage: xoomle_google2csv.pl "{query}" [> results.csv]

# Your Google API developer's key
my $google_key = 'insert key here';

use strict;

# Uses our home-brewed XooMLe Perl module
# use SOAP::Lite
use XooMLe;

$ARGV[0] or die qq{usage: perl xoomle_search2csv.pl "{query}"\n};

# Create a new XooMLe object rather than using SOAP::Lite
# my $google_search = SOAP::Lite->service("file:$google_wdsl");
my $google_search = new XooMLe;

my $results = $google_search -> doGoogleSearch(
  $google_key, shift @ARGV, 0, 10, "false", "",
  "false", "", "latin1", "latin1"
);

@{$results->{'resultElements'}} or warn 'No results';

print qq{"title","url","snippet"\n};

foreach (@{$results->{'resultElements'}}) {
  $_->{title} =~ s!"!""!g;
  # double escape " marks
  $_->{snippet} =~ s!"!""!g;
  my $output = qq{"$_->{title}","$_->{URL}","$_->{snippet}"\n};
  # drop all HTML tags
  $output =~ s!<.+?>!!g;
  print $output;
}
```

Running the Hack

Run the script from the command line, providing a query and sending the output to a CSV file you wish to create or to which you wish to append additional results. For example, using "restful SOAP" as our query and results.csv as our output:

```
$ perl xoomle_google2csv.pl "restful SOAP" > results.csv
```

Leaving off the > and CSV filename sends the results to the screen for your perusal.

Applicability

In the same manner, you can adapt just about any SOAP::Lite-based hack in this book and those you've made up yourself to use the XooMLe module.

1. Place *XooMLe.pm* in the same directory as the hack at hand.

2. Replace use SOAP::Lite; with use XooMLe;.

3. Replace my $google_search = SOAP::Lite->service("file:$google_wdsl"); with my $google_search = new XooMLe;.

In general, bear in mind that your mileage may vary and don't be afraid to tweak.

See Also

- PoXML [Hack #53], a plain old XML alternative to SOAP::Lite
- NoXML [Hack #54], a regular expressions-based, XML Parser–free SOAP::Lite alternative

—Beau Lebens and Rael Dornfest

HACK
#37

Google by Email

Access 10 of Google's search results at a time via email.

Long before the Web existed, there was email. And now, thanks to the Google API, there's Google email. Created by the team at Cape Clear (*http://capescience.capeclear.com/google/*), CapeMail queries Google via email. Send email to *google@capeclear.com* with the query you want on the subject line. You'll receive a message back with the estimated results count and the first 10 results. Here's an excerpt from a search for Frankenstein:

```
Estimated Total Results Number = 505000
URL  = "http://www.nlm.nih.gov/hmd/Frankenstein/frankhome.html"
Title = "Frankenstein Exhibit Home Page"
Snippet = "Table of Contents Introduction The Birth of Frankenstein,
The Celluloid Monster. Promise and Peril, Frankenstein: The Modern
Prometheus. ... "
URL  = "http://www.literature.org/authors/shelley-mary/Frankenstein/"
Title = "Online Literature Library - Mary Shelley - Frankenstein"
```

```
Snippet = "Next Back Contents Home Authors Contact, Frankenstein. Mary
Shelley. Preface; Chapter 1; Chapter 2; Chapter 3; Chapter 4;
Chapter 5; Chapter ...   "
```

Like many other Google API applications, CapeMail may be used only 1,000 times per day; the Google API allows the use of the API key only 1,000 times a day. Don't rely on this to the exclusion of other ways to access Google. But if you're in a situation where web searching is not as easy as email—you're using a mobile phone or PDA, for example—this is a quick and easy way to interface with Google.

CapeMail Tricks

CapeMail comes in handy with the combination of an email application and a way to automate sending messages (cron, for example). Say you're researching a particular topic—a relatively obscure topic but one that does generate web page results. You could set up your scheduler (or even your email program if able to send timed messages) to fire off a message to Cape-Mail once a day, gather, and archive the search results. Further, you could use your email's filtering rules to divert the CapeMail pages to their own folder for offline browsing. Make sure your search is fairly narrow, though, because CapeMail returns only 10 results at a time.

HACK #38 Simplifying Google Groups URLs

If the Google Groups URLs are a little too unwieldy, the Google Groups Simplifier will cut them down to size.

Google Groups [Hack #30] can produce some rather abominable URLs for individual posts. One message can generate a URL the likes of:

```
http://groups.google.com/groups?q=O%27reilly+%22mac+os+x%22
&hl=en&lr=&ie=UTF-8&oe=utf-8&scoring=d
&selm=ujaotqldn50oo4%40corp.supernews.com&rnum=37
```

This is a difficult URL to save and reference—not to mention emailing to a colleague.

Andrew Flegg's Google Groups Simplifier (*http://www.bleb.org/google/*) munges Groups URLs, compacting them down into something more manageable yet still allowing them to function as before.

This is a handy little tool. To use, it copy the URL that you want to make smaller and paste it into the form on the Google Groups Simplifier page. The URL above simplifies to:

```
http://groups.google.com/groups?selm=ujaotqldn50oo4%40
corp.supernews.com
```

Note that this URL is from an individually viewed message and not from a message thread (which is several messages in a framed page). If you try to simplify a thread's URL, you'll get an error message from the Google Groups Simplifier.

How does this work? The Google Groups Simplifier chops off everything but the &selm= part. Not very difficult to do, but the URLs are so large that it's handy to have an automated way to do it so you don't remove more of the URL than you need to.

If you plan to use this tool a lot, the Simplifer also offers a bookmarklet from the front page.

Other URL-Shortening Options

The Google Groups Simplifier is handy, because it shortens the URL while still making clear where the URL comes from. A glance at it and you know that the URL is from Google Groups. However, in some cases you might find that the URL is still too long and you need to shorten it still further. In that case, you might want to use one of the URL-shortening services.

URL-shortening services generate unique codes for each URL provided, allowing extremely long URLs to be compressed into much shorter, unique URLs. For example, Yahoo! News URLs can be terribly long, but with TinyURL, they can be shortened to something like *http://tinyurl.com/2ph8*. (Note: these URLs are not private so don't treat them as such. TinyURL whacking—*http://marnanel.org/writing/tinyurl-whacking*—covers making up TinyURLs to find sites other people have fed to the system.)

Don't use these services unless you absolutely have to, though; they obscure the origin of the URL, making the URLs difficult to track for research. They do come in handy if you have to reference a page cached by Google. For example, here's an URL for a cached version of oreilly.com: *http://216.239.39.100/search?q=cache:TbOF_622vaYC:www.oreilly.com/+oreilly&hl=en&ie=UTF-8*. While it's not as long as a typical Google Groups message URL, it's long enough to be difficult to paste into an email and otherwise distribute.

TinyURL (*http://www.tinyurl.com*) shortens URLs to 23 characters. A bookmarklet is available. The service converted the Google Groups URL at the beginning of this hack to *http://tinyurl.com/180q*.

MakeAShorterLink (*http://www.makeashorterlink.com/*) shortens URLs to about 40 characters, which when clicked, take the browser to "gateway" pages with details of where they're about to be sent, after which the browser is redirected to the desired URL. MakeAShorterLink converted that Google Groups URL to *http://makeashorterlink.com/?A2FD145A1*.

Shorl (*http://www.shorl.com*), in addition to shorting URLs to about 35 characters, tracks click-through statistics for the generated URL. These stats may only be accessed by the person creating the Shorl URL using a password generated at the time. Shorl turned the Groups URL above into *http://www. shorl.com/jasomykuprystu*, with the stats page at *http://shorl.com/stat. php?id=jasomykuprystu&pwd=jirafryvukomuha*. Note the embedded password (pwd=jirafryvukomuha).

HACK #39 · What Does Google Think Of...

What does Google think of you, your friends, your neighborhood, or your favorite movie?

If you've ever wondered what people think of your home town, your favorite band, your favorite snack food, or even you, Googlism (*http://www. googlism.com/*) may provide you something useful.

The Interface

The interface is dirt simple. Enter your query and check the appropriate radio button to specify whether you're looking for a who, a what, a where, or a when. You can also use the tabs to see what other objects people are searching for and what searched-for objects are the most popular. A word of warning: some of these are not work-safe.

What You Get Back

Googlism will respond with a list of things Google believes about the query at hand, be it a person, place, thing, or moment in time. For example, a search for Perl and "What" returns, along with a laundry list of others:

```
Perl is a fairly straightforward
Perl is aesthetically pleasing
Perl is just plain fun
```

Among the more humorous results for Steve Jobs and "Who" are:

```
steve jobs is my new idol
steve jobs is at it again
steve jobs is apple's focus group
```

To figure out what page any particular statement comes from, simply copy and paste it into a plain old Google search. That last statement, for instance, came from an article titled "Innovation: How Apple does it" at *http://www. gulker.com/ra/appleinnovation.html*.

Practical Uses

For the most part this is a party hack—a good party hack. Its a fun way to aggregate related statements into a silly (and occasionally profound) list.

But that's just for the most part. Googlism also works as a handy ready-reference application, allowing you to quickly find answers to simple or simply-asked questions. Just ask them of Googlism in a way that can end with the word is. For example, to discover the capital of Virginia enter The capital of Virginia. To learn why the sky is blue try The reason the sky is blue. Sometimes this doesn't work very well; try the oldest person in the world and you'll immediately be confronted with a variety of contradictory information. You'd have to visit each page represented by a result and see which answer, if any, best suited your research needs.

Expanding the Application

This application is a lot of fun, but it could be expanded. The trick is to determine how web page creators generate statements.

For example, when initially describing an acronym, many writers use the words "stands for." So you could add a Googlism that searches for your keyword and the phrase "stands for." Do a Google search for "SETI stands for" and "DDR stands for" and you'll see what I mean.

When referring to animals, plants, and even stones, the phrase "are found" is often used, so you could add a Googlism that located things. Do a Google search for sapphires are found and jaguars are found and see what you find.

See if you can think of any phrases that are in common usage, and then check those phrases in Google too see how many results each phrase has. You might get some ideas for a topic-specific Googlism tool yourself.

HACK #40   GooglePeople

People who need GooglePeople are the luckiest people in the world.

Sometimes on the Web it's hard to separate the signal from the noise. It's also hard to separate information about people from information about everything else. That's where GooglePeople (*http://www.avaquest.com/demos/GooglePeople/GooglePeople.cgi*) comes in. GooglePeople takes a "Who Is" or "Who Was" query (e.g., "Who was the first man on the moon?" or "Who was the fifth president of the United States?") and offers a list of possible candidates. It works well for some questions, but for others it's way off base.

Using GooglePeople

GooglePeople is simple: enter a "Who Is" or "Who Was" question in the query box. GooglePeople will think about it for a minute or three and provide you with a list of possible candidates to answer your question, with the most likely candidate on top, the other candidates listed underneath and rated for relevance with a series of asterisks.

Click a candidate name for a Google query integrating your original query and the candidate's name; this provides a quick test of the validity and usefulness of the GooglePeople query at hand.

Tips for Using GooglePeople

I found that for some questions GooglePeople worked very well. Who was the first African American woman in space? was answered perfectly. But some questions had GooglePeople perplexed.

Books and authors. GooglePeople seems to have a bit of trouble with identifying the authors of fiction books. For example, asking Who is the author of "Galahad at Blandings", GooglePeople will not confidently give an answer but will suggest that the most likely person is Bertie Wooster. Bertie is close, but no cigar; he's a fictional character created by the same author of *Galahad at Blandings*—P. G. Wodehouse—but he's far from an author. GooglePeople was able to state with confidence that Mark Twain was the author of *Huckleberry Finn*.

Numbers. Sometimes expressing numbers as numbers (1st) rather than words (first) makes a lot of difference in results. Asking GooglePeople about the first person to do something versus the "1st" person to do something can lead to very different results, so be sure to try both versions.

Mind your questions. Finally, don't try subjective questions if you seriously expect a good answer. Asking GooglePeople, Who's the most popular singer? or Who is the smartest person in the world? can net you some wild answers.

Using GooglePeople

While GooglePeople can appear to be a toy, it does come in handy for ready-reference questions. Obviously, you should be sure to double-check any answers you get against the full list of web answers for your question. And remember, just because it's on the Web doesn't mean it's credible!

CHAPTER FOUR

Non-API Google Applications
Hacks #41–49

As you've seen so far in this book, amazing things can be done with Google data access without ever using the Google API. This section of the book deals with Google applications that scrape Google's HTML to access its data rather than use the sanctioned Google API.

Scraping Versus the API

What is scraping and how is it different from using the Google API? Scraping is the act of using a program to pull information from an HTML page.

The Google API, on the other hand, allows you to query Google's search data directly, instead of pulling information from saved HTML as the scrapers in this section do.

Why Scrape Google Data?

Why have Google scrapers in this book anyway? Can't you do everything with the Google API? Alas, you can't. The Google API is a great way to search Google's main body of web pages, but it doesn't go much further than that. It's even limited in what it can pull from Google's main web search. For example, the Google API can't do a phonebook search. And it can't access the data from Google News, Google Catalogs, or most of Google's other specialty search properties.

That's too bad, because cool things can be done with the data from those searches. Need to track news stories for a certain topic? It's a lot easier to access several compiled searches from a spreadsheet than to manually scan HTML pages. Plus, once the information is loaded into a spreadsheet, you can resort and manipulate the data just about any way you please.

Things to Keep in Mind While Scraping

Though the programs provided in this section will provide you with hours of fun Google scraping, there are a few things you'll need to keep in mind.

Scrapers break. These scrapers are built based on the format of the Google results at this writing. If the format of results changes significantly, scrapers can, and will, break.

Don't automate your scraping. It might be tempting to go one step further and create programs that automate retrieving and scraping of Google pages.

Don't do it. Retrieving Google pages by any automated methods other than Google's API is against Google's Terms of Service (TOS). So what, you might think. After all, they can't find you, right? They might not be able to find you specifically, but they can ban access from an entire block of IP addresses based on your IP address, affecting you and others around you. Would they do this? They would and they have. See *http://news.com.com/2100-1023-883558.html* for information about a Comcast block that took place in early 2002.

Search results have limits. Remember that even though you're scraping saved result pages, you're still subject to the limitations of Google's search—you can't get more than 1,000 results for a web search, for example. That said, make sure that you've set up your web search to get the most out of each scraped page. Make sure you're getting 100 results per page.

Using Scraped Data Files

Once you've got some results, scraped them, and saved them to a comma-delimited file, what use are they?

Most of the time, you think of comma-delimited files as spreadsheet files, but they're more versatile than that. Comma-delimited files can be loaded into databases and different data-handling programs. You could even write a Perl program that did something interesting with comma-delimited files (or get a geek friend to write it for you).

But the best thing about comma-delimited files is that they age well. They're just text files. You can use them with several different programs, you don't have to worry about compatibility issues, and they're small.

Not Fancy but Handy

Google scraping applications aren't as complicated as Google API applications, nor are they anywhere near as glamorous. But if you're trying to save search results from a variety of Google's properties, they really do come in handy.

H·A·C·K #41 Don't Try This at Home
Google tools that violate Google's Terms of Service.

Despite all that the Google API does, there are folks (myself included) who wish it would do more. Then there are those who started building programmatic access to Google long before an the API became available. This survey covers a few of them.

We present them here for two reasons: to give you an idea what software you don't want to use if you have a concern about being banned from Google, and to inspire you. This software wasn't written because someone was sitting around trying to violate Google's TOS; it was written because someone simply wanted to get something done. They're creative and pragmatic and well worth a look.

> Google's Terms of Service (TOS) prohibit automated querying of the database except in conjunction with the Google API. Automatic searching for whatever reason is a big no-no. Google can react to this very strongly; in fact, they have temporarily banned whole IP address blocks based on the actions of a few, so be careful what you use to query Google.

Don't Try These at Home

Here is a list of tools to avoid, unless you don't mind getting yourself banned:

Gnews2RSS (http://www.voidstar.com/gnews2rss.php?q=news&num=15)
  Turns a Google News search into a form suitable for syndication.

WebPosition Gold (http://www.webposition.com/)
  Performs a range of tasks for web wranglers, including designing more search engine–friendly pages, supporting automated URL submissions, and analyzing search engine traffic to a site. Unfortunately, their automated rank-checking feature violates Google's Terms of Service. This program does so many things, however, that you could consider using it for some position-checking tasks alone.

AgentWebRanking (http://www.agentwebranking.com/)
Checks your web page's ranking with dozens of major search engines all over the world. That search engine list also includes Google, though the program violates Google's Terms of Service by going around the Google API.

Other Programs to Be Concerned About

When reviewing search engine tools, keep an eye out for those that:

- Offer an automated check of rankings in Google without requiring a developer's key
- Offer an automated search and retrieval of special collections not covered by the Google API, such as Google News and Google Catalogs
- Frame, metasearch, or otherwise use Google's content without apparent agreement or partnership with Google

Building a Custom Date-Range Search Form
Search only Google pages indexed today, yesterday, the last 7 days, or last 30 days.

Google has a date-based search [Hack #11] but uses Julian dates. Most people can't convert Gregorian to Julian in their heads. But with a conversion formula and a little Perl scripting, you can have a Google search form that offers to let users search Google pages indexed today, yesterday, the last seven days, or the last 30 days.

The Form

The frontend to the script is a simple HTML form:

```
<form action="http://path/to/cgi-bin/goofresh.cgi"
method="get">
Search for:<br />
<input type="text" name="query" size="30" />
<p />
Search for pages indexed how many days back?<br />
<select name="days_back">
<option value="0">Today</option>
<option value="1">Yesterday</option>
<option value="7">Last 7 Days</option>
<option value="30">Last 30 Days</option>
</select>
<p />
<input type="submit" value="Search">
</form>
```

The form prompts for two user inputs. The first is a Google query, replete with support for special syntaxes [in "The Special Syntaxes" in Chapter 1] and syntax mixing [Hack #8]; after all, we'll just be passing your query along to Google itself. The second input, a pull-down list, prompts for how many days' worth of search the form should perform.

 This hack requires an additional module, Time::JulianDay, and won't run without it (*http://search.cpan.org/ search?query=Time%3A%3AJulianDay*).

The Code

Note that this script just does a couple of date translations in Perl and redirects the browser to Google, altered query in tow. It's just a regular query as far as Google is concerned and so doesn't require a developer's API key.

```perl
#!/usr/local/bin/perl
# goofresh.cgi
# searches for recently-Indexed files on google
# usage: goofresh.cgi is called as a CGI with form input,
# redirecting the browser to Google, altered query in tow

use CGI qw/:standard/;
use Time::JulianDay;

# build a URL-escaped query
(my $query = param('query')) =~ s#(\W)#sprintf("%%%02x", ord($1))#ge;

# how many days back?
my $days_back = int param('days_back') || 0;

# what's the current julian date?
my $julian_date = int local_julian_day(time);

# redirect the browser to Google with query in tow
print redirect(
    'http://www.google.com/search?num=100' .
    "&q=$query" .
    "+daterange%3A" . ($julian_date - $days_back) . "-$julian_date"
);
```

Hacking the Hack

If you don't like the date ranges hardcoded into the form, make up your own and adjust the form accordingly:

```html
<form action="http://path/to/cgi-bin/goofresh.cgi"
method="get">
Search for:<br />
<input type="text" name="query" size="30" />
```

```
<p />
Search for pages indexed how many days back?<br />
<select name="days_back">
<option value="0">Today</option>
<option value="30">Around 1 Month</option>
<option value="60">Around 2 Months</option>
<option value="90">Around 3 Months</option>
<option value="365">1 Year</option>
</select>
<p />
<input type="submit" value="Search">
</form>
```

Or simply let the user specify how many days to go back in a text field:

```
<form action="http://path/to/cgi-bin/goofresh.cgi"
method="get">
Search for:<br />
<input type="text" name="query" size="30" />
<p />
Search for pages indexed how many days back?<br />
<input type="text" name="days_back" size="4"
maxlength="4" />
<p />
<input type="submit" value="Search">
</form>
```

Building Google Directory URLs

#43 This hack uses ODP category information to build URLs for the Google Directory.

The Google Directory (*http://directory.google.com/*) overlays the Open Directory Project (or "ODP" or "DMOZ," *http://www.dmoz.org/*) ontology onto the Google core index. The result is a Yahoo!-like directory hierarchy of search results and their associated categories with the added magic of Google's popularity algorithms.

The ODP opens its entire database of listings to anybody—provided you're willing to download a 205 MB file (and that's compressed!). While you're probably not interested in all the individual listings, you might want particular ODP categories. Or you may be interested in watching new listings flowing into certain categories.

Unfortunately, the ODP does not offer a way to search by keyword sites added within a recent time period. (Yahoo! does offer this.) So instead of searching for recently added sites, the best way to get new site information from the ODP is to monitor categories.

Because the Google Directory does build its directory based on the ODP information, you can use the ODP category hierarchy information to generate Google Directory URLs. This hack searches the ODP category hierarchy information for keywords you specify, then builds Google Directory URLs and checks them to make sure they're active.

You'll need to download the category hierarchy information from the ODP to get this hack to work. The compressed file containing this information is available from *http://dmoz.org/rdf.html*. The specific file you're after is *http://dmoz.org/rdf/structure.rdf.u8.gz*. Before using it, you must uncompress it using a decompression application specific to your operating system. In the Unix environment, this looks something like:

```
% gunzip structure.rdf.u8.gz
```

Bear in mind that the full category hierarchy is over 35 MB. If you just want to experiment with the structure, you can get a excerpt at *http://dmoz.org/rdf/structure.example.txt*. This version is a plain text file and does not require uncompressing.

The Code

```perl
#!/usr/bin/perl
# google_dir.pl
# Uses ODP category information to build URLs into the Google Directory.
# Usage: perl google_dir.pl "keywords" < structure.rdf.u8

use strict;

use LWP::Simple;

# Turn off output buffering
$|++;

my $directory_url = "http://directory.google.com";

$ARGV
   or die qq{usage: perl google_dir.pl "{query}" < structure.rdf.u8\n};

# Grab those command-line specified keywords and build a regular expression
my $keywords = shift @ARGV;
$keywords =~ s!\s+!\||!g;

# A place to store topics
my %topics;

# Loop through the DMOZ category file, printing matching results
while (<>) {
  /"(Top\/.*$keywords.*)"/i and !$topics{$1}++
     and print "$directory_url/$1\n";
}
```

Running the Hack

Run the script from the command line, along with a query and the piped-in contents of the DMOZ category file:

```
% perl googledir.pl "keywords" < structure.rdf.u8
```

If you're using the shorter category excerpt, *structure.example.txt*, use:

```
% perl googledir.pl "keywords" < structure.example.txt
```

The Results

Feeding this hack the keyword mosaic would look something like:

```
% perl googledir.pl "mosaic" < structure.rdf.u8
http://directory.google.com/Top/Arts/Crafts/Mosaics
http://directory.google.com/Top/Arts/Crafts/Mosaics/Glass
http://directory.google.com/Top/Arts/Crafts/Mosaics/Ceramic_and_Broken_China
http://directory.google.com/Top/Arts/Crafts/Mosaics/Associations_and_
Directories
http://directory.google.com/Top/Arts/Crafts/Mosaics/Stone
http://directory.google.com/Top/Shopping/Crafts/Mosaics
http://directory.google.com/Top/Shopping/Crafts/Supplies/Mosaics
...
```

Hacking the Hack

There isn't much hacking you can do to this hack; it's designed to take ODP data, create Google URLs, and verify those URLs. How well you can get this to work for you really depends on the types of search words you choose.

Do choose words that are more general. If you're interested in a particular state in the U.S., for example, choose the name of the state and major cities, but don't choose the name of a very small town or of the governor. Do choose the name of a company and not of its CFO. A good rule of thumb is to choose the keywords that you might find as entry names in an encyclopedia or almanac. You can easily imagine finding a company name as an encyclopedia entry, but it's a rare CFO who would rate an entry to themselves in an encyclopedia.

HACK Scraping Google Results
#44

Scraping the results of a Google search into a comma-delimited file.

Because you can use the Google API to get results and put them in any format you like, why in the world would you bother to do a manual search result on Google, save the results, and then scrape them with a Perl program? You might not want, or indeed be able, to do anything as fancy as the

Google API allows; you might just want to grab some results, drop them into a spreadsheet, and go.

Just like we did in Peeling Phone Numbers [Hack #49], you can save Google web search results to a file, and then process them into a comma-delimited text file with a short Perl script.

> Be sure to set your preferences [Hack #1] to 100 results per page to get the most out of this hack.

The Code

```perl
#!/usr/bin/perl
# google2csv.pl # Google Web Search Results exported to CSV suitable
# for import into Excel
# Usage: perl google2csv.pl < results.html > results.csv

print qq{"title","url","size","domain suffix"\n};

my($results) = (join '', <>) =~
  m!<div>(.*?)</div>!mis;

while ( $results =~
m!<p><a href="?(.+?)"?>(.+?)</a>.+?\s+-\s+(\d+k)?!mgis
) {
  my($url,$title, $size) = ($1||'',$2||'',$3||'');
  my($suffix) = $url =~ m!\.(\w+)/!;
  $title =~ s!"!""!g;          # double escape " marks
  $title =~ s!<.+?>!!g; # drop all HTML tags
  print qq{"$title","$url","$size","$suffix"\n};
}
```

Running the Script

Run the script from the command line, specifying the result's HTML file-name and name of the CSV file you wish to create or to which you wish to append additional results. For example, using *results.html* as input and *results.csv* as output:

```
$ perl google2csv.pl < results.html > results.csv
```

Leaving off the > and CSV filename sends the results to the screen for your perusal:

```
$ perl google2csv.pl < results.html
```

The Results

Here's a sample run on the results of a search for Mac OS X:

```
$ perl google2csv.pl < results.html
"title","url","size","domain suffix"
"Apple - Mac OS X","http://www.apple.com/macosx/","","com"
"Apple - Software - Mac OS X Server","http://www.apple.com/server/",
"29k","com"
"Mac OS X Development","http://developer.apple.com/macosx/","28k","com"
"Mac OS X Hints - Get the most from X!","http://www.macosxhints.com/",
"","com"
"Mac OS X Apps - The Source For Mac OS X Software",
"http://www.macosxapps.com/","39k","com"
"VersionTracker.com - free Macintosh software downloads for Mac
OS ... ","http://www.versiontracker.com/macosx/","101k","com"
"O'Reilly Mac OS X Conference",
"http://conferences.oreillynet.com/macosx2002/","25k","com"
"MacNN | OS X","http://osx.macnn.com/","94k","com"
"???? - Mac OS X","http://www.apple.co.jp/macosx/","43k","jp"
"Apple - Support - Mac OS X",
"http://www.info.apple.com/usen/macosx/","36k","com"
```

You'll see that the program records four attributes to the CSV file: title, URL, size (when available), and top-level domain. The "snippet" of web page usually included with a Google result was omitted, because it's difficult to read in a spreadsheet format.

So why include the page size and domain? Research. If you're generating a set of results to be referred to later, it's handy to be able to sort them by suffix. "edu" results tend to be different from "org" results, which tend to be different from "com" results, and so on. Not to mention differing result sets by country, *.uk* versus *.jp*, for instance. And if you're generating links to contact later (to ask for a reciprocal link, for example), it's handy to be able to set apart the less-commercial suffixes such as *.edu* and *.org*.

HACK #45   Scraping Google AdWords

Scrape the AdWords from a saved Google results page into a form suitable for importing into a spreadsheet or database.

Google's AdWords™—the text ads that appear to the right of the regular search results—are delivered on a cost-per-click basis, and purchasers of the AdWords are allowed to set a ceiling on the amount of money they spend on their ad. This means if even if you run a search for the same query word multiple times, you won't necessarily get the same set of ads each time.

Scraping Google AdWords

If you're considering using Google AdWords to run ads, you might want to gather up and save the ads that are running for the query words you're interested in. Google AdWords are not provided by the Google API; of course you can't automatically scrape Google's results outside the Google API, because it's against Google's Terms of Service.

This hack will let you scrape the AdWords from a saved Google results page and export them to a CSV (comma-separated value) file, which you can then import into Excel or your favorite spreadsheet program.

 This hack requires an additional Perl module, HTML::
TokeParser (*http://search.cpan.org/search?query=htmL %3A%3Atokeparser&mode=all*). You'll need to install it before the hack will run.

The Code

```perl
#!/usr/bin/perl
# usage: perl adwords.pl results.html

use strict;
use HTML::TokeParser;
die "I need at least one file: $!\n"
    unless @ARGV;
my @Ads;
for my $file (@ARGV){
  # skip if the file doesn't exist
  # you could add more file testing here.
  # errors go to STDERR so they won't
  # pollute our csv file
    unless (-e $file) {
        warn "What??: $file -- $! \n-- skipping --\n";
        next;
    }
  # now parse the file
  my $p = HTML::TokeParser->new($file);
  # $p is a kind of iterator and everything
  # in the given file is a token. We are going to
  # iterate through them all but we might throw them away
  # if they aren't what we are looking for.
  # run this: perldoc HTML::TokeParser
  while(my $token = $p->get_token) {
      # look for a start token whose name is 'td'
      # and has an attribute named 'id' and that
      # attribute's value is 'taw' followed by one
      # or more digits.
      next unless $token->[0] eq 'S'
          and $token->[1] eq 'td'
          and $token->[2]{id} =~ /taw\d+/;
      # $ad is a hash ref that will hold our
```

```perl
        # data for this ad.
        my $ad;
        # if we are here we found the td tag. It also has
        # the url we want
        # we strip off the 'go to' stuff
        ($ad->{url}) = $token->[2]{onmouseover} =~ /go to ([^']+)'/;
        # now go directly to the next anchor tag
        my $link = $p->get_tag('a');
        # grab the href attribute and clean it up
        $ad->{href} = $link->[1]{href};
        $ad->{href} =~ s|/url\?q=||;
        # the adwords are the text upto the closing </a> tag
        $ad->{adwords} = $p->get_trimmed_text('/a');
        # Now look at every token looking for text.
        # Unless the text matches 'Interest:' it is
        # description text so we add it to the description.
        # If it is the 'Interest:' token then
        # we want to move to the next img token
        # and grab the 'width' attribute's value
        while( my $token = $p->get_token ) {
            # this will skip all the <br> and <font> tags
            next unless $token->[0] eq 'T';
            unless($token->[1] =~ /Interest:/) {
                $ad->{desc} .= ' ' . $token->[1];
                next;
            }
            my $img = $p->get_tag('img');
            $ad->{interest} = $img->[1]{width};
            last; # we are done
        }
        # the url is also in this description but
        # we don't need it. We already found it.
        $ad->{desc} =~ s/$ad->{url}.*//;
        # change two or more whitespace characters into one space.
        $ad->{desc} =~ s/\s{2,}/ /g;
        # there is nothing else to look for so
        # we add this ad to our list of ads.
        push(@Ads,$ad);
    }
}
print quoted( qw( AdWords HREF Description URL Interest ) );
for my $ad (@Ads) {
    print quoted( @$ad{qw( adwords href desc url interest )} );
}
# we want a csv (comma separated values)
# so excel will open it without asking
# any questions. So we have to print quote marks
sub quoted {
    return join( ",", map { "'$_'" } @_ )."\n";
}
```

How It Works

Call this script on the command line, providing the name of the saved Google results page and a file in which to put the CSV results:

```
% perl adword input.html > output.csv
```

input.html is the name of the Google results page you've saved. *output.csv* is the name of the comma-delimited file to which you want to save your results. You can also provide multiple input files on the command line if you'd like:

```
% perl adword input.html input2.html > output.csv
```

The Results

The results will appear in a comma-delimited format that looks like this:

```
"AdWords","HREF","Description","URL","Interest"
"Free Blogging Site","http://www.1sound.com/ix",
" The ultimate blog spot Start your journal now ","www.1sound.com/ix","40"
"New Webaga Blog","http://www.webaga.com/blog.php",
" Fully customizable. Fairly inexpensive. ","www.webaga.com","24"
"Blog this","http://edebates.e-thepeople.org/a-national/article/10245/
view&",
" Will online diarists rule the Net strewn with failed dotcoms? ",
"e-thePeople.org","26"
"Ford - Ford Cars","http://quickquote.forddirect.com/FordDirect.jsp",
" Build a Ford online here and get a price quote from your local dealer! ",
"www.forddirect.com","40"
"See Ford Dealer's Invoice","http://buyingadvice.com/search/",
" Save $1,400 in hidden dealership profits on your next new car. ",
"buyingadvice.com","28"
"New Ford Dealer Prices","http://www.pricequotes.com/",
" Compare Low Price Quotes on a New Ford from Local Dealers and Save! ",
"www.pricequotes.com","25"
```

(Each line was prematurely broken for the purposes of publication.)

You'll see that the hack returns the AdWords headline, the link URL, the description in the ad, the URL on the ad (this is the URL that appears in the ad text, while the HREF is what the URL links to), and the Interest, which is the size of the Interest bar on the text ad. The Interest bar gives an idea of how many click-throughs an ad has had, showing how popular it is.

Hacking the Hack

You might find that the hack as it's written provides too much information. Instead of the information above, you might want a little less information, or you might want it in a different order.

The code you'll need to change is in one section.

```
my @headers = qw( AdWords HREF Description URL Interest );
print '"',join('","',@headers),'"',"\n";
for my $ad (@Ads) {
    print '"', join('","',
            $ad->{adwords},
            $ad->{href},
            $ad->{desc},
            $ad->{url},
            $ad->{interest}),'"',"\n";
```

The first part you'll need to change is the lower part, beginning with print "", join. As you see, each line corresponds to part of the data written to the comma-delimited file. Simply rearrange the lines in the order you want them, omitting the information you don't want.

For example, you might want the Adwords title, the URL, and the description, in that order. Your code would look like this:

```
print '"',join('","',@headers),'"',"\n";
for my $ad (@Ads) {
    print '"', join('","',
            $ad->{adwords},
            $ad->{url},
            $ad->{desc}),'"',"\n";
```

Once you've made the changes to that you'll have to change the "header line" that tells Excel what each field is. That's at the top of the code snippet:

```
my @headers = qw( AdWords HREF Description URL Interest);
```

You'll need to rearrange the words in parentheses to match the information that you're outputting to the CSV file. In the case above, where I'm saving just the AdWords title, URL, and description, the line would look like this:

```
my @headers = qw( AdWords URL Description);
```

See Also

- Getting the Most out of AdWords [Hack #99]

—Tara Calishain and Tim Allwine

Scraping Google Groups
#46 Pulling results from Google Groups searches into a comma-delimited file.

It's easy to look at the Internet and say it's web pages, or it's computers, or it's networks. But look a little deeper and you'll see that the core of the Internet is discussions: mailing lists, online forums, and even web sites, where people hold forth in glorious HTML, waiting for people to drop by, consider their philosophies, make contact, or buy their products and services.

Nowhere is the Internet-as-conversation idea more prevalent than in Usenet newsgroups. Google Groups has an archive of over 700 million messages from years of Usenet traffic. If you're doing timely research, searching and saving Google Groups message pointers comes in really handy.

Because Google Groups is not searchable by the current version of the Google API, you can't build an automated Google Groups query tool without violating Google's TOS. However, you can scrape the HTML of a page you visit personally and save to your hard drive.

Saving Pages

The first thing you need to do is run a Google Groups search. See the Google Groups [Hack #30] discussion for some hints on best practices for searching this message archive.

It's best to put pages you're going to scrape in order of date; that way if you're going to scrape more pages later, it's easy to look at them and check the last date the search results changed. Let's say you're trying to keep up with uses of Perl in programming the Google API; your query might look like this:

```
perl group:google.public.web-apis
```

On the righthand side of the results page is an option to sort either by relevance or date. Sort it by date. Your results page should look something like Figure 4-1.

Save this page to your hard drive, naming it something memorable like *groups.html*.

Scraping Caveats

There are a couple of things to keep in mind when it comes to scraping pages, Google or not:

Scraping is brittle. A scraper is based on the way a page is formatted at the time the scraper is written. This means one minor change in the page, and things break down rather quickly.

There are myriad ways of scraping any particular page. This is just one of them, so experiment!

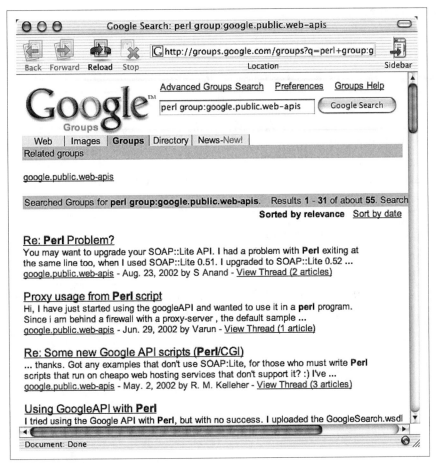

Figure 4-1. Results of a Google Groups search

The Code

```
# groups2csv.pl
# Google Groups results exported to CSV suitable for import into Excel
# Usage: perl groups2csv.pl < groups.html > groups.csv

# The CSV Header
print qq{"title","url","group","date","author","number of articles"\n};

# The base URL for Google Groups
my $url = "http://groups.google.com";

# Rake in those results
my($results) = (join '', <>);

# Perform a regular expression match to glean individual results
while ( $results =~ m!<p><a href="?(.+?)"?>(.+?)</a><font size=-1(.+?)<br>
```

```
<font color=green><a href=.+?>(.+?)</a>\s+-\s+(.+?)\s+by\s+(.+?)\s+-.+?\(((\
d+) articles!mgis ) {
    my($path, $title, $snippet, $group, $date, $author, $articles) =
        ($1||'',$2||'',$3||'',$4||'',$5||'',$6||'',$7||'');
    $title =~ s!"!""!g; # double escape " marks
    $title =~ s!<.+?>!!g; # drop all HTML tags
    print qq{"$title","$url$path","$group","$date","$author","$articles"\n};
}
```

Running the Hack

Run the script from the command line, specifying the Google Groups results
filename you saved earlier and name of the CSV file you wish to create or to
which you wish to append additional results. For example, using *groups.html*
as your input and *groups.csv* as your output:

```
$ perl groups2csv.pl < groups.html > groups.csv
```

Leaving off the > and CSV filename sends the results to the screen for your
perusal.

Using a double >> before the CSV filename appends the current set of results
to the CSV file, creating it if it doesn't already exist. This is useful for combining more than one set of results, represented by more than one saved
results page:

```
$ perl groups2csv.pl < results_1.html > results.csv
$ perl groups2csv.pl < results_2.html >> results.csv
```

The Results

Scraping the results of a search for perl group:google.public.web-apis , anything mentioning the Perl programming language on the Google APIs discussion forum, looks like:

```
$ perl groups2csv.pl < groups.html
"title","url","group","date","author","number of articles"
"Re: Perl Problem?",
"http://groups.google.com/groups?q=perl+group:google.public.
web-apis&hl=en&lr=&ie=UTF-8&output=search&selm=5533bb12.0208230215.
365a093d%40po sting.google.com&rnum=1",
"google.public.web-apis","Aug. 23, 2002","S Anand","2"
"Proxy usage from Perl script",
"http://groups.google.com/groups?q=perl+group:goo
gle.public.web-apis&hl=en&lr=&ie=UTF-8&output=search&selm=575db61f.
0206290446.1d fe4ea7%40posting.google.com&rnum=2",
"google.public.web-apis","Jun. 29, 2002","Varun","3"
...
"The Google Velocity",
"http://groups.google.com/groups?q=perl+group:google.public.web-apis&hl
=en&lr=&ie=UTF-8&output=search&selm=18a1ac72.0204221336.47fdee71%
40posting.google.com&rnum=29",
"google.public.web-apis","Apr. 22, 2002","John Graham-Cumming","2"
```

Scraping Google News

#47 Scrape Google News search results to get at the latest from thousands of aggregated news sources.

Since Google added thousands of sources to its Google News [Hack #32] search engine, it's become an excellent source for any researcher. However, because you can't access Google News through the Google API, you'll have to scrape your results from the HTML of a Google News results page. This hack does just that, gathering up results into a comma-delimited file suitable for loading into a spreadsheet or database. For each news story, it extracts the title, URL, source (i.e., news agency), publication date or age of the news item, and an excerpted description.

Because Google's Terms of Service prohibits the automated access of their search engines except through the Google API, this hack does not actually connect to Google. Instead, it works on a page of results that you've saved from a Google News search you've run yourself. Simply save the results page as HTML source using your browser's File → Save As... command.

Make sure the results are listed by date instead of relevance. When results are listed by relevance some of the descriptions are missing, because similar stories are clumped together. You can sort results by date by choosing the "Sort By Date" link on the results page or by adding &scoring=d to the end of the results URL. Also make sure you're getting the maximum number of results by adding &num=100 to the end of the results URL. For example, Figure 4-2 shows results of a query for monk detective, hoping to find out more about the new popular feel-good detective show, "Monk."

The Code

```perl
#!/usr/bin/perl
# news2csv.pl
# Google News Results exported to CSV suitable for import into Excel
# Usage: perl news2csv.pl < news.html > news.csv

print qq{"title","link","source","date or age", "description"\n};

my %unescape = ('&lt;'=>'<', '&gt;'=>'>', '&amp;'=>'&',
   '&quot;'=>'"', ' '=>' ');
my $unescape_re = join '|' => keys %unescape;
my($results) = (join '', <>) =~ m!(.*)!mis;
$results =~ s/($unescape_re)/$unescape{$1}/migs; # unescape HTML
$results =~ s![\n\r]! !migs; # drop spurious newlines

while ( $results =~ m!(.+?)(.+?) - (.+?)(.+?)!migs ) {
  my($url, $title, $source, $date_age, $description) =
  ($1||'',$2||'',$3||'',$4||'', $5||'');
  $title =~ s!"!""!g; # double escape " marks
```

```
    $description =~ s!"!""!g;
    my $output =
        qq{"$title","$url","$source","$date_age","$description"\n};
    $output =~ s!<.+?>!!g; # drop all HTML tags
    print $output;
}
```

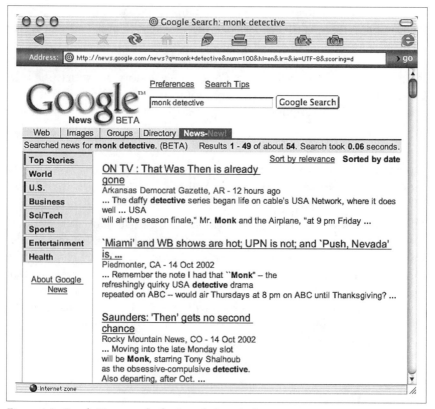

Figure 4-2. Google News results for "monk detective"

Running the Script

Run the script from the command line, specifying the Google News results HTML filename and name of the CSV file you wish to create or to which you wish to append additional results. For example, using *news.html* as our input and *news.csv* as our output:

```
$ perl news2csv.pl < news.html > news.csv
```

Leaving off the > and CSV filename sends the results to the screen for your perusal.

The Results

The following are some of the 54 results returned by a Google News search for monk detective and using the HTML page of results shown in Figure 4-2:

```
"title","link","source","date or age", "description"
"ON TV : That Was Then is already gone",
"http://www.nwanews.com/adg/story_style.php?storyid=9127",
"Arkansas Democrat Gazette, AR",
"12 hours ago",
" ... The daffy detective series began life on cable<92>s USA Network,
where it does well ... USA will air the season finale,"" Mr. Monk ... "
"`Miami' and WB shows are hot; UPN is not; and `Push, Nevada' is, ... ",
"http://www.bayarea.com/mld/bayarea/entertainment/television/...",
"Piedmonter, CA",
"14 Oct 2002",
" ... Remember the note I had that ``Monk'' -- the refreshingly quirky
USA detective dramarepeated on ABC -- would air Thursdays ... "
...
"Indie Film Fest hits New Haven",
"http://www.yaledailynews.com/article.asp?AID=19740",
"Yale Daily News",
"20 Sep 2002",
" ... The Tower of Babble,"" directed by Beau Bauman '99, and
""Made-Up,"" which was directed by Tony Shalhoub DRA '80, who
also stars in the USA detective show ""Monk."". ... "
```

(Each listing actually occurs on its own line; lines are broken and occasionally shortened for the purposes of publication.)

Hacking the Hack

Most of this program you want to leave alone. It's been built to make sense out of the Google News formatting. But if you don't like the way the program organizes the information that's taken out of the results page, you can change it. Just rearrange the variables on the following line, sorting them any way you want them. Be sure to you keep a comma between each one.

```
my $output =
    qq{"$title","$url","$source","$date_age","$description"\n};
```

For example, perhaps you want only the URL and title. The line should read:

```
my $output =
    qq{"$url","$title"\n};
```

That \n specifies a newline, and the $ characters specify that $url and $title are variable names; keep them intact.

Of course, now your output won't match the header at the top of the CSV file, by default:

```
print qq{"title","link","source","date or age", "description"\n};
```

As before, simply change this to match, as follows:

```
print qq{"url","title"\n};
```

HACK #48 Scraping Google Catalogs

Scrape and save Google catalog search results to a comma-delimited file.

The December-Holiday-of-Your-Choice comes but once a year, but catalog shopping is a year-round joy. And Google Catalogs [Hack #33] makes it easier than ever.

Of course, just because you spend a rainy winter afternoon finding the perfect shawl for Aunt Prunella doesn't mean that you'll be able to replicate the search when you need it. Or maybe you want to do a search for several things and browse them at your leisure later.

Because Google Catalogs aren't supported by the Google API, this hack scrapes finds from the HTML of a Google Catalogs results page. It saves the catalog title, date or season, page number, and even a link to an image of the page itself at Google. Results are saved in CSV format, ready for import into a database or spreadsheet application.

Because Google's Terms of Service prohibits the automated access of their search engines except through the Google API, this hack does not actually connect to Google. Instead, it works on a page of results that you've saved from a Google Catalogs search you've run yourself. Simply save the results page as HTML source using your browser's File → Save As... command.

As with the Google News hack [Hack #47], you can optimize the effectiveness of this hack by changing the results URL ever so slightly to tweak the order of and data displayed. By adding a &num=100 to the end of the catalog search results URL, you'll get up to 100 results instead of only the first.

For example, Figure 4-3 shows results of a query for the perfect shawl for that aunt.

The Code

```
#!/usr/bin/perl
# catalogs2csv.pl
# Google Catalogs Results exported to CSV suitable for import into Excel
# Usage: perl catalogs2csv.pl < catalogs.html > catalogs.csv

print qq{"title","link","date","page"\n};

my($results) = join '', <>;
```

```
while ( $results =~ m!<td>(.+?)   <font size=-1>(.+?) - Pa
ge (\w+?) -.+?<a href="(/catalogs.+?)"><img src=.+?></a>  !migs )
{
    my($title, $date, $page, $url) = ($1||'',$2||'',$3||'',$4||'');
    $title =~ s!"!""!g;  # double escape " marks
    my $output = qq{"$title","$url","$date","$page"\n};
    $output =~ s! ! !g;  # clean spaces
    print $output;
}
```

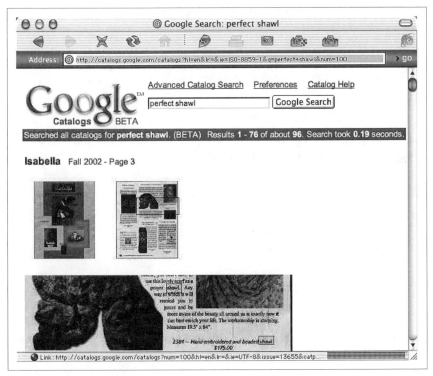

Figure 4-3. Google Catalogs results for "perfect shawl"

Running the Script

Run the script from the command line, specifying the Google Catalogs results HTML filename and name of the CSV file you wish to create or to which you wish to append additional results. For example, using *catalogs.html* as our input and *catalogs.csv* as our output:

```
$ perl catalogs2csv.pl < catalogs.html > catalogs.csv
```

Leaving off the > and CSV filename sends the results to the screen for your perusal.

The Results

You (and your aunt) appear to be in luck; there's an abundance of perfect shawls to be found in the Google Catalogs:

```
"title","link","date","page"
"Isabella","http://catalogs.google.com/catalogs?num=100
&hl=en&lr=&ie=UTF-8&issue=13655&catpage=cover","Fall 2002","3"
"Sovietski Collection","http://catalogs.google.com/catalogs?num=100
&hl=en&lr=&ie=UTF-8&issue=9447&catpage=cover","Summer 2002","37"
"Rego","http://catalogs.google.com/catalogs?num=100&hl=en
&lr=&ie=UTF-8&issue=12484&catpage=cover","2002","21"
"Crazy Crow Trading Post","http://catalogs.google.com/catalogs?num=100
&hl=en&lr=&ie=UTF-8&issue=12346&catpage=cover","2002","39"
"Winter Silks - Sale","http://catalogs.google.com/catalogs?num=100
&hl=en&lr=&ie=UTF-8&issue=10002&catpage=cover","Summer 2002","11"
...
"Previews","http://catalogs.google.com/catalogs?num=100
&hl=en&lr=&ie=UTF-8&issue=14468&catpage=cover","Oct 2002","381"
```

(Each listing actually occurs on its own line; lines are broken and occasionally shortened for the purposes of publication.)

Hacking the Hack

The output format may be altered to suit your fancy; see the Google News Scraper [Hack #47] for details on hacking the hack.

Scraping the Google Phonebook

Create a comma-delimited file from a list of phone numbers returned by Google.

Just because Google's API doesn't support the phonebook: [Hack #17] syntax doesn't mean that you can't make use of Google phonebook data.

This simple Perl script takes a page of Google phonebook: results and produces a comma-delimited text file suitable for import into Excel or your average database application. The script doesn't use the Google API, though, because the API doesn't yet support phonebook lookups. Instead, you'll need to run the search in your trusty web browser and save the results to your computer's hard drive as an HTML file. Point the script at the HTML file and it'll do it's thing.

Which results should you save? You have two choices depending on which syntax you're using:

- If you're using the phonebook: syntax, save the second page of results, reached by clicking the "More business listings..." or "More residential listings..." links on the initial results page.

- If you're using the bphonebook: or rphonebook: syntax, simply save the first page of results. Depending on how many pages of results you have, you might have to run the program several times.

Because this program is so simple, you might be tempted to plug this code into a program that uses LWP::Simple to automatically grab result pages from Google, automating the entire process. You should know that accessing Google with automated queries outside of the Google API is against their Terms of Service.

The Code

```
#!/usr/bin/perl
# phonebook2csv
# Google Phonebook results in CSV suitable for import into Excel
# Usage: perl phonebook2csv.pl < results.html > results.csv

# CSV header
print qq{"name","phone number","address"\n};

my @listings = split /<hr size=1>/, join '', <>;

foreach (@listings[1..($#listings-1)]) {
        s!\n!!g; # drop spurious newlines
        s!<.+?>!!g; # drop all HTML tags
        s!"!""!g; # double escape " marks
        print '"' . join('","', (split /\s+-\s+/)[0..2]) . "\"\n";
}
```

Running the Hack

Run the script from the command line, specifying the phonebook results HTML filename and name of the CSV file you wish to create or to which you wish to append additional results. For example, using *results.html* as our input and *results.csv* as our output:

```
$ perl phonebook2csv.pl < results.html > results.csv
```

Leaving off the > and CSV filename sends the results to the screen for your perusal:

```
$ perl phonebook2csv.pl < results.html > results.csv
"name","phone number","address"
"John Doe","(555) 555-5555","Wandering, TX 98765"
"Jane Doe","(555) 555-5555","Horsing Around, MT 90909"
```

```
"John and Jane Doe","(555) 555-5555","Somewhere, CA 92929"
"John Q. Doe","(555) 555-5555","Freezing, NE 91919"
"Jane J. Doe","(555) 555-5555","1 Sunnyside Street, "Tanning, FL 90210""
"John Doe, Jr.","(555) 555-5555","Beverly Hills, CA 90210"
"John Doe","(555) 555-5555","1 Lost St., Yonkers, NY 91234"
"John Doe","(555) 555-5555","1 Doe Street, Doe, OR 99999"
"John Doe","(555) 555-5555","Beverly Hills, CA 90210"
```

Using a double >> before the CSV filename appends the current set of results to the CSV file, creating it if it doesn't already exist. This is useful for combining more than one set of results, represented by more than one saved results page:

```
$ perl phonebook2csv.pl < results_1.html > results.csv
$ perl phonebook2csv.pl < results_2.html >> results.csv
```

## CHAPTER FIVE

Introducing the
Google Web API
Hacks #50–59

A first look at the Google API and how to sign up.

Why an API?

When search engines first appeared on the scene, they were more open to being spidered, scraped, and aggregated. Sites like Excite and AltaVista didn't worry too much about the odd surfer using Perl to grab a slice of page, or meta–search engines including their results in their aggregated search results. Sure, egregious data suckers might get shut out, but the search engines weren't worried about sharing their information on a smaller scale.

Google never took that stance. Instead, they have regularly prohibited meta–search engines from using their content without a license, and they try their best to block unidentified web agents like Perl's LWP::Simple module or even wget on the command line. Google has further been known to block IP-address ranges for running automated queries.

Google had every right to do this; after all, it is their search technology, database, and computer power. Unfortunately, however, these policies meant that casual researchers and Google nuts, like you and I, don't have the ability to play their rich data set in any automated way.

In the Spring of 2002, Google changed all that with the release of the Google Web API (*http://api.google.com/*). The Google Web API doesn't allow you to do every kind of search possible, for example, it doesn't support the phonebook: [Hack #17] syntax, but it does make the lion's share of Google's rich and massive database available for developers to create their own interfaces and use Google search results to their liking.

 API stands for "Application Programming Interface," a doorway for programmatic access to a particular resource or application, in this case, the Google index.

So how can you participate in all this Google API goodness?

You'll have to register for a developer's key, a login of sorts to the Google API. Each key affords its owner 1,000 Google Web API queries per day, after which you're out of luck until tomorrow. In fact, even if you don't plan on writing any applications, it's still useful to have a key at your disposal. There are various third-party applications built on the Google API that you may wish to visit and try out; some of these ask that you use your own key and alotted 1,000 queries.

Signing Up and Google's Terms

Signing up for a Google Web API developer's key is simple. First you'll have to create a Google account, which at the moment is good only for the Google Web APIs and Google Answers. Google promises more applications associated with Google accounts in the future. The requirements are only a valid email address and made-up password.

You will, of course, have to agree to Google's Terms & Conditions (*http://www.google.com/apis/download.html*) before you can to proceed. In broad strokes, this says:

- Google exercises no editorial control over the sites that appear in its index. The Google API might return some results you might find offensive.

- The Google API may be used for personal use only. It may not be used to sell a product or service, or to drive traffic to a site for the sake of advertising sales.

- You can't noodle with Google's intellectual property marks that appear within the API.

- Google does not accept any liability for the use of their API. This is a beta program.

- You may indicate that the program you create uses the Google API, but not if the application(s) "(1) tarnish, infringe, or dilute Google's trademarks, (2) violate any applicable law, and (3) infringe any third party rights." Any other use of Google's trademark or logo requires written consent.

Once you've entered your email address, created a password, and agreed to the Terms of Service, Google sends you an email message to confirm the legitimacy of your email address. The message includes a link for final activation of the account. Click the link to activate your account and Google will email you your very own license key.

You've signed in, you've generated a key, you're all set! What now? If you don't intend to do any programming, just stop here. Put your key in a safe place and keep it on hand to use with any cool third-party Google API-based services you come across.

The Google Web APIs Developer's Kit

If you are interested in doing some programming, download the Google Web APIs Developer's Kit (*http://www.google.com/apis/download.html*). While not strictly necessary to any Google API programming you might do, the kit contains much that is useful:

- A cross-platform WSDL file (see below)
- A Java wrapper library abstracting away some of the SOAP plumbing
- A sample .NET application
- Documentation, including JavaDoc and SOAP XML samples

Simply click the download link, unzip the file, and take a look at the *README.txt* file to get underway.

Using the Key in a Hack

Every time you send a request to the Google server in a program, you have to send your key along with it. Google checks the key and determines if it's valid, and you're still within your daily 1,000 query limit; if so, Google processes the request.

All the programs in this book, regardless of language and platform, provide a place to plug in your key. The key itself is just a string of random-looking characters (e.g., 12BuCK13mY5hOE/34KNOcK@ttH3DoOR).

A Perl hack usually includes a line like the following:

```
...
# Your Google API developer's key
my $google_key='insert key here';
...
```

The Java *GoogleAPIDemo* included in the Google Web APIs Developer's Kit is invoked on the command line like so:

```
% java -cp googleapi.jar com.google.soap.search.GoogleAPIDemo
insert_key_here search ostrich
```

In both cases, *insert key here* or *insert_key_here* should be substituted with your own Google Web API key. For example, I'd plug my made-up key into the Perl script as follows:

```
...
# Your Google API developer's key
my $google_key='12BuCK13mY5hOE/34KNOcK@ttH3DoOR';
...
```

What's WSDL?

Pronounced "whiz-dill," WSDL stands for Web Services Description Language, an XML format for describing web services. The most useful bit of the Google Web APIs Developer's Kit is *GoogleSearch.wsdl*, a WSDL file describing the Google API's available services, method names, and expected arguments to your programming language of choice.

For the most part, it's easiest simply to keep the *GoogleSearch.wsdl* file in the same directory as the scripts you're writing. This is, in most cases, assumed in the hacks in this book. If you prefer to keep it elsewhere, be sure to alter the path in the script at hand. A Perl hack usually specifies the location of the WSDL file like so:

```
...
# Location of the GoogleSearch WSDL file
my $google_wdsl = "./GoogleSearch.wsdl";
...
```

I like to keep such files together in a *library* directory and so would make the following adjustment to the above code snippet:

```
...
# Location of the GoogleSearch WSDL file
my $google_wdsl = "/home/me/lib/GoogleSearch.wsdl";
...
```

Understanding the Google API Query

The core of a Google application is the query. Without the query, there's no Google data, and without that, you don't have much of an application. Because of its importance, it's worth taking a little time to look into the anatomy of a typical query.

Query Essentials

The command in a typical Perl-based Google API application that sends a query to Google looks like:

```
my $results = $google_search ->
  doGoogleSearch(
    key, query, start, maxResults,
    filter, restrict, safeSearch, lr,
    ie, oe
  );
```

Usually the items within the parentheses are variables, numbers, or Boolean values (true or false). In the example above, I've included the names of the arguments themselves rather than sample values so you can see their definitions here:

key

This is where you put your Google API developer's key [Chapter 1]. Without a key, the query won't get very far.

query

This is your query, composed of keywords, phrases, and special syntaxes.

start

Also known as the offset, this integer value specifies at what result to start counting when determining which 10 results to return. If this number were 16, the Google API would return results 16–25. If 300, results 300–309 (assuming, of course, that your query found that many results). This is what's known as a "zero-based index"; counting starts at 0, not 1. The first result is result 0, and the 999th, 998. It's a little odd, admittedly, but you get used to it quickly—especially if you go on to do much programming. Acceptable values are 0 to 999, because Google only returns up to a thousand results for a query.

maxResults

This integer specifies the number of results you'd like the API to return. The API returns results in batches of up to ten, so acceptable values are 1 through 10.

filter

You might think the filter option concerns the SafeSearch filter for adult content. It doesn't. This Boolean value (true or false) specifies whether your results go through automatic query filtering, removing near-duplicate content (titles and snippets are very similar) and multiple (more than two) results from the same host or site. With filtering enabled, only the first two results from each host are included in the result set.

restrict

No, restrict doesn't have anything to do with SafeSearch either. It allows for restricting your search to one of Google's topical searches or to a specific country. Google has four topic restricts: U.S. Government (unclesam), Linux (linux), Macintosh (mac), and FreeBSD (bsd). You'll find the complete country list in the Google Web API documentation. To leave your search unrestricted, leave this option blank (usually signified by empty quotation marks, "").

safeSearch

> Now here's the SafeSearch filtering option. This Boolean (`true` or `false`) specifies whether results returned will be filtered for questionable (read: adult) content.

lr

> This stands for "language restrict" and it's a bit tricky. Google has a list of languages in its API documentation to which you can restrict search results, or you can simply leave this option blank and have no language restrictions.
>
> There are several ways you can restrict to language. First, you can simply include a language code. If you wanted to restrict results to English, for example, you'd use lang_en. But you can also restrict results to more than one language, separating each language code with a | (pipe), signifying OR. lang_en|lang_de, then, constrains results to only those "in English or German."
>
> You can omit languages from results by prepending them with a - (minus sign). -lang_en returns all results but those in English.

ie

> This stands for "input encoding," allowing you to specify the character encoding used in the query you're feeding the API. Google's documentation says, "Clients should encode all request data in UTF-8 and should expect results to be in UTF-8." In the first iteration of Google's API program, the Google API documenation offered a table of encoding options (latin1, cyrillic, etc.) but now everything is UTF-8. In fact, requests for anything other than UTF-8 are summarily ignored.

oe

> This stands for "output encoding." As with input encoding, everything's UTF-8.

A Sample

Enough with the placeholders; what does an actual query look like?

Take for example a query that uses variables for the key and the query, requests 10 results starting at result number 100 (actually the hundred-and-first result), and specifies filtering and SafeSearch be turned on. That query in Perl would look like this:

```
my $results = $google_search ->
doGoogleSearch(
$google_key, $query, 100, 10,
"true", "", "true", "",
"utf8", "utf8"
);
```

Note that the key and query could just as easily have been passed along as quote-delimited strings:

```
my $results = $google_search ->
doGoogleSearch(
"12BuCK13mY5hOE/34KNOcK@ttH3DoOR", "+paloentology +dentistry" , 100, 10,
"true", "", "true", "",
"utf8", "utf8"
);
```

While things appear a little more complex when you start fiddling with the language and topic restrictions, the core query remains mostly unchanged; only the values of the options change.

Intersecting Country, and Topic Restrictions

Sometimes you might want to restrict your results to a particular language in a particular country, or a particular language, particular country, and particular topic. Now here's where things start looking a little on the odd side.

Here are the rules:

- Omit something by prepending it with a - (minus sign).
- Separate restrictions with a . (period, or full stop)—spaces are not allowed.
- Specify an OR relationship between two restrictions with a | (pipe).
- Group restrictions with parentheses.

Let's say you want a query to return results in French, draw only from Canadian sites, and focus only within the Linux topic. Your query would look something like this:

```
my $results = $google_search ->
   doGoogleSearch(
      $google_key, $query, 100, 10,
      "true", "linux.countryCA", "true", "lang_fr",
      "utf8", "utf8"
   );
```

For results from Canada or from France, you'd use:

```
"linux.(countryCA|countryFR)"
```

Or maybe you want results in French, yet from anywhere but France:

```
"linux.(-countryFR)"
```

Putting Query Elements to Use

You might use the different elements of the query as follows:

Using SafeSearch

If you're building a program that's for family-friendly use, you'll probably want to have SafeSearch turned on as a matter of course. But you can also use it to compare safe and unsafe results. The "SafeSearch Certifying URLs" [Hack #81] hack does just that. You could create a program that takes a word from a web form and checks its counts in filtered and unfiltered searches, providing a "naughty rating" for the word based on the counts.

Setting search result numbers

Whether you request 1 or 10 results, you're still using one of your developer key's daily dose of a thousand Goole Web API queries. Wouldn't it then make sense to always request ten? Not necessarily; if you're only using the top result—to bounce the browser to another page, generate a random query string for a password, or whatever—you might as well add even the minutest amount of speed to your application by not requesting results you're just going to throw out or ignore.

Searching different topics

With four different specialty topics available for searching through the Google API, dozens of different languages, and dozens of different countries, there are thousands of combinations of topic/language/country restriction that you would work through.

Consider an "open source country" application. You could create a list of keywords very specific to open source (like linux, perl, etc.) and create a program that cycles through a series of queries that restricts your search to an open source topic (like linux) and a particular country. So you might discover that perl was mentioned in France in the linux topic 15 times, in Germany 20 times, etc.

You could also concentrate less on the program itself and more on an interface to access these variables. How about a form with pull-down menus that allowed you to restrict your searches by continent (instead of country)? You could specify which continent in a variable that's passed to the query. Or how about an interface that lets the user specify a topic and cycles through a list of countries and languages, pulling result counts for each one?

Understanding the Google API Response

While the Google API grants you programmatic access to the lion's share of Google's index, it doesn't provide all the functionality available through the Google.com web site's search interface.

Can Do

The Google API, in addition to simple keyword queries, supports the following *special syntaxes* [in "The Special Syntaxes" in Chapter 1]:

```
site:
daterange:
intitle:
inurl:
allintext:
allinlinks:
filetype:
info:
link:
related:
cache:
```

Can't Do

The Google API does not support these special syntaxes:

```
phonebook:
rphonebook:
bphonebook:
stocks:
```

While queries of this sort provide no individual results, aggregate result data is sometimes returned and can prove rather useful. *kincount.cgi* [Hack #70], one of the hacks in this book, takes advantage of result counts returned for phonebook: queries.

The 10-Result Limit

While searches through the standard Google.com home page can be tuned [Hack #1] to return 10, 20, 30, 50, or 100 results per page, the Google Web API limits the number to 10 per query. This doesn't mean, mind you, that the rest are not available to you, but it takes a wee bit of creative programming entailing looping through results, 10 at a time [Hack #1].

What's in the Results

The Google API provides both aggregate and per-result data in its result set.

Aggregate data. The aggregate data, information on the query itself and on the kinds and number of results that query turned up, consists of:

<documentFiltering>
   A Boolean (true/false) value specifying whether or not results were filtered for very similar results or those that come from the same web host

<directoryCategories>
A list of directory categories, if any, associated with the query

Individual search result data. The "guts" of a search result—the URLs, page titles, and snippets—are returned in a <resultElements> list. Each result consists of the following elements:

<summary>
The Google Directory summary, if available

<URL>
The search result's URL; consistently starts with http://

<snippet>
A brief excerpt of the page with query terms highlighted in bold (HTML <b> </b> tags)

<title>
The page title in HTML

<cachedSize>
The size in kilobytes (K) of the Google-cached version of the page, if available

You'll notice the conspicuous absence of PageRank [Hack #95]. Google does not make PageRank available through anything but the official Google Toolbar [Hack #24]. You can get a general idea of a page's popularity by looking over the "popularity bars" in the Google Directory.

HACK #50 Programming the Google Web API with Perl

A simple script illustrating the basics of programming the Google Web API with Perl and laying the groundwork for the lion's share of hacks to come.

The vast majority of hacks in this book are written in Perl. While the specifics vary from hack to hack, much of the busy work of querying the Google API and looping over the results remain essentially the same. This hack is utterly basic, providing a foundation on which to build more complex and interesting applications. If you haven't done anything of the sort before, this hack is a good starting point for experimentation. It simply submits a query to Google and prints out the results.

The Code

```
#!/usr/local/bin/perl
# googly.pl
# A typical Google Web API Perl script
# Usage: perl googly.pl <query>
```

```
# Your Google API developer's key
my $google_key='insert key here';

# Location of the GoogleSearch WSDL file
my $google_wdsl = "./GoogleSearch.wsdl";

use strict;

# Use the SOAP::Lite Perl module
use SOAP::Lite;

# Take the query from the command-line
my $query = shift @ARGV or die "Usage: perl googly.pl <query>\n";

# Create a new SOAP::Lite instance, feeding it GoogleSearch.wsdl
my $google_search = SOAP::Lite->service("file:$google_wdsl");

# Query Google
my $results = $google_search ->
    doGoogleSearch(
      $google_key, $query, 0, 10, "false", "",   "false",
      "", "latin1", "latin1"
    );

# No results?
@{$results->{resultElements}} or exit;

# Loop through the results
foreach my $result (@{$results->{resultElements}}) {
 # Print out the main bits of each result
 print
   join "\n",
   $result->{title} || "no title",
   $result->{URL},
   $result->{snippet} || 'no snippet',
   "\n";
}
```

Running the Hack

Run this script from the command line, passing it your preferred query keywords:

```
$ perl googly.pl "query keywords"
```

The Results

Here's a sample run. The first attempt doesn't specify a query and so triggers a usage message and doesn't go any further. The second searches for
learning perl and loops through the results.

```
% perl googly.pl
Usage: perl googly.pl <query>
% perl googly.pl "learning perl"
oreilly.com -- Online Catalog: Learning
Perl, 3rd Edition
http://www.oreilly.com/catalog/lperl3/
... learning perl, 3rd Edition Making Easy Things Easy and Hard Things
Possible By Randal L. Schwartz, Tom Phoenix 3rd Edition July
2001 0-596-00132-0
...
Amazon.com: buying info: learning perl (2nd Edition)
http://www.amazon.com/exec/obidos/ASIN/1565922840
... learning perl takes common programming idioms and expresses them
in "perlish"<br> terms. ... (learning perl,
Programming Perl, Perl Cookbook).
```

See Also

- Looping Around the 10-Result Limit [Hack #51]

Looping Around the 10-Result Limit
HACK #51
If you want more than 10 results, you'll have to loop.

The Google API returns only 10 results per query. Ten results is plenty for some queries, but for most applications, 10 results barely scratches the surface. If you want more than 10 results, you're going to have to loop, querying for the next set of 10 each time. The first query returns the top ten. The next, 11 through 20. And so forth.

This hack builds on the basic query shown in "Programming the Google Web API with Perl" [Hack #50]. To get at more than the top 10 results, no matter the programming language you're using, you'll have to create a loop. The example is in Perl, because that's what most of the hacks in this book are written in. Alterations to support looping are shown in bold.

The Code

```
#!/usr/local/bin/perl
# looply.pl
# A typical Google Web API Perl script
# Usage: perl looply.pl <query>

# Your Google API developer's key
my $google_key='insert key here';

# Location of the GoogleSearch WSDL file
my $google_wdsl = "./GoogleSearch.wsdl";
```

```
# Number of times to loop, retrieving 10 results at a time
my $loops = 3; # 3 loops x 10 results per loop = top 30 results

use strict;

# Use the SOAP::Lite Perl module
use SOAP::Lite;

# Take the query from the command-line
my $query = shift @ARGV or die "Usage: perl looply.pl <query>\n";

# Create a new SOAP::Lite instance, feeding it GoogleSearch.wsdl

my $google_search = SOAP::Lite->service("file:$google_wdsl");

# Keep track of result number
my $number = 0;

for (my $offset = 0; $offset <= ($loops-1)*10; $offset += 10) {
  # Query Google
  my $results = $google_search ->
   doGoogleSearch(
     $google_key, $query, $offset, 10, "false", "", "false",
     "", "latin1", "latin1"
   );

  # No sense continuing unless there are more results
  last unless @{$results->{resultElements}};

  # Loop through the results
  foreach my $result (@{$results->{'resultElements'}}) {

   # Print out the main bits of each result
   print
    join "\n",
    ++$number,
    $result->{title} || "no title",
    $result->{URL},
    $result->{snippet} || 'no snippet',
    "\n";

  }
}
```

Notice that the script tells Google which set of 10 results it's after by passing an offset ($offset). The offset is increased by 10 each time ($offset += 10).

Running the Script

Run this script from the command line, passing it your preferred query:

```
$ perl looply.pl "query"
```

The Results

```
% perl looply.pl
Usage: perl looply.pl <query>
% perl looply.pl "learning perl"
1
oreilly.com -- Online Catalog: Learning Perl, 3rd Edition
http://www.oreilly.com/catalog/lperl3/
... Learning Perl, 3rd Edition Making Easy Things
Easy and Hard Things Possible By Randal<br> L. Schwartz, Tom Phoenix
3rd Edition July 2001 0-596-00132-0, Order Number ...

...
29
Intro to Perl for CGI
http://hotwired.lycos.com/webmonkey/98/47/index2a.html
... Some people feel that the benefits of learning
Perl scripting are few.<br> But ... part. That's right.
Learning Perl is just like being a cop. ...
30
WebDeveloper.com ®: Where Web Developers and Designers Learn How ...
http://www.webdeveloper.com/reviews/book6.html
... Registration CreditCard Processing Compare Prices.
Learning Perl. Learning<br> Perl, 2nd Edition.
Publisher: O'Reilly Author: Randal Schwartz ...
```

See Also

- Programming the Google Web API with Perl [Hack #50]

HACK #52 The SOAP::Lite Perl Module

Installing the SOAP::Lite Perl module, backbone of the vast majority of hacks in this book.

SOAP::Lite (*http://www.soaplite.com*) is the defacto standard for interfacing with SOAP-based web services from Perl. As such, it is used extensively throughout this book; just about all the hacks in the Google Web API Applications [Chapter 6] section are written in Perl using SOAP::Lite.

SOAPing your ISP

It's unfortunately not that common for internet service providers (ISPs) to make SOAP::Lite available to their users. In many cases, ISPs are rather restrictive in general about what modules they make available and scripts they allow users to execute. Others are rather more accomodating and more than willing to install Perl modules upon request. Before taking up your time and brainpower installing SOAP::Lite yourself, check with your service provider.

Installing SOAP::Lite

Probably the easiest way to install SOAP::Lite is via another Perl module, CPAN, included with just about every modern Perl distribution. The CPAN module automates the installation of Perl modules, fetching components and any prerequisites from the Comprehensive Perl Archive Network (thus the name, CPAN) and building the whole kit-and-kaboodle on the fly.

CPAN installs modules into standard system-wide locations and, therefore, assumes you're running as the root user. If you have no more than regular user access, you'll have to install SOAP::Lite and its prerequisites by hand (see "Unix installation by hand").

Unix and Mac OS X installation via CPAN. Assuming you have the CPAN module, have root access, and are connected to the Internet, installation should be no more complicated than:

```
% su
Password:
# perl -MCPAN -e shell
cpan shell -- CPAN exploration and modules installation (v1.52)
ReadLine support available (try ``install Bundle::CPAN'')
cpan> install SOAP::Lite
```

Or, if you prefer one-liners:

```
% sudo perl -MCPAN -e 'install SOAP::Lite'
```

In either case, go grab yourself a cup of coffee, meander the garden, read the paper, and check back once in a while. Your terminal's sure to be riddled with incomprehensible gobbledegook that you can, for the most part, summarily ignore. You may be asked a question or three; in most cases, simply hitting return to accept the default answer will do the trick.

Unix installation by hand. If CPAN installation didn't quite work as expected, you can of course install SOAP::Lite by hand. Download the latest version from SOAPLite.com (*http://www.soaplite.com/*), unpack, and build it like so:

```
% tar xvzf SOAP-Lite-latest.tar.gz
SOAP-Lite-0.55
SOAP-Lite-0.55/Changes
...
SOAP-Lite-0.55/t/37-mod_xmlrpc.t
SOAP-Lite-0.55/t/TEST.pl
% cd SOAP-Lite-0.55
% perl Makefile.PL
We are about to install SOAP::Lite and for your convenience will
provide you with list of modules and prerequisites, so you'll be able
```

```
to choose only modules you need for your configuration.
XMLRPC::Lite, UDDI::Lite, and XML::Parser::Lite are included by default.
Installed transports can be used for both SOAP::Lite and XMLRPC::Lite.
Client HTTP support (SOAP::Transport::HTTP::Client)        [yes]
Client HTTPS support (SOAP::Transport::HTTPS::Client...    [no]
...
SSL support for TCP transport (SOAP::Transport::TCP)       [no]
Compression support for HTTP transport (SOAP::Transport... [no]
Do you want to proceed with this configuration? [yes]
During "make test" phase we may run tests with several SOAP servers
that may take long and may fail due to server/connectivity problems.
Do you want to perform these tests in addition to core tests? [no]
Checking if your kit is complete...
Looks good
...
% make
mkdir blib
mkdir blib/lib
...
% make test
PERL_DL_NONLAZY=1 /usr/bin/perl -Iblib/arch -Iblib/lib
-I/System/Library/Perl/darwin -I/System/Library/Perl -e 'use
Test::Harness qw(&runtests $verbose); $verbose=0; runtests @ARGV;'
t/01-core.t t/02-payload.t t/03-server.t t/04-attach.t t/05-customxml.t
t/06-modules.t t/07-xmlrpc_payload.t t/08-schema.t t/01-core...........
...
% su
Password:
# make install
Installing /Library/Perl/XMLRPC/Lite.pm
Installing /Library/Perl/XMLRPC/Test.pm
...
```

If, during the perl Makefile.PL phase, you run into any warnings about
installing prerequisites, you'll have to install each in turn before attempting
to install SOAP::Lite again. A typical prerequisite warning looks something
like this:

```
Checking if your kit is complete...
Looks good
Warning: prerequisite HTTP::Daemon failed to load: Can't locate
HTTP/Daemon.pm in @INC (@INC contains: /System/Library/Perl/darwin
/System/Library/Perl /Library/Perl/darwin /Library/Perl /Library/Perl
/Network/Library/Perl/darwin /Network/Library/Perl
/Network/Library/Perl .) at (eval 8) line 3.
```

If you've little more than user access to the system and still insist on installing SOAP::Lite yourself, you'll have to install it and all its prerequisites

somewhere in your home directory. *~/lib*, a *lib* directory in your home directory, is as good a place as any. Inform Perl of your preference like so:

```
% perl Makefile.PL LIB=/home/login/lib
```

Replace */home/login/lib* with an appropriate path.

Windows installation via PPM. If you're running Perl under Windows, chances are its ActiveState's ActivePerl (*http://www.activestate.com/Products/ActivePerl/*). Thankfully, ActivePerl's outfitted with a CPAN-like module installation utility. The Programmer's Package Manager (PPM, *http://aspn.activestate.com/ASPN/Downloads/ActivePerl/PPM/*) grabs nicely packaged module bundles from the ActiveState archive and drops them into place on your Windows system with little need of help from you.

Simply launch PPM from inside a DOS terminal window and tell it to install the SOAP::Lite bundle.

```
C:\>ppm
PPM interactive shell (2.1.6) - type 'help' for available commands.
PPM> install SOAP::Lite
```

If you're running a reasonably recent build, you're probably in for a pleasant surprise:

```
C:\>ppm
PPM interactive shell (2.1.6) - type 'help' for available commands.
PPM> install SOAP::Lite
Version 0.55 of 'SOAP-Lite' is already installed.
```

SOAP::Lite Alternatives

Having trouble? Perhaps your ISP doesn't deem SOAP::Lite worthy. Attempts at installing it yourself have you pulling out your hair?

While SOAP::Lite is the preferred method for interfacing with the Google Web API—and, indeed, web services in general. That said, it'd hardly be fair of us to leave you high and dry, unable to tuck in to this comprehensive collection of Google Hacks.

Never fear, there's more hackery afoot. PoXML [Hack #53], our home-brewed, lightweight Perl module treats Google's SOAP as plain old XML, using the LWP::UserAgent module to make HTTP requests and XML::Simple to parse the XML response. Going one step further, our NoXML [Hack #54] doesn't even require an XML parser (gasp!), doing all its work with regular expressions. And then there's XooMLe [Hack #36], a third-party service offering an intermediary plain old XML interface to the Google Web API. Each of these alternatives provides a drop-in replacement for SOAP::Lite with little more than a two-line alteration to the hack.

Plain Old XML, a SOAP::Lite Alternative

PoXML is a drop-in replacement, of sorts, for the SOAP::Lite-less.

PoXML is a bit of home-brewed hackery for those who don't have the SOAP::Lite [Hack #52] Perl module at their disposal. Perhaps you had more than enough trouble installing it yourself.

> Any Perl guru will insist that module installation is as simple as can be. That said, any other Perl guru will be forced to admit that it's an inconsistent experience and often harder than it should be.

PoXML is a drop-in replacement—to a rather decent degree—for SOAP:: Lite. It treats Google's SOAP as plain old XML, using the LWP::UserAgent module to make HTTP requests and XML::Simple to parse the XML response. And best of all, it requires little more than a two-line alteration to the target hack.

The Code

The heart of this hack is *PoXML.pm*, a little Perl module best saved into the same directory as your hacks.

```perl
# PoXML.pm
# PoXML [pronounced "plain old xml"] is a dire-need drop-in
# replacement for SOAP::Lite designed for Google Web API hacking.

package PoXML;

use strict;
no strict "refs";

# LWP for making HTTP requests, XML for parsing Google SOAP
use LWP::UserAgent;
use XML::Simple;

# Create a new PoXML
  sub new {
  my $self = {};
  bless($self);
  return $self;
}

# Replacement for the SOAP::Lite-based doGoogleSearch method
sub doGoogleSearch {
   my($self, %args);
   ($self, @args{qw/ key q start maxResults filter restrict
   safeSearch lr ie oe /}) = @_;
```

```
# grab SOAP request from __DATA__
my $tell = tell(DATA);
my $soap_request = join '', ;
seek(DATA, $tell, 0);
$soap_request =~ s/\$(\w+)/$args{$1}/ge; #interpolate variables

# Make (POST) a SOAP-based request to Google
my $ua = LWP::UserAgent->new;
my $req = HTTP::Request->new(
  POST => 'http://api.google.com/search/beta2');
$req->content_type('text/xml');
$req->content($soap_request);
my $res = $ua->request($req);
my $soap_response = $res->as_string;

# Drop the HTTP headers and so forth until the initial xml element
$soap_response =~ s/^.+?(<\?xml)/$1/migs;

# Drop element namespaces for tolerance of future prefix changes
$soap_response =~ s!(<\/?)[\w-]+?:([\w-]+?)!$1$2!g;

# Parse the XML
my $results = XMLin($soap_response);

# Normalize and drop the unnecessary encoding bits
my $return = $results->{'Body'}->{'doGoogleSearchResponse'}->{return};
foreach ( keys %{$return} ) {
  $return->{$_}->{content} and
  $return->{$_} = $return->{$_}->{content} || '';
}

my @items;
foreach my $item ( @{$return->{resultElements}->{item}} ) {
  foreach my $key ( keys %$item ) {
    $item->{$key} = $item->{$key}->{content} || '';
  }
  push @items, $item;
}

$return->{resultElements} = \@items;

my @categories;
foreach my $key ( keys %{$return->{directoryCategories}->{item}} ) {
  $return->{directoryCategories}->{$key} =
  $return->{directoryCategories}->{item}->{$key}->{content} || '';
}

# Return nice, clean, usable results
return $return;
}

1;
```

```
# This is the SOAP message template sent to api.google.com. Variables
# signified with $variablename are replaced by the values of their
# counterparts sent to the doGoogleSearch subroutine.

__DATA__
<?xml version='1.0' encoding='UTF-8'?>
<SOAP-ENV:Envelope
 xmlns:SOAP-ENV="http://schemas.xmlsoap.org/soap/envelope/"
 xmlns:xsi="http://www.w3.org/1999/XMLSchema-instance"
 xmlns:xsd="http://www.w3.org/1999/XMLSchema">
  <SOAP-ENV:Body>
   <ns1:doGoogleSearch xmlns:ns1="urn:GoogleSearch"
    SOAP-ENV:encodingStyle="http://schemas.xmlsoap.org/soap/encoding/">
     <key xsi:type="xsd:string">$key</key>
     <q xsi:type="xsd:string">$q</q>
     <start xsi:type="xsd:int">$start</start>
     <maxResults xsi:type="xsd:int">$maxResults</maxResults>
     <filter xsi:type="xsd:boolean">$filter</filter>
     <restrict xsi:type="xsd:string">$restrict</restrict>
     <safeSearch xsi:type="xsd:boolean">$safeSearch</safeSearch>
     <lr xsi:type="xsd:string">$lr</lr>
     <ie xsi:type="xsd:string">$ie</ie>
     <oe xsi:type="xsd:string">$oe</oe>
   </ns1:doGoogleSearch>
  </SOAP-ENV:Body>
</SOAP-ENV:Envelope>
```

Here's a little script to show PoXML in action. Its no different, really, from any number of hacks in this book. The only minor alterations necessary to make use of PoXML instead of SOAP::Lite are highlighted in bold.

```
#!/usr/bin/perl
# poxml_google2csv.pl
# Google Web Search Results via PoXML ("plain old xml") module
# exported to CSV suitable for import into Excel
# Usage: poxml_google2csv.pl "{query}" [> results.csv]

# Your Google API developer's key
my $google_key = 'insert key here';

use strict;

# use SOAP::Lite;
use PoXML;

$ARGV[0]
  or die qq{usage: perl poxml_search2csv.pl "{query}"\n};

# my $google_search = SOAP::Lite->service("file:$google_wdsl");
my $google_search = new PoXML;

my $results = $google_search ->
  doGoogleSearch(
    $google_key, shift @ARGV, 0, 10, "false",
```

```
      "", "false", "", "latin1", "latin1"
    );

  @{$results->{'resultElements'}} or die('No results');

  print qq{"title","url","snippet"\n};

  foreach (@{$results->{'resultElements'}}) {
    $_->{title} =~ s!"!""!g; # double escape " marks
    $_->{snippet} =~ s!"!""!g;
    my $output = qq{"$_->{title}","$_->{URL}","$_->{snippet}"\n};
    $output =~ s!<.+?>!!g; # drop all HTML tags
    print $output;
  }
```

Running the Hack

Run the script from the command line, providing a query on the command line and piping the output to a CSV file you wish to create or to which you wish to append additional results. For example, using "plain old xml" as our query and *results.csv* as our output:

```
$ perl poxml_google2csv.pl "plain old xml" > results.csv
```

Leaving off the > and CSV filename sends the results to the screen for your perusal.

The Results

```
% perl poxml_google2csv.pl "plain old xml"
"title","url","snippet"
"XML.com: Distributed XML [Sep. 06, 2000]",
"http://www.xml.com/pub/2000/09/06/distributed.html",
" ... extensible. Unlike plain old XML, there's no sense of
constraining what the document can describe by a DTD or schema.
This means ... "
...
"Plain Old Documentation",
"http://axkit.org/wiki/view/AxKit/PlainOldDocumentation",
" ... perlpodspec - Plain Old Documentation: format specification
and notes. ... Examples: =pod This is a plain Pod paragraph. ...
encodings in Pod parsing would be as in XML ... "
```

Applicability and Limitations

In the same manner, you can adapt just about any SOAP::Lite-based hack in this book and those you've made up yourself to use PoXML.

1. Place *PoXML.pm* in the same directory as the hack at hand.

2. Replace use SOAP::Lite; with use PoXML;.

3. Replace my $google_search = SOAP::Lite->service("file:$google_wdsl"); with my $google_search = new PoXML;.

There are, however, some limitations. While PoXML works nicely to extract results and aggregate results the likes of <estimatedTotalResultsCount />, it falls down on gleaning some of the more advanced result elements like <directoryCategories />, an array of categories turned up by the query.

In general, bear in mind that your mileage may vary, and don't be afraid to tweak.

See Also

- NoXML [Hack #54], a regular expressions–based, XML Parser–free SOAP::Lite alternative
- XooMLE [Hack #36], a third-party service offering an intermediary plain old XML interface to the Google Web API

NoXML, Another SOAP::Lite Alternative
#54

NoXML is a regular expressions–based, XML Parser–free drop-in alternative to SOAP::Lite.

XML jockeys might well want to avert their eyes for this one. What is herein suggested is something just so preposterous that it just might prove useful—and indeed it does. NoXML is a drop-in alternative to SOAP::Lite. As its name suggests, this home-brewed module doesn't make use of an XML parser of any kind, relying instead on some dead-simple regular expressions and other bits of programmatic magic.

If you have only a basic Perl installation at your disposal and are lacking both the SOAP::Lite [Hack #52] and XML::Parser Perl modules, NoXML will do in a pinch, playing nicely with just about every Perl hack in this book.

> As any XML guru will attest, there's simply no substitute for an honest-to-goodness XML parser. And they'd be right. There are encoding and hierarchy issues that a regular expression–based parser simply can't fathom. NoXML is simplistic at best. That said, it does what needs doing, the very essence of "hacking."

Best of all, NoXML can fill in for SOAP::Lite with little more than a two-line alteration to the target hack.

The Code

The heart of this hack is *NoXML.pm*, which should be saved into the same directory as your hacks themselves.

```perl
# NoXML.pm
# NoXML [pronounced "no xml"] is a dire-need drop-in
# replacement for SOAP::Lite designed for Google Web API hacking.

package NoXML;

use strict;
no strict "refs";

# LWP for making HTTP requests, XML for parsing Google SOAP
use LWP::UserAgent;
use XML::Simple;

# Create a new NoXML
sub new {
  my $self = {};
  bless($self);
  return $self;
}

# Replacement for the SOAP::Lite-based doGoogleSearch method
sub doGoogleSearch {
  my($self, %args);
  ($self, @args{qw/ key q start maxResults filter restrict
  safeSearch lr ie oe /}) = @_;

  # grab SOAP request from __DATA__
  my $tell = tell(DATA);
  my $soap_request = join '', ;
  seek(DATA, $tell, 0);
  $soap_request =~ s/\$(\w+)/$args{$1}/ge; #interpolate variables

  # Make (POST) a SOAP-based request to Google
  my $ua = LWP::UserAgent->new;
  my $req = HTTP::Request->new(POST => 'http://api.google.com/search/
beta2');
  $req->content_type('text/xml');
  $req->content($soap_request);
  my $res = $ua->request($req);
  my $soap_response = $res->as_string;

  # Drop the HTTP headers and so forth until the initial xml element
  $soap_response =~ s/^.+?(<\?xml)/$1/migs;

  # Drop element namespaces for tolerance of future prefix changes
  $soap_response =~ s!(<\/?)[\w-]+?:([\w-]+?)!$1$2!g;

  # Set up a return dataset
  my $return;
```

```perl
    # Unescape escaped HTML in the resultset
    my %unescape = ('<'=>'<', '>'=>'>', '&'=>'&', '"'=>'"', '&apos;'=>"'");
    my $unescape_re = join '|' => keys %unescape;

    # Divide the SOAP response into the results and other metadata
    my($before, $results, $after) = $soap_response =~
      m#(^.+)(.+?)(.+$)#migs ;
    my $before_and_after = $before . $after;

    # Glean as much metadata as possible (while being somewhat lazy ;-)
    while ($before_and_after =~ m#([^<]*?)<#migs) {
      $return->{$1} = $3; # pack the metadata into the return dataset
    }

    # Glean the results
    my @results;
    while ($results =~ m#(.+?)#migs) {
      my $item = $1;
      my $pairs = {};
      while ( $item =~ m#([^<]*)#migs ) {
        my($element, $value) = ($1, $2);
        $value =~ s/($unescape_re)/$unescape{$1}/g;
        $pairs->{$element} = $value;
      }
      push @results, $pairs;
    }

    # Pack the results into the return dataset
    $return->{resultElements} = \@results;

    # Return nice, clean, usable results
    return $return;
}

1;

# This is the SOAP message template sent to api.google.com. Variables
# signified with $variablename are replaced by the values of their
# counterparts sent to the doGoogleSearch subroutine.

__DATA__
<?xml version='1.0' encoding='UTF-8'?>
<SOAP-ENV:Envelope
 xmlns:SOAP-ENV="http://schemas.xmlsoap.org/soap/envelope/"
 xmlns:xsi="http://www.w3.org/1999/XMLSchema-instance"
 xmlns:xsd="http://www.w3.org/1999/XMLSchema">
  <SOAP-ENV:Body>
    <ns1:doGoogleSearch xmlns:ns1="urn:GoogleSearch"
     SOAP-ENV:encodingStyle="http://schemas.xmlsoap.org/soap/encoding/">
      <key xsi:type="xsd:string">$key</key>
      <q xsi:type="xsd:string">$q</q>
      <start xsi:type="xsd:int">$start</start>
      <maxResults xsi:type="xsd:int">$maxResults</maxResults>
```

```
    <filter xsi:type="xsd:boolean">$filter</filter>
    <restrict xsi:type="xsd:string">$restrict</restrict>
    <safeSearch xsi:type="xsd:boolean">$safeSearch</safeSearch>
    <lr xsi:type="xsd:string">$lr</lr>
    <ie xsi:type="xsd:string">$ie</ie>
    <oe xsi:type="xsd:string">$oe</oe>
  </ns1:doGoogleSearch>
 </SOAP-ENV:Body>
</SOAP-ENV:Envelope>
```

Here's a little script to show NoXML in action. It's no different, really, from
any number of hacks in this book. The only minor alterations necessary to
make use of NoXML instead of SOAP::Lite are highlighted in bold.

```
#!/usr/bin/perl
# noxml_google2csv.pl
# Google Web Search Results via NoXML ("no xml") module
# exported to CSV suitable for import into Excel
# Usage: noxml_google2csv.pl "{query}" [> results.csv]

# Your Google API developer's key
my $google_key='insert key here';

use strict;

# use SOAP::Lite;
use NoXML;

$ARGV[0]
  or die qq{usage: perl noxml_search2csv.pl "{query}"\n};

# my $google_search = SOAP::Lite->service("file:$google_wdsl");
my $google_search = new NoXML;

my $results = $google_search ->
  doGoogleSearch(
    $google_key, shift @ARGV, 0, 10, "false",
    "", "false", "", "latin1", "latin1"
  );
@{$results->{'resultElements'}} or die('No results');

print qq{"title","url","snippet"\n};

foreach (@{$results->{'resultElements'}}) {
  $_->{title} =~ s!"!""!g; # double escape " marks
  $_->{snippet} =~ s!"!""!g;
  my $output = qq{"$_->{title}","$_->{URL}","$_->{snippet}"\n};
  $output =~ s!<.+?>!!g; # drop all HTML tags
  print $output;
}
```

Running the Hack

Run the script from the command line, providing a query on the command line and piping the output to a CSV file you wish to create or to which you wish to append additional results. For example, using "no xml" as our query and *results.csv* as your output:

```
$ perl noxml_google2csv.pl "no xml" > results.csv
```

Leaving off the > and CSV filename sends the results to the screen for your perusal.

The Results

```
% perl noxml_google2csv.pl "no xml"
"title","url","snippet"
"site-comments@w3.org from January 2002: No XML specifications",
"http://lists.w3.org/Archives/Public/site-comments/2002Jan/0015.html",
"No XML specifications. From: Prof. ... Next message: Ian B. Jacobs:
&quot;Re: No XML specifications&quot;; Previous message: Rob Cummings:
&quot;Website design...&quot;; ...   "
...
"Re: [xml] XPath with no XML Doc",
"http://mail.gnome.org/archives/xml/2002-March/msg00194.html",
" ... Re: [xml] XPath with no XML Doc. From: &quot;Richard Jinks&quot;
<cyberthymia yahoo co uk>; To: <xml gnome org>; Subject:
Re: [xml] XPath with no XML Doc; ...   "
```

Applicability and Limitations

In the same manner, you can adapt just about any SOAP::Lite-based hack in this book and those you've made up yourself to use NoXML.

1. Place *NoXML.pm* in the same directory as the hack at hand.

2. Replace use SOAP::Lite; with use NoXML;.

3. Replace my $google_search = SOAP::Lite->service("file:$google_wdsl"); with my $google_search = new NoXML;.

There are, however, some limitations. While NoXML works nicely to extract results and aggregate results the likes of <estimatedTotalResultsCount />, it falls down on gleaning some of the more advanced result elements like <directoryCategories />, an array of categories turned up by the query.

In general, bear in mind that your mileage may vary and don't be afraid to tweak.

See Also

- PoXML [Hack #53], a plain old XML alternative to SOAP::Lite
- XooMLE [Hack #36], a third-party service offering an intermediary plain old XML interface to the Google Web API

Programming the Google Web API with PHP
A simple example of programming the Google Web API with PHP and the NuSOAP module.

PHP (*http://www.php.net/*), a recursive acronym for "PHP Hypertext Processing," has seen wide use as the HTML-embedded scripting language for web development. Add to that the NuSOAP PHP module for creating and consuming SOAP-based web services (*http://dietrich.ganx4.com/nusoap*) and you've a powerful combination.

This hack illustrates basic use of PHP and NuSOAP in concert to interact with the Google Web API.

The Code

```
<!--
# googly.php
# A typical Google Web API php script
# Usage: googly.php?query=<query>
-->
<html>
<head>
 <title>googly.php</title>
</head>
<body>
<?
# Use the NuSOAP php library
require_once('nusoap.php');

# Set parameters
$parameters = array(
  'key'=>'insert key here',
  'q' => $HTTP_GET_VARS['query'],
  'start' => '0',
  'maxResults' => '10',
  'filter' => 'false',
  'restrict' => '',
  'safeSearch' => 'false',
  'lr' => '',
  'ie' => 'latin',
  'oe' => 'latin'
);
```

```
# Create a new SOAP client, feeding it GoogleSearch.wsdl on Google's site
$soapclient = new soapclient('http://api.google.com/GoogleSearch.wsdl',
'wsdl');

# query Google
$results = $soapclient->call('doGoogleSearch',$parameters);

# Results?
if ( is_array($results['resultElements']) ) {
  print "<p>Your Google query for '" . $HTTP_GET_VARS['query'] . "' found "
. $results['estimatedTotalResultsCount'] . " results, the top ten of which
are:</p>";
  foreach ( $results['resultElements'] as $result ) {
    print
      "<p><a href='" . $result['URL'] . "'>" .
      ( $result['title'] ? $result['title'] : 'no title' ) .
      "</a><br />" . $result['URL'] . "<br />" .
      ( $result['snippet'] ? $result['snippet'] : 'no snippet' ) .
      "</p>";
  }
}

# No Results
else {
  print "Your Google query for '" . $HTTP_GET_VARS['query'] . "' returned no
results";
}
?>
</body>
</html>
```

Running the Hack

Invoke this hack from your browser in the same manner you would a CGI
script. It accepts one named argument, query with your preferred Google
search:

```
http://localhost/googly.php?query=your google query
```

The Results

A search for php looks something like Figure 5-1.

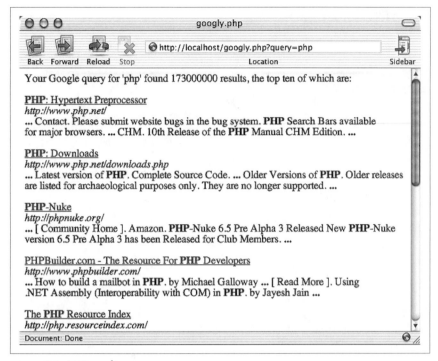

```
    000                          googly.php

    Back  Forward  Reload  Stop              Location                    Sidebar

    Your Google query for 'php' found 173000000 results, the top ten of which are:

    PHP: Hypertext Preprocessor
    http://www.php.net/
    ... Contact. Please submit website bugs in the bug system. PHP Search Bars available
    for major browsers. ... CHM. 10th Release of the PHP Manual CHM Edition. ...

    PHP: Downloads
    http://www.php.net/downloads.php
    ... Latest version of PHP. Complete Source Code. ... Older Versions of PHP. Older releases
    are listed for archaeological purposes only. They are no longer supported. ...

    PHP-Nuke
    http://phpnuke.org/
    ... [ Community Home ]. Amazon. PHP-Nuke 6.5 Pre Alpha 3 Released New PHP-Nuke
    version 6.5 Pre Alpha 3 has been Released for Club Members. ...

    PHPBuilder.com - The Resource For PHP Developers
    http://www.phpbuilder.com/
    ... How to build a mailbot in PHP. by Michael Galloway ... [ Read More ]. Using
    .NET Assembly (Interoperability with COM) in PHP. by Jayesh Jain ...

    The PHP Resource Index
    http://php.resourceindex.com/

    Document: Done
```

Figure 5-1. PHP results page

Programming the Google Web API with Java
#56 Programming the Google Web API in Java is a snap, thanks to all the functionality packed into the Google Web API Developer's Kit.

Thanks to the Java Archive (JAR) file included in the Google Web API Developer's Kit [in "The Google Web APIs Developer's Kit"], programming to the Google API in Java couldn't be simpler. The *googleapi.jar* archive includes *com.google.soap.search*, a nice clean wrapper around the underlying Google SOAP, along with the Apache Software Foundation's open source Crimson (*http://xml.apache.org/crimson*) XML parser and Apache SOAP (*http://xml.apache.org/soap/*) stack, among others.

You'll need a copy of the Java 2 Platform, Standard Edition (J2SE, *http://java.sun.com/downloads/*) to compile and run this hack.

The Code

```
// Googly.java
// Bring in the Google SOAP wrapper
import com.google.soap.search.*;
import java.io.*;
public class Googly {
  // Your Google API developer's key
  private static String googleKey = "insert key here";
  public static void main(String[] args) {
    // Make sure there's a Google query on the command-line
    if (args.length != 1) {
      System.err.println("Usage: java [-classpath classpath] Googly <query>
");
      System.exit(1);
    }
    // Create a new GoogleSearch object
    GoogleSearch s = new GoogleSearch();
    try {

      s.setKey(googleKey);
      s.setQueryString(args[0]); // Google query from the command-line
      s.setMaxResults(10);
      // Query Google
      GoogleSearchResult r = s.doSearch();
      // Gather the results
      GoogleSearchResultElement[] re = r.getResultElements();

      // Output
      for ( int i = 0; i < re.length; i++ ) {
      System.out.println(re[i].getTitle());
      System.out.println(re[i].getURL());
      System.out.println(re[i].getSnippet() + "\n");
      }

      // Anything go wrong?
    } catch (GoogleSearchFault f) {
      System.out.println("GoogleSearchFault: " + f.toString());
    }
  }

}
```

Be sure to drop in your own Google developer's key [in "Using the Key in a Hack"]
(e.g., 12BuCK13mY5hOE/34KNOcK@ttH3DoOR) in place of "*insert key here*":

```
// Your Google API developer's key
private static String googleKey = "12BuCK13mY5hOE/34KNOcK@ttH3DoOR";
```

Compiling the Code

To successfully compile the Googly application, you'll need that *googleapi.
jar* archive. I chose to keep it in the same directory as as my *Googly.java*

source file; if you've put it elsewhere, adjust the path after -classpath accordingly.

```
% javac -classpath googleapi.jar Googly.java
```

This should leave you with a brand new *Googly.class* file, ready to run.

Running the Hack

Run Googly on the command line, passing it your Google query, like so:

```
% java -classpath .:googleapi.jar Googly "query words"
```

The Results

```
% java -classpath .:googleapi.jar Googly "Learning Java"
oreilly.com -- Online Catalog: Learning Java
http://www.oreilly.com/catalog/learnjava/
For programmers either just migrating to Java or already working
steadily in the forefront of Java development, Learning Java gives
a clear, systematic   ...
oreilly.com -- Online Catalog:   Learning    Java  , 2nd Edition
http://www.oreilly.com/catalog/learnjava2/
This new edition of Learning Java has been expanded and updated for
Java 2 Standard Edition SDK 1.4. It comprehensively addresses ...
...
Java Programming...From the Grounds Up / Web Developer
http://www.webdeveloper.com/java/java_programming_grounds_up.html
... WebDeveloper.com. Java Programming... From the Grounds Up. by
Mark C. Reynolds ... Java Classes and Methods. Java utilizes the
basic object technology found in C++. ...
```

HACK #57   Programming the Google Web API with Python

Programming the Google Web API with Python is simple and clean, as these scripts and interactive examples demonstrate.

Programming to the Google Web API from Python is a piece of cake, thanks to Mark Pilgrim's PyGoogle wrapper module (*http://diveintomark.org/ projects/pygoogle/*). PyGoogle abstracts away much of the underlying SOAP, XML, and request/response layers, leaving you free to spend your time with the data itself.

PyGoogle Installation

Download a copy of PyGoogle and follow the installation instructions (*http:/ /diveintomark.org/projects/pygoogle/readme.txt*). Assuming all goes to plan, this should be nothing more complex than:

```
% python setup.py install
```

Alternately, if you want to give this a whirl without installing PyGoogle or don't have permissions to install it globally on your system, simply put the included *SOAP.py* and *google.py* files into the same directory as the *googly.py* script itself.

The Code

```python
#!/usr/bin/python
# googly.py
# A typical Google Web API Python script using Mark Pilgrim's
# PyGoogle Google Web API wrapper
# [http://diveintomark.org/projects/pygoogle/]
# Usage: python googly.py <query>

import sys, string, codecs

# Use the PyGoogle module
import google

# Grab the query from the command-line
if sys.argv[1:]:
  query = sys.argv[1]
else:
  sys.exit('Usage: python googly.py <query>')

# Your Google API developer's key
google.LICENSE_KEY = 'insert key here'

# Query Google
data = google.doGoogleSearch(query)

# Teach standard output to deal with utf-8 encoding in the results
sys.stdout = codecs.lookup('utf-8')[-1](sys.stdout)

# Output
for result in data.results:
  print string.join( (result.title, result.URL, result.snippet), "\n"), "\n"
```

Running the Hack

Invoke the script on the command line as follows:

```
% python googly.py "query words"
```

The Results

```
% python googly.py "learning python"
oreilly.com -- Online Catalog: <b>Learning</b>
<b>Python</b>
http://www.oreilly.com/catalog/lpython/
<b>Learning</b> <b>Python</b> is an
  introduction to the increasingly popular interpreted programming
```

language that's portable, powerful, and remarkably easy to use in both
...
...
Book Review: Learning Python
http://www2.linuxjournal.com/lj-issues/issue66/3541.html
... Issue 66: Book Review: Learning
Python ... Enter
Learning Python. My executive summary
is that this is the right book for me and probably for many others
as well. ...

Hacking the Hack

Python has a marvelous interface for working interactively with the inter-
preter. It's a good place to experiment with modules such as PyGoogle, querying the Google API on the fly and digging through the data structures it
returns.

Here's a sample interactive PyGoogle session demonstrating use of the
doGoogleSearch, doGetCachedPage, and doSpellingSuggestion functions.

```
% python
Python 2.2 (#1, 07/14/02, 23:25:09)
[GCC Apple cpp-precomp 6.14] on darwin
Type "help", "copyright", "credits" or "license" for more information.
>>> import google
>>> google.LICENSE_KEY = 'insert key here'
>>> data = google.doGoogleSearch("Learning Python")
>>> dir(data.meta)
['__doc__', '__init__', '__module__', 'directoryCategories',
'documentFiltering', 'endIndex', 'estimateIsExact',
'estimatedTotalResultsCount', 'searchComments', 'searchQuery',
'searchTime', 'searchTips', 'startIndex']
>>> data.meta.estimatedTotalResultsCount
115000
>>> data.meta.directoryCategories
[{u'specialEncoding': '', u'fullViewableName': "Top/Business/Industries/
Publishing/Publishers/Nonfiction/Business/O'Reilly_and_Associates/
Technical_Books/Python"}]
>>> dir(data.results[5])
['URL', '__doc__', '__init__', '__module__', 'cachedSize',
'directoryCategory', 'directoryTitle', 'hostName',
'relatedInformationPresent', 'snippet', 'summary', 'title']
>>> data.results[0].title
'oreilly.com -- Online Catalog: <b>Learning</b> <b>Python</b>'
>>> data.results[0].URL
'http://www.oreilly.com/catalog/lpython/'
>>> google.doGetCachedPage(data.results[0].URL)
'<meta http-equiv="Content-Type" content="text/html; charset=ISO-8859-1">\n
<BASE HREF="http://www.oreilly.com/catalog/lpython/"><table border=1
...
>>> google.doSpellingSuggestion('lurn piethon')
'learn python'
```

Programming the Google Web API with C# and .NET

HACK
#58

Create GUI and console Google search applications with C# and the .NET framework.

The Google Web APIs Developer's Kit [in "The Google Web APIs Developer's Kit"] includes a sample C# Visual Studio .NET (*http://msdn.microsoft.com/ vstudio/*) project for a simple GUI Google search application (take a look in the *dotnet/CSharp* folder). The functional bits you'd probably find most interesting are in the *Form1.cs* code.

This hack provides basic code for a simple console Google search application similar in function (and, in the case of Java [Hack #56], form, too) to those in Perl [Hack #50], Python [Hack #57], et al.

Compiling and running this hack requires that you have the .NET Framework (*http://msdn.microsoft.com/library/default. asp?url=/nhp/default.asp?contentid=28000519*) installed.

The Code

```
// googly.cs
// A Google Web API C# console application
// Usage: googly.exe <query>
// Copyright (c) 2002, Chris Sells.
// No warranties extended. Use at your own risk.
using System;
class Googly {
  static void Main(string[] args) {
    // Your Google API developer's key
    string googleKey = "insert key here";
    // Take the query from the command-line
    if( args.Length != 1 ) {
      Console.WriteLine("Usage: google.exe <query>");
      return;
    }
    string query = args[0];
    // Create a Google SOAP client proxy, generated by:
    // c:\> wsdl.exe http://api.google.com/GoogleSearch.wsdl
    GoogleSearchService googleSearch = new GoogleSearchService( );
    // Query Google
    GoogleSearchResult results = googleSearch.doGoogleSearch(googleKey,
query, 0, 10, false, "", false, "", "latin1", "latin1");
    // No results?
    if( results.resultElements == null ) return;
    // Loop through results
    foreach( ResultElement result in results.resultElements ) {
      Console.WriteLine( );
```

```
        Console.WriteLine(result.title);
        Console.WriteLine(result.URL);
        Console.WriteLine(result.snippet);
        Console.WriteLine( );
      }
    }
  }
}
```

Remember to insert your Google developer's key [in "Using the Key in a Hack"] (e.g.,
12BuCK13mY5hOE/34KNOcK@ttH3DoOR) in place of "insert key here":

```
// Your Google API developer's key
string googleKey = "12BuCK13mY5hOE/34KNOcK@ttH3DoOR";
```

Compiling the Code

Before compiling the C# code itself, you must create a Google SOAP client
proxy. The proxy is a wodge of code custom built to the specifications of the
GoogleSearch.wsdl file, an XML-based description of the Google Web Service, all its methods, parameters, and return values. Thankfully, you don't
have to do this by hand; the .NET Framework kit includes an application,
wsdl.exe, that does all the coding for you.

> This is a remarkable bit of magic if you think about it: the
> lion's share of interfacing to a web service autogenerated
> from a description thereof.

Call *wsdl.exe* with the location of your *GoogleSearch.wsdl* file like so:

```
C:\GOOGLY.NET>wsdl.exe GoogleSearch.wsdl
```

If you don't happen to have the WSDL file handy, don't fret. You can point
wsdl.exe at its location on Google's web site:

```
C:\GOOGLY.NET\CS>wsdl.exe http://api.google.com/GoogleSearch.wsdl
Microsoft (R) Web Services Description Language Utility
[Microsoft (R) .NET Framework, Version 1.0.3705.0]
Copyright (C) Microsoft Corporation 1998-2001. All rights reserved.
Writing file 'C:\GOOGLY.NET\CS\GoogleSearchService.cs'.
```

The end result is a *GoogleSearchService.cs* file that looks something like:

```
//----------------------------------------------------------------------
// <autogenerated>
//     This code was generated by a tool.
//     Runtime Version: 1.0.3705.288
//
//     Changes to this file may cause incorrect behavior and will be lost if
//     the code is regenerated.
// </autogenerated>
//----------------------------------------------------------------------
//
```

```
// This source code was auto-generated by wsdl, Version=1.0.3705.288.
//
using System.Diagnostics;
using System.Xml.Serialization;
using System;
using System.Web.Services.Protocols;
using System.ComponentModel;
using System.Web.Services;
...
    public System.IAsyncResult BegindoGoogleSearch(string key,
    string q, int start, int maxResults, bool filter, string restrict,
    bool safeSearch, string lr, string ie, string oe,
    System.AsyncCallback callback, object asyncState) {
        return this.BeginInvoke("doGoogleSearch", new object[] {
                        key,
                        q,
                        start,
                        maxResults,
                        filter,
                        restrict,
                        safeSearch,
                        lr,
                        ie,
                        oe}, callback, asyncState);
    }
...
```

Now on to *googly.cs* itself:

```
C:\GOOGLY.NET\CS>csc /out:googly.exe *.cs
Microsoft (R) Visual C# .NET Compiler version 7.00.9466
for Microsoft (R) .NET Framework version 1.0.3705
Copyright (C) Microsoft Corporation 2001. All rights reserved.
```

Running the Hack

Run Googly on the command line, passing it your Google query:

```
C:\GOOGLY.NET\CS>googly.exe "query words"
```

 The DOS command window isn't the best at displaying and allowing scrollback of lots of output. To send the results of your Google query to a file for perusal in your favorite text editor, append: > results.txt.

The Results

```
% googly.exe "WSDL while you work"
Axis/Radio interop, actual and potential
http://www.intertwingly.net/stories/2002/02/08/
axisradioInteropActualAndPotential.html <b>...</b> But
<b>you</b> might find more exciting services here
```

```
<b>...</b> Instead, we should <b>work</b>
together and<br> continuously strive to <b>...</b>
<b>While</b> <b>WSDL</b> is certainly far from
perfect and has many <b>...</b>
...
Simplified <b>WSDL</b>
http://capescience.capeclear.com/articles/simplifiedWSDL/
<b>...</b> So how does it <b>work</b>?
<b>...</b> If <b>you</b> would like to edit
<b>WSDL</b> <b>while</b> still avoiding<br> all
those XML tags, check out the <b>WSDL</b> Editor in
CapeStudio. <b>...</b>
```

—Chris Sells and Rael Dornfest

 HACK
#59 Programming the Google Web API with VB.NET

Create GUI and console Google search applications with Visual Basic and the .NET framework.

Along with the functionally identical C# [Hack #58] version, the Google Web APIs Developer's Kit [in "The Google Web APIs Developer's Kit"] (*dotnet/Visual Basic* folder) includes a sample Google search in Visual Basic. While you can probably glean just about all you need from the *Google Demo Form.vb* code, this hack provides basic code for a simple console Google search application without the possibile opacity of a full-blown Visual Studio .NET project.

 Compiling and running this hack requires that you have the .NET Framework (*http://msdn.microsoft.com/library/default. asp?url=/nhp/default.asp?contentid=28000519*) installed.

The Code

```vb
' googly.vb
' A Google Web API VB.NET console application
' Usage: googly.exe <query>
' Copyright (c) 2002, Chris Sells.
' No warranties extended. Use at your own risk.
Imports System
Module Googly
  Sub Main(ByVal args As String())
    ' Your Google API developer's key
    Dim googleKey As String = "insert key here"
    ' Take the query from the command-line
    If args.Length <> 1 Then
      Console.WriteLine("Usage: google.exe <query>")
      Return
```

```
       End If
       Dim query As String = args(0)
       ' Create a Google SOAP client proxy, generated by:
       ' c:\> wsdl.exe /l:vb http://api.google.com/GoogleSearch.wsdl
       Dim googleSearch As GoogleSearchService = New GoogleSearchService( )
       ' Query Google
       Dim results As GoogleSearchResult = googleSearch.
   doGoogleSearch(googleKey, query, 0, 10, False, "", False, "", "latin1",
   "latin1")
         ' No results?
         If results.resultElements Is Nothing Then Return
         ' Loop through results
         Dim result As ResultElement
         For Each result In results.resultElements
           Console.WriteLine( )
           Console.WriteLine(result.title)
           Console.WriteLine(result.URL)
           Console.WriteLine(result.snippet)
           Console.WriteLine( )
         Next
       End Sub
     End Module
```

You'll need to replace "insert key here" with your Google developer's key
[in "Using the Key in a Hack"] (e.g., 12BuCK13mY5h0E/34KN0cK@ttH3D0oR). Your code
should look something like:

```
' Your Google API developer's key
Dim googleKey As String = "12BuCK13mY5h0E/34KN0cK@ttH3D0oR"
```

Compiling the Code

Before compiling the VB application code itself, you must create a Google
SOAP client proxy. The proxy is a wodge of code custom built to the specifications of the GoogleSearch.wsdl [in "What's WSDL?"] file, an XML-based
description of the Google Web Service, all its methods, parameters, and
return values. Thankfully, you don't have to do this by hand; the .NET
Framework kit includes an application, *wsdl.exe* to do all the coding for you.

> This is a remarkable bit of magic if you think about it: the
> lion's share of interfacing to a web service autogenerated
> from a description thereof.

Call *wsdl.exe* with the location of your *GoogleSearch.wsdl* file and specify
that you'd like Visual Basic proxy code:

```
C:\GOOGLY.NET\VB>wsdl.exe /l:vb GoogleSearch.wsdl
```

If you don't happen to have the WSDL file handy, don't fret. You can point *wsdl.exe* at its location on Google's web site:

```
C:\GOOGLY.NET\VB>wsdl.exe /l:vb http://api.google.com/GoogleSearch.wsdl
Microsoft (R) Web Services Description Language Utility
[Microsoft (R) .NET Framework, Version 1.0.3705.0]
Copyright (C) Microsoft Corporation 1998-2001. All rights reserved.
Writing file 'C:\GOOGLY.NET\VB\GoogleSearchService.vb'.
```

What you get is a *GoogleSearchService.vb* file with all that underlying Google SOAP-handling ready to go:

```
'------------------------------------------------------------------------
' <autogenerated>
'     This code was generated by a tool.
'     Runtime Version: 1.0.3705.288
'
'     Changes to this file may cause incorrect behavior and will be lost if
'     the code is regenerated.
' </autogenerated>
'------------------------------------------------------------------------
Option Strict Off
Option Explicit On
Imports System
Imports System.ComponentModel
Imports System.Diagnostics
Imports System.Web.Services
Imports System.Web.Services.Protocols
Imports System.Xml.Serialization
...
    Public Function BegindoGoogleSearch(ByVal key As String, ByVal q As
String, ByVal start As Integer, ByVal maxResults As Integer, ByVal
filter As Boolean, ByVal restrict As String, ByVal safeSearch As
Boolean, ByVal lr As String, ByVal ie As String, ByVal oe As String,
ByVal callback As System.AsyncCallback, ByVal asyncState As Object) As
System.IAsyncResult
        Return Me.BeginInvoke("doGoogleSearch", New Object() {key, q,
start, maxResults, filter, restrict, safeSearch, lr, ie, oe}, callback,
asyncState) End Function

    '<remarks/>
    Public Function EnddoGoogleSearch(ByVal asyncResult As System.
IAsyncResult) As GoogleSearchResult
        Dim results() As Object = Me.EndInvoke(asyncResult)
        Return CType(results(0),GoogleSearchResult)
    End Function
End Class
...
```

Now to compile that *googly.vb*:

```
C:\GOOGLY.NET\VB>vbc /out:googly.exe *.vb
Microsoft (R) Visual Basic .NET Compiler version 7.00.9466
for Microsoft (R) .NET Framework version 1.00.3705
Copyright (C) Microsoft Corporation 1987-2001. All rights reserved.
```

Running the Hack

Run Googly on the command line, passing it your Google query:

```
C:\GOOGLY.NET\VB>googly.exe "query words"
```

> The DOS command window isn't the best at displaying and allowing scrollback of lots of output. To send the results of your Google query to a file for perusal in your favorite text editor, append: > results.txt

The Results

Functionally identical to its C# counterpart [Hack #58], running this Visual Basic hack should turn up about the same results—Google index willing.

—*Chris Sells and Rael Dornfest*

Google Web API Applications
Hacks #60–85

It's funny how people look at things in different ways. Nowhere is that more apparent than with this section. In this part of the book, we're going to look at several different Google applications, which run the gamut from date-range searching with a client-side application (an application that you run from the desktop instead of from a web site) to a program that runs from a web form to count the number of different suffixes in a search result page.

The Ingenuity of Millions

The release of the Google API in April 2002 inspired hundreds of people all over the Web to try their hand at tapping Google's data source, including yours truly. Some of the earliest applications were tapping into Google's results and including them on a web page, or integrating Google results with content management tools like Movable Type and Radio Userland. Then as more people experimented with the API, the variety of applications grew from the seriously useful to the amazingly silly. (We've created a special section of the book for the amazingly silly ones.)

Learning to Code

Want to learn to code? Are you a barely beginning programmer who wants to learn more? This isn't the Camel Book (O'Reilly's best selling *Programming Perl*, at *http://www.oreilly.com/catalog/pperl3/*, in case you're not yet in the know), but if you're interested in Perl, spend some time browsing through this section. You can use these programs as they are, or use the "Hacking the Hack" sections to tweak and fiddle with the scripts. This is a useful way to get more Perl knowledge if you're a searching nut, and you want to play with programs that do something useful right out of the gate.

What You'll Find Here

You'll find a variety of applications in this section, from visualizing Google results to creating a "neighborhood" to restricting searches to top-level results. But bear in mind that even though these are API programs, they're not the only ones in the book. You'll find applications using the Google API in many sections of this book.

Finding More Google API Applications

The hacks in this book are only a few of the myriad applications available online. Where to go if you want to find more?

Google Directory
Start with Google. The Google Directory offers a category for the Google API at *http://directory.google.com/Top/Computers/Internet/Searching/Search_Engines/Google/Web_APIs/*.

Soapware.org
Soapware.org has a brief list of API applications, available at *http://www.soapware.org/directory/4/services/googleApi/applications*.

Daypop
Daypop (*http://www.daypop.com*) is a search engine for news and weblog sites. If there's something buzzing about the weblog community, it's sure to be on Daypop. Search for "Google API" or "Google API Applications" for pointers to Google API applications that people have made mention of in their weblogs or web sites.

The Possibilities Aren't Endless, but They're Expanding

The Google API is still in beta. Furthermore, it's still pretty limited in what it offers. You can't get data from Google News, for example. That said, the ingenuity of those fiddling with the Google API knows no bounds. Watch the Web as the API expands, and more and more programmers take advantage of its power.

 HACK
#60 **Date-Range Searching with a Client-Side Application**

Monitor a set of queries for new finds added to the Google index yesterday.

The GooFresh [Hack #42] hack is a simple web form–driven CGI script for building date range [Hack #11] Google queries. A simple web-based interface is fine when you want to search for only one or two items at a time. But what of performing multiple searches over time, saving the results to your computer for comparative analysis?

A better fit for this task is a client-side application that you run from the comfort of your own computer's desktop. This Perl script feeds specified queries to Google via the Google Web API, limiting results to those indexed yesterday. New finds are appended to a comma-delimited text file per query, suitable for import into Excel or your average database application.

 This hack requires an additional Perl module, Time::Julian-Day (*http://search.cpan.org/author/MUIR/*); it just won't work until you have the module installed.

The Queries

First, you'll need to prepare a few queries to feed the script. Try these out via the Google search interface itself first to make sure you're receiving the kind of results you're expecting. Your queries can be anything you'd be interested in tracking over time: topics of long-lasting or current interest, searches for new directories of information [Hack #21] coming online, unique quotes from articles or other sources that you want to monitor for signs of plagiarism.

Use whatever special syntaxes you like except for link:; as you might remember, link: can't be used in concert with any other special syntax like daterange:, upon which this hack relies. If you insist on trying anyway (e.g., link:www.yahoo.com daterange:2452421-2452521), Google will simply treat link as yet another query word (e.g., link www.yahoo.com), yielding some unexpected and useless results.

Put each query on its own line. A sample query file will look something like this:

```
"digital archives"
intitle:"state library of"
intitle:directory intitle:resources
"now * * time for all good men * come * * aid * * party"
```

Save the text file somewhere memorable; alongside the script you're about to write is as good a place as any.

The Code

```
#!/usr/local/bin/perl -w
# goonow.pl
# feeds queries specified in a text file to Google, querying
# for recent additions to the Google index.  The script appends
# to CSV files, one per query, creating them if they don't exist.
# usage: perl goonow.pl [query_filename]
```

```perl
# My Google API developer's key
my $google_key='insert key here';

# Location of the GoogleSearch WSDL file
my $google_wdsl = "./GoogleSearch.wsdl";

use strict;

use SOAP::Lite;
use Time::JulianDay;

$ARGV[0] or die "usage: perl goonow.pl [query_filename]\n";

my $julian_date = int local_julian_day(time) - 2;

my $google_search  = SOAP::Lite->service("file:$google_wdsl");

open QUERIES, $ARGV[0] or die "Couldn't read $ARGV[0]: $!";

while (my $query = <QUERIES>) {
  chomp $query;
  warn "Searching Google for $query\n"

  $query .= " daterange:$julian_date-$julian_date";
  (my $outfile = $query) =~ s/\W/_/g;
  open (OUT, ">> $outfile.csv")
    or die "Couldn't open $outfile.csv: $!\n";

  my $results = $google_search ->
    doGoogleSearch(
      $google_key, $query, 0, 10, "false", "",  "false",
      "", "latin1", "latin1"
    );
  foreach (@{$results->{'resultElements'}}) {
    print OUT '"' . join('","', (
      map {
        s!\n!!g; # drop spurious newlines
        s!<.+?>!!g; # drop all HTML tags
        s!"!""!g; # double escape " marks
        $_;
      } @$_{'title','URL','snippet'}
    ) ) . "\"\n";
  }
}
```

You'll notice that GooNow checks the day before yesterday's rather than yesterday's additions (my $julian_date = int local_julian_day(time) - 2;). Google indexes some pages very frequently; these show up in yesterday's additions and really bulk up your search results. So if you search for yesterday's results, in addition to updated pages you'll get a lot of noise, pages that Google indexes every day, rather than the fresh content you're after. Skipping back one more day is a nice hack to get around the noise.

Running the Hack

This script is invoked on the command line like so:

```
$ perl goonow.pl query_filename
```

Where *query_filename* is the name of the text file holding all the queries to be fed to the script. The file can be located either in the local directory or elsewhere; if the latter, be sure to include the entire path (e.g., */mydocu~1/ hacks/queries.txt*).

Bear in mind that all output is directed to CSV files, one per query. So don't expect any fascinating output on the screen.

The Results

Taking a quick look at one of the CSV output files created, *intitle__state_ library_of_.csv*:

```
"State Library of Louisiana","http://www.state.lib.la.us/"," ...
Click
here if you have any questions or comments. Copyright <C2><A9>
1998-2001 State Library of Louisiana Last modified: August 07,
2002. "
"STATE LIBRARY OF NEW SOUTH WALES, SYDNEY
AUSTRALIA","http://www.slnsw.gov.au/", " ... State Library of New
South
Wales Macquarie St, Sydney NSW Australia 2000 Phone: +61 2 9273
1414
Fax: +61 2 9273 1255. Your comments You could win a prize! ...  "
"State Library of Victoria","http://www.slv.vic.gov.au/"," ...
clicking
on our logo. State Library of Victoria Logo with link to homepage
State
Library of Victoria. A world class cultural resource ...  "
...
```

Hacking the Hack

The script keeps appending new finds to the appropriate CVS output file. If you wish to reset the CVS files associated with particular queries, simply delete them and the script will create them anew.

Or you can make one slight adjustment to have the script create the CSV files anew each time, overwriting the previous version, like so:

```
...
(my $outfile = $query) =~ s/\W/_/g;
open (OUT, "> $outfile.csv")
   or die "Couldn't open $outfile.csv: $!\n";
my $results = $google_search ->
   doGoogleSearch(
```

```
        $google_key, $query, 0, 10, "false", "", "false",
        "", "latin1", "latin1"
    );
    ...
```

Notice the only change in the code is the removal of one of the > characters when the output file is created—open (OUT, "> $outfile.csv") instead of open (OUT, ">> $outfile.csv").

HACK #61   Adding a Little Google to Your Word

Use Google with Microsoft Word for better spelling suggestions than the traditional dictionary.

Some of the hacks we cover in this book are very useful, some are weird, and some of them are not exactly useful but have a definite cool factor. The first version of CapeSpeller (*http://www.capescience.com/google/spell.shtml*) fit into that last category. Send a word via email and receive a spelling suggestion in return.

While cool, there weren't many scenarios where you'd absolutely need to use it. But the newer version of CapeSpeller is far more useful; it's now designed to integrate with Microsoft Word and provide spelling suggestions powered by Google as an alternative to the standard Word/Office dictionary.

Now, why in the world would you want another spellchecker in Word? Doesn't it already have a rather good one? Indeed it does, but it employs a traditional dictionary, which falls over when faced with certain proper nouns, jargon, and acronyms. Google's dictionary [Hack #16] is chock-full of these sorts of up-to-the-minute, hip, and non-traditional suggestions.

Using CapeSpeller

There are several steps to acquiring and installing CapeSpeller.

1. First, you'll need to have the Microsoft SOAP Toolkit installed (*http://msdn.microsoft.com/downloads/default.asp?URL=/code/sample.asp?url=/msdn-files/027/001/580/msdncompositedoc.xml*). It's a fairly small download but may take a little wrangling to get squared away. You must be running Internet Explorer 5 or later. You may also have to update your Windows Installer depending on what version of Windows you're using. The CapeSpeller site (*http://www.capescience.com/google/spell.shtml*) provides more details.

2. Once you've got the SOAP toolkit squared away, you'll have to get two code items from CapeScience. The first is a zipped executable that's available from *http://www.capescience.com/google/download/CapeSpeller.zip*. Download that one, unzip it, and run the executable.

3. After you've downloaded and installed the executable, download the source code. The source code contains a place for you to copy and paste your API. Unless you've got a legit developer's key there, you won't be able to get spelling suggestions from Google.

4. The final thing you'll need to do to get CapeSpeller to work with Word is to set up a macro. CapeScience offers instructions for setting up a spellcheck macro at *http://www.capescience.com/google/spelltoword.shtml*.

HACK #62 Permuting a Query

Run all permutations of query keywords and phrases to squeeze the last drop of results from the Google index.

Google, ah, Google. Search engine of over 3 billion pages and 3 zillion possibilities. One of Google's charms, if you're a search engine geek like me, is trying various tweaks with your Google search to see what exactly makes a difference to the results you get.

It's amazing what makes a difference. For example, you wouldn't think that word order would make much of an impact but it does. In fact, buried in Google's documentation is the admission that the word order of a query will impact search results.

While that's an interesting thought, who has time to generate and run every possible iteration of a multiword query? The Google API to the rescue! This hack takes a query of up to four keywords or "quoted phrases" (as well as supporting special syntaxes) and runs all possible permutations, showing result counts by permutation and the top results for each permutation.

You'll need to have the Algorithm::Permute Perl module for this program to work correctly (*http://search.cpan.org/ search?query=algorithm%3A%3Apermute&mode=all*).

The Code

```perl
#!/usr/local/bin/perl
# order_matters.cgi
# Queries Google for every possible permutation of up to 4 query keywords,
# returning result counts by permutation and top results across
permutations.
# order_matters.cgi is called as a CGI with form input

# Your Google API developer's key
my $google_key='insert key here';

# Location of the GoogleSearch WSDL file
my $google_wdsl = "./GoogleSearch.wsdl";
```

```
use strict;

use SOAP::Lite;
use CGI qw/:standard *table/;
use Algorithm::Permute;

print
  header(),
  start_html("Order Matters"),
  h1("Order Matters"),
  start_form(-method=>'GET'),
  'Query:   ', textfield(-name=>'query'),
  '   ',
  submit(-name=>'submit', -value=>'Search'), br(),
  '<font size="-2" color="green">Enter up to 4 query keywords or "quoted
phrases"</font>',
  end_form(), p();

if (param('query')) {

  # Glean keywords
  my @keywords = grep !/^\s*$/,  split /([+-]?".+?")|\s+/, param('query');

  scalar @keywords > 4 and
    print('<font color="red">Only 4 query keywords or phrases allowed.</font>
'), last;

  my $google_search = SOAP::Lite->service("file:$google_wdsl");

  print
    start_table({-cellpadding=>'10', -border=>'1'}),
    Tr([th({-colspan=>'2'}, ['Result Counts by Permutation' ])]),
    Tr([th({-align=>'left'}, ['Query', 'Count'])]);

  my $results = {}; # keep track of what we've seen across queries

  # Iterate over every possible permutation
  my $p = new Algorithm::Permute( \@keywords );
  while (my $query = join(' ', $p->next)) {

    # Query Google
    my $r = $google_search ->
     doGoogleSearch(
      $google_key,
      $query,
      0, 10, "false", "",  "false", "", "latin1", "latin1"
     );
       print Tr([td({-align=>'left'}, [$query, $r->
{'estimatedTotalResultsCount'}] )]);
     @{$r->{'resultElements'}} or next;
```

```
      # Assign a rank
      my $rank = 10;
      foreach (@{$r->{'resultElements'}}) {
        $results->{$_->{URL}} = {
          title => $_->{title},
          snippet => $_->{snippet},
          seen => ($results->{$_->{URL}}->{seen}) + $rank
        };
        $rank--;
      }
    }

    print
      end_table(), p(),
      start_table({-cellpadding=>'10', -border=>'1'}),
      Tr([th({-colspan=>'2'}, ['Top Results across Permutations' ])]),
      Tr([th({-align=>'left'}, ['Score', 'Result'])]);

    foreach ( sort { $results->{$b}->{seen} <=> $results->{$a}->{seen} } keys
    %$results ) {
      print Tr(td([
        $results->{$_}->{seen},
        b($results->{$_}->{title}||'no title') . br() .
        a({href=>$_}, $_) . br() .
        i($results->{$_}->{snippet}||'no snippet')
      ]));
    }

      print end_table(),
    }
    print end_html();
```

Running the Hack

The hack runs via a web form that is integrated into the code. Call the CGI
and enter the query you want to check (up to four words or phrases). The
script will first search for every possible combination of the search words
and phrases, as Figure 6-1 shows.

The script then displays top 10 search results across all permutations of the
query, as Figure 6-2 shows.

Using the Hack

At first blush, this hack looks like a novelty with few practical applications.
But if you're a regular researcher or a web wrangler, you might find it of
interest.

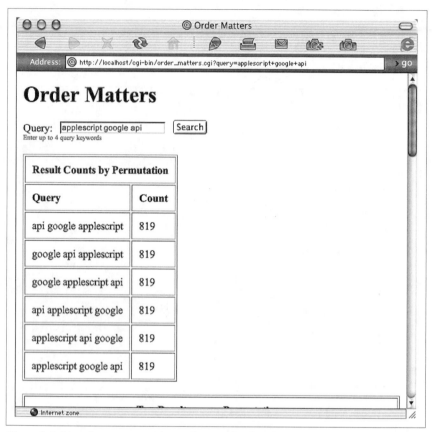

Figure 6-1. List of permutations for applescript google api

If you're a regular researcher—that is, there are certain topics that you research on a regular basis—you might want to spend some time with this hack and see if you can detect a pattern in how your regular search terms are impacted by changing word order. You might need to revise your searching so that certain words always come first or last in your query.

If you're a web wrangler, you need to know where your page appears in Google's search results. If your page loses a lot of ranking ground because of a shift in a query arrangement, maybe you want to add some more words to your text or shift your existing text.

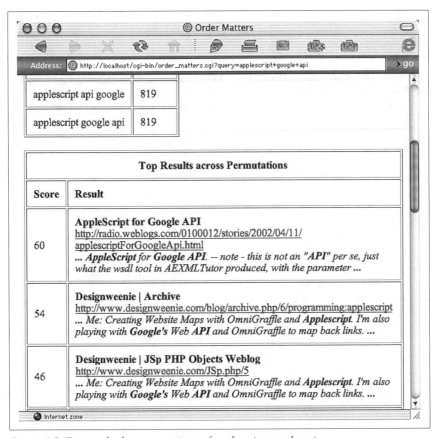

applescript api google	819
applescript google api	819

Top Results across Permutations	
Score	**Result**
60	**AppleScript for Google API** http://radio.weblogs.com/0100012/stories/2002/04/11/ applescriptForGoogleApi.html *... **AppleScript** for **Google API**. – note - this is not an "API" per se, just what the wsdl tool in AEXMLTutor produced, with the parameter ...*
54	**Designweenie | Archive** http://www.designweenie.com/blog/archive.php/6/programming:applescript *... Me: Creating Website Maps with OmniGraffle and **Applescript**. I'm also playing with **Google's** Web **API** and OmniGraffle to map back links. ...*
46	**Designweenie | JSp PHP Objects Weblog** http://www.designweenie.com/JSp.php/5 *... Me: Creating Website Maps with OmniGraffle and **Applescript**. I'm also playing with **Google's** Web **API** and OmniGraffle to map back links. ...*

Figure 6-2. Top results for permutations of applescript google api

HACK #63 Tracking Result Counts over Time

Query Google for each day of a specified date range, counting the number of results at each time index.

Sometimes the results of a search aren't of as much interest as knowing the number thereof. How popular is a particular keyword? How many times is so-and-so mentioned? How do differing phrases or spellings stack up against each other?

You may also wish to track the popularity of a term over time to watch its ups and downs, spot trends, and notice tipping points. Combining the Google API and `daterange:` [Hack #11] syntax is just the ticket.

This hack queries Google for each day over a specified date range, counting the number of results for each day. This leads to a list of numbers that you could enter into Excel and chart, for example.

There are a couple of caveats before diving right into the code. First, the average keyword will tend to show more results over time as Google ads more pages to its index. Second, Google doesn't stand behind its date-range search; results shouldn't be taken as gospel.

> This hack requires the Time::JulianDay (*http://search.cpan. org/search?query=Time%3A%3AJulianDay*) Perl module.

The Code

```perl
#!/usr/local/bin/perl
# goocount.pl
# Runs the specified query for every day between the specified
# start and end dates, returning date and count as CSV.
# usage: goocount.pl query="{query}" start={date} end={date}\n}
# where dates are of the format: yyyy-mm-dd, e.g. 2002-12-31

# Your Google API developer's key
my $google_key='insert key here';

# Location of the GoogleSearch WSDL file
my $google_wdsl = "./GoogleSearch.wsdl";

use SOAP::Lite;
use Time::JulianDay;
use CGI qw/:standard/;

# For checking date validity
my $date_regex = '(\d{4})-(\d{1,2})-(\d{1,2})';

# Make sure all arguments are passed correctly
( param('query') and param('start') =~ /^(?:$date_regex)?$/
  and param('end') =~ /^(?:$date_regex)?$/ ) or
    die qq{usage: goocount.pl query="{query}" start={date} end={date}\n};

# Julian date manipulation
my $query = param('query');
my $yesterday_julian = int local_julian_day(time) - 1;
my $start_julian = (param('start') =~ /$date_regex/)
  ? julian_day($1,$2,$3) : $yesterday_julian;
my $end_julian = (param('end') =~ /$date_regex/)
  ? julian_day($1,$2,$3) : $yesterday_julian;

# Create a new Google SOAP request
my $google_search  = SOAP::Lite->service("file:$google_wdsl");
```

```
print qq{"date","count"\n};

# Iterate over each of the Julian dates for your query
foreach my $julian ($start_julian..$end_julian) {
  $full_query = "$query daterange:$julian-$julian";
  # Query Google
  my $result = $google_search ->
    doGoogleSearch(
      $google_key, $full_query, 0, 10, "false", "",  "false",
      "", "latin1", "latin1"
    );

  # Output
  print
    '"',
    sprintf("%04d-%02d-%02d", inverse_julian_day($julian)),
    qq{,"$result->{estimatedTotalResultsCount}"\n};
}
```

Running the Hack

Run the script from the command line, specifying a query, start, and end dates. Perhaps you'd like to see track mentions of the latest Macintosh operating system (code name "Jaguar") leading up to, on, and after its launch (August 24, 2002). The following invocation sends its results to a comma-separated (CSV) file for easy import into Excel or a database:

```
% perl goocount.pl query="OS X Jaguar" \
start=2002-08-20 end=2002-08-28 > count.csv
```

Leaving off the > and CSV filename sends the results to the screen for your perusal:

```
% perl goocount.pl query="OS X Jaguar" \
start=2002-08-20 end=2002-08-28
```

If you want to track results over time, you could run the script every day (using cron under Unix or the scheduler under Windows), with no date specified, to get the information for that day's date. Just use >> filename.csv to append to the filename instead of writing over it. Or you could get the results emailed to you for your daily reading pleasure.

The Results

Here's that search for Jaguar, the new Macintosh operating system:

```
% perl goocount.pl query="OS X Jaguar" \
start=2002-08-20 end=2002-08-28
"date","count"
"2002-08-20","18"
"2002-08-21","7"
```

```
"2002-08-22","21"
"2002-08-23","66"
"2002-08-24","145"
"2002-08-25","38"
"2002-08-26","94"
"2002-08-27","55"
"2002-08-28","102"
```

Notice the expected spike in new finds on release day, August 24th.

Working with These Results

If you have a fairly short list, it's easy to just look at the results and see if there are any spikes or particular items of interest about the result counts. But if you have a long list or you want a visual overview of the results, it's easy to use these numbers to create a graph in Excel or your favorite spreadsheet program.

Simply save the results to a file, and then open the file in Excel and use the chart wizard to create a graph. You'll have to do some tweaking but just generating the chart generates an interesting overview, as shown in Figure 6-3.

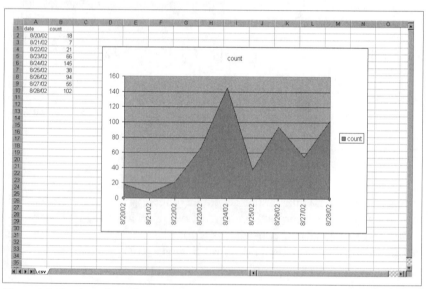

Figure 6-3. Excel graph tracking mentions of OS X Jaguar

Hacking the Hack

You can render the results as a web page by altering the code ever so slightly (changes are in bold) and directing the output to an HTML file (>> filename.html):

```
...
print
  header( ),
  start_html("GooCount: $query"),
  start_table({-border=>undef}, caption("GooCount:$query")),
  Tr([ th(['Date', 'Count']) ]);

foreach my $julian ($start_julian..$end_julian) {
  $full_query = "$query daterange:$julian-$julian";
  my $result = $google_search ->
    doGoogleSearch(
      $google_key, $full_query, 0, 10, "false", "",  "false",
      "", "latin1", "latin1"
    );

  print
    Tr([ td([
      sprintf("%04d-%02d-%02d", inverse_julian_day($julian)),
      $result->{estimatedTotalResultsCount}
    ]) ]);
}

print
  end_table( ),
  end_html;
```

HACK
#64 ## Visualizing Google Results

The TouchGraph Google Browser is the perfect Google complement for those
who appreciate visual displays of information.

Some people are born text crawlers. They can retrieve the mostly text
resources of the Internet and browse them happily for hours. But others are
more visually oriented and find that the flat text results of the Internet leave
something to be desired, especially when it comes to search results.

If you're the type who appreciates visual displays of information, you're
bound to like the TouchGraph Google Browser (*http://www.touchgraph.
com/TGGoogleBrowser.html*). This Java applet allows you to start with the
pages that are similar to one URL, and then expand outward to pages that
are similar to the first set of pages, on and on, until you have a giant map of
"nodes" (a.k.a. URLs) on your screen.

Note that what you're finding here are URLs that are similar to another
URL. You aren't doing a keyword search, and you're not using the link:
syntax. You're searching by Google's measure of similarity.

Starting to Browse

Start your journey by entering a URL on the TouchGraph home page and clicking the "Graph It" link. Your browser will launch the TouchGraph Java applet, covering your window with a large mass of linked nodes, as shown in Figure 6-4.

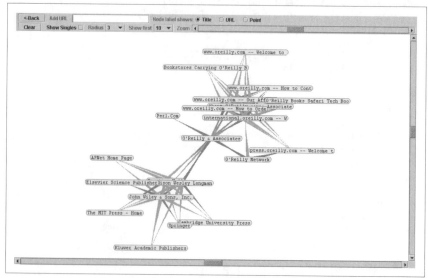

Figure 6-4. Mass of linked nodes generated by TouchGraph

 You'll need a web browser capable of running Java applets. If Java support in your preferred browser comes in the form of a plug-in, your browser should have the smarts to launch a plug-in locator/downloader and walk you through the installation process.

If you're easily entertained like me, you might amuse yourself for a while just by clicking and dragging the nodes around. But there's more to do than that.

Expanding Your View

Hold your mouse over one of items in the group of pages. You'll notice that a little box with an H pops up. Click on that and you'll get a box of information about that particular node, as shown in Figure 6-5.

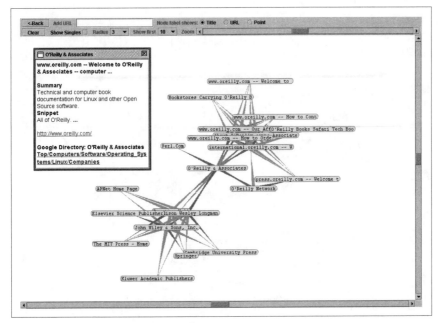

Figure 6-5. Node information pop-up box

The box of information contains title, snippet, and URL—pretty much everything you'd get from a regular search result. Click on the URL in the box to open that URL's web page itself in another browser window.

Not interested in visiting web pages just yet? Want to do some more search visualization? Double-click on one of the nodes. TouchGraph uses the API to request from Google pages similar to the URL of the node you double-clicked. Keep double-clicking at will; when no more pages are available, a green C will appear when you put your mouse over the node (no more than 30 results are available for each node). If you do it often enough, you'll end up with a whole screen full of nodes with lines denoting their relationship to one-another, as Figure 6-6 shows.

Visualization Options

Once you've generated similarity page listings for a few different sites, you'll find yourself with a pretty crowded page. TouchGraph has a few options to change the look of what you're viewing.

For each node, you can show page title, page URL, or "point" (the first two letters of the title). If you're just browsing page relationships, the title's probably best. However, if you've been working with the applet for a while

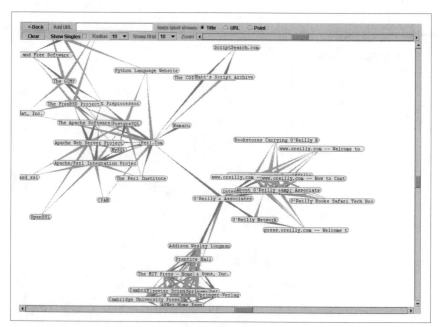

Figure 6-6. Node mass expanded by double-clicking on nodes

and have mapped out a plethora of nodes, the "point" or URL options can save some space. The URL option removes the *www* and *.com* from the URL, leaving the other domain suffixes. For example, *www.perl.com* will show as *perl*, while *www.perl.org* shows as *perl.org*.

Speaking of saving space, there's a zoom slider on the upper-right side of the applet window. When you've generated several distinct groups of nodes, zooming out allows you to see the different groupings more clearly. However, it also becomes difficult to see relationships between the nodes in the different groups.

TouchGraph offers the option to view the "singles," the nodes in a group that have a relationship with only one other node. This option is off by default; check the Show Singles checkbox to turn it on. I find it's better to leave them out; they crowd the page and make it difficult to establish and explore separate groups of nodes.

The Radius setting specifies how many nodes will show around the node you've clicked on. A radius of 1 will show all nodes directly linked to the node you've clicked, a radius of 2 will show all nodes directly linked to the node you've clicked as well as all nodes directly linked to those nodes, and so on. The higher the radius, the more crowded things get. The groupings do, however, tend to settle themselves into nice little discernable clumps, as shown in Figure 6-7.

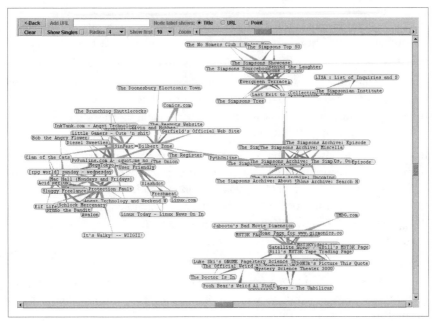

Figure 6-7. Node mass with Radius set to 4

A drop-down menu beside the Radius setting specifies how many search results—how many connections—are shown. A setting of 10 is, in my experience, optimal.

Making the Most of These Visualizations

Yes, it's cool. Yes, it's unusual. And yes, it's fun dragging those little nodes around. But what exactly is the TouchGraph good for?

TouchGraph does two rather useful things. First, it allows you to see at a glance the similarity relationship between large groups of URLs. You can't do this with several flat results to similar URL queries. Second, if you do some exploration you can sometimes get a list of companies in the same industry or area. This comes in handy when you're researching a particular industry or topic. It'll take some exploration, though, so keep trying.

TouchGraph Google Browser created by Alex Shapiro (*http://www. touchgraph.com/*).

Meandering Your Google Neighborhood

HACK
#65

Google Neighborhood attempts to detangle the Web by building a "neighborhood" of sites around a URL.

It's called the World Wide Web, not the World Wide Straight Line. Sites link to other sites, building a "web" of sites. And what a tangled web we weave.

Google Neighborhood attempts to detangle some small portion of the Web by using the Google API to find sites related to a URL you provide, scraping the links on the sites returned, and building a "neighborhood" of sites that link both the original URL and each other.

If you'd like to give this hack a whirl without having to run it yourself, there's a live version available at *http://diveintomark.org/archives/2002/06/04.html#who_are_the_people_in_your_neighborhood*. The source code (included below) for Google Neighborhood is available for download from *http://diveintomark.org/projects/misc/neighbor.py.txt*.

The Code

Google Neighborhood is written in the Python (*http://www.python.org*) programming language. Your system will need to have Python installed for you to run this hack.

```
"""
neighbor.cgi
Blogroll finder and aggregator
"""

__author__ = "Mark Pilgrim (f8dy@diveintomark.org)"
__copyright__ = "Copyright 2002, Mark Pilgrim"
__license__ = "Python"
try:
    import timeoutsocket # http://www.timo-tasi.org/python/timeoutsocket.py
    timeoutsocket.setDefaultSocketTimeout(10)
except:
    pass
import urllib, urlparse, os, time, operator, sys, pickle, re, cgi, time
from sgmllib import SGMLParser
from threading import *
BUFFERSIZE = 1024
IGNOREEXTS = ('.xml', '.opml', '.rss', '.rdf', '.pdf', '.doc')
INCLUDEEXTS = ('', '.html', '.htm', '.shtml', '.php', '.asp', '.jsp')
IGNOREDOMAINS = ('cgi.alexa.com', 'adserver1.backbeatmedia.com',
'ask.slashdot.org', 'freshmeat.net', 'readroom.ipl.org', 'amazon.com',
'ringsurf.com')
def prettyURL(url):
    protocol, domain, path, params, query, fragment = urlparse.urlparse(url)
    if path == '/':
        path = ''
```

```
    return urlparse.urlunparse(('',domain,path,'','','')).replace('//','')

def simplifyURL(url):
    url = url.replace('www.', '')
    url = url.replace('/coming.html', '/')
    protocol, domain, path, params, query, fragment = urlparse.urlparse(url)
    if path == '':
        url = url + '/'
    return url
class MinimalURLOpener(urllib.FancyURLopener):
    def __init__(self, *args):
        apply(urllib.FancyURLopener.__init__, (self,) + args)
        self.addheaders = [('User-agent', '')]
    def http_error_401(self, url, fp, errcode, errmsg, headers, data=None):
        pass
class BlogrollParser(SGMLParser):
    def __init__(self, url):
        SGMLParser.__init__(self)
        self.url = url
        self.reset()

    def reset(self):
        SGMLParser.reset(self)
        self.possible = []
        self.blogroll = []
        self.ina = 0

    def _goodlink(self, href):
        protocol, domain, path, params, query, fragment = urlparse.
urlparse(href)
        if protocol.lower() <> 'http': return 0
        if self.url.find(domain) <> -1: return 0
        if domain in IGNOREDOMAINS: return 0
        if domain.find(':5335') <> -1: return 0
        if domain.find('.google') <> -1: return 0
        if fragment: return 0
        shortpath, ext = os.path.splitext(path)
        ext = ext.lower()
        if ext in INCLUDEEXTS: return 1
        if ext.lower() in IGNOREEXTS: return 0
        # more rules here?
        return 1

    def _confirmpossibles(self):
        if len(self.possible) >= 4:
            for url in self.possible:
                if url not in self.blogroll:
                    self.blogroll.append(url)
        self.possible = []

    def start_a(self, attrs):
        self.ina = 1
        hreflist = [e[1] for e in attrs if e[0]=='href']
```

```
                if not hreflist: return
                href = simplifyURL(hreflist[0])
                if self._goodlink(href):
                    self.possible.append(href)
        def end_a(self):
            self.ina = 0

        def handle_data(self, data):
            if self.ina: return
            if data.strip():
                self._confirmpossibles()

        def end_html(self, attrs):
            self.confirmpossibles()
    def getRadioBlogroll(url):
        try:
            usock = MinimalURLOpener().open('%s/gems/mySubscriptions.opml' %
    url)
            opmlSource = usock.read()
            usock.close()
        except:
            return []
        if opmlSource.find('<opml') == -1: return []
        radioBlogroll = []
        start = 0
        while 1:
            p = opmlSource.find('htmlUrl="', start)
            if p == -1: break
            refurl = opmlSource[p:p+100].split('"')[1]
            radioBlogroll.append(refurl)
            start = p + len(refurl) + 10
        return radioBlogroll
    def getBlogroll(url):
        if url[:7] <> 'http://':
            url = 'http://' + url
        radioBlogroll = getRadioBlogroll(url)
        if radioBlogroll:
            return radioBlogroll
        parser = BlogrollParser(url)
        try:
            usock = MinimalURLOpener().open(url)
            htmlSource = usock.read()
            usock.close()
        except:
            return []
        parser.feed(htmlSource)
        return parser.blogroll
    class BlogrollThread(Thread):
        def __init__(self, master, url):
            Thread.__init__(self)
            self.master = master
            self.url = url
        def run(self):
```

```
            self.master.callback(self.url, getBlogroll(self.url))
class BlogrollThreadMaster:
    def __init__(self, url, recurse):
        self.blogrollDict = {}
        self.done = 0
        if type(url)==type(''):
            blogroll = getBlogroll(url)
        else:
            blogroll = url
        self.run(blogroll, recurse)

    def callback(self, url, blogroll):
        if not self.done:
            self.blogrollDict[url] = blogroll

    def run(self, blogroll, recurse):
        start = 0
        end = 5
        while 1:
            threads = []
            for url in blogroll[start:end]:
                if not self.blogrollDict.has_key(url):
                    t = BlogrollThread(self, url)
                    threads.append(t)
            for t in threads:
                t.start()
                time.sleep(0.000001)
            for t in threads:
                time.sleep(0.000001)
                t.join(10)
            start += 5
            end += 5
            if start > len(blogroll): break
        if recurse > 1:
            masterlist = reduce(operator.add, self.blogrollDict.values())
            newlist = [url for url in masterlist if not self.blogrollDict.
has_key(url)]
            self.run(newlist, recurse - 1)
        else:
            self.done = 1
def sortBlogrollData(blogrollDict):
    sortD = {}
    for blogroll in blogrollDict.values():
        for url in blogroll:
            sortD[url] = sortD.setdefault(url, 0) + 1
    sortI = [(v, k) for k, v in sortD.items()]
    sortI.sort()
    sortI.reverse()
    return sortI
def trimdata(sortI, cutoff):
    return [(c, url) for c, url in sortI if c >= cutoff]
def getRelated(url):
    import google
```

```
        results = []
        start - 0
        for i in range(3):
            data = google.doGoogleSearch('related:%s' % url, start)
            results.extend([oneResult.URL for oneResult in data.results])
            start += 10
            if len(data.results) < 10: break
        return results
def getNeighborhood(baseURL):
        relatedList = getRelated(baseURL)
        blogrollDict = BlogrollThreadMaster(relatedList, 1).blogrollDict
        neighborhood = sortBlogrollData(blogrollDict)
        neighborhood = trimdata(neighborhood, 2)
        neighborhood = [(c,url, prettyURL(url)) for c,url in neighborhood]
        return neighborhood

def render_html(baseURL, data):
        output = []
        output.append("""
<table class="socialnetwork" summary="neighborhood for %s">
<caption>Neighborhood for %s</caption>
<thead>
<tr>
<th scope="col">Name</th>
<th scope="col">Links</th>
<th shope="col">Explore</th>
</tr>
</thead>
<tbody>""" % (cgi.escape(prettyURL(baseURL)), cgi.
escape(prettyURL(baseURL))))
        for c, url, title in data:
            output.append("""<tr><td><a href="%s">%s</a></td><td>%s</td><td><a
href="%s">explore</a></td></tr>""" % (url, title, c, 'http://diveintomark.
org/cgi-bin/neighborhood.cgi?url=%s' % cgi.escape(url)))
        output.append("""
</tbody>
</table>""")
        return "".join(output)
def render_rss(baseURL, data):
        title = prettyURL(baseURL)
        channeltitle = "%s neighborhood" % title
        localtime = time.strftime('%Y-%m-%dT%H:%M:%S-05:00', time.localtime())
        output = []
        output.append("""<?xml version="1.0"?>
<rdf:RDF xmlns="http://purl.org/rss/1.0/"
xmlns:rdf="http://www.w3.org/1999/02/22-rdf-syntax-ns#" xmlns:dc="http://
purl.org/dc/elements/1.1/" xmlns:sy="http://purl.org/rss/1.0/modules/
syndication/" xmlns:admin="http://webns.net/mvcb/">
<channel rdf:about="%(baseURL)s">
<title>%(channeltitle)s</title>
<link>%(baseURL)s</link>
<description>Sites in the virtual neighborhood of %(title)s</description>
<language>en-us</language>
```

```
<lastBuildDate>%(localtime)s</lastBuildDate>
<pubDate>%(localtime)s</pubDate>
<admin:generatorAgent rdf:resource="http://divintomark.org/cgi-bin/
neighborhood.cgi/?v=1.1" />
<admin:errorReportsTo rdf:resource="mailto:f8dy@diveintomark.org"/>
<sy:updatePeriod>weekly</sy:updatePeriod>
<sy:updateFrequency>1</sy:updateFrequency>
<sy:updateBase>2000-01-01T12:00+00:00</sy:updateBase>
<items>
<rdf:Seq>
""" % locals())
##"""
    for c, url, title in data:
        output.append("""<rdf:li rdf:resource="%s" />
""" % url)
    output.append("""</rdf:Seq>
</items>
</channel>
""")
    for c, url, title in data:
        output.append("""<item rdf:about="%(url)s">
<title>%(title)s</title>
<link>%(url)s</link>
<description>%(c)s links</description>
</item>
""" % locals())
    output.append("""</rdf:RDF>""")
    return "".join(output)

if __name__ == '__main__':
    print render_html(getNeighborhood(sys.argv[1]))
```

Running the Hack

Google Neighborhood runs as a CGI script in your browser. Provide it the
URL you're interested in using as the center, select HTML or RSS output
(see also "Syndicating Google Search Results" [Hack #82]), and hit the "Meander" button.

You'll need an HTML form to call Google Neighborhood. Here's a simple
one:

```
<form action="/cgi-bin/neighborhood.cgi" method="get">
URL: <input name="url" type="text" />
<br />
Output as: <input name="fl" type="radio" value="html" checked="true" /> HTML
<input name="fl" type="radio" value="rss" checked="true" /> RSS
<br />
<input type="submit" value="Meander" />
</form>
```

Of course, you should alter the `action=` to point at the location in which you installed the CGI script.

Figure 6-8 shows a representation of Rael's (raelity.org's, to be precise) Google Neighborhood. Clicking on any of the links on the left transports you to the URL shown. More interestingly, the "explore" link shifts your point-of-view, centering the neighborhood on the associated URL. You can thus meander a neighborhood to your heart's content; don't be surprised, especially in the blogging world, if you keep coming across the same links. Speaking of links, the number listed beneath the "Links" heading represents the number of links the associated site has to the currently focused site.

Figure 6-8. raelity.org's Google Neighborhood

Hacking the Hack

If you want to hack this hack you can concentrate your efforts on a small block of code specifying what file extensions you want to include and exclude, as well as what domains you want to exclude when calculating your neighborhoods:

```
IGNOREEXTS = ('.xml', '.opml', '.rss', '.rdf', '.pdf', '.doc')
INCLUDEEXTS = ('', '.html', '.htm', '.shtml', '.php', '.asp', '.jsp')
IGNOREDOMAINS = ('cgi.alexa.com', 'adserver1.backbeatmedia.com', 'ask.
slashdot.org','freshmeat.net', 'readroom.ipl.org', 'amazon.com',
'ringsurf.com')
```

Noticing/ignoring file extensions. The way the hack is currently written, the neighborhood is built around pretty standard files. However, you could create a neighborhood of sites served by PHP (*http://www.php.net/*), including only URLs with a PHP (*.php*) extension. Or perhaps your interest lies in Word documents and PDF files. You'd alter the code as follows:

```
IGNOREEXTS = ('.xml', '.opml', '.rss', '.rdf', '.html', '.htm', '.shtml',
'.php', '.asp', '.jsp')
INCLUDEEXTS = ('', '.pdf', '.doc')
```

Ignoring domains. Sometimes when you're building a neighborhood you might notice that the same links are popping up again and again. They're not really part of the neighborhood but tend to be places that the web pages making up your neighborhood often link to. For example, most Blogger-based weblogs include a link to Blogger.com as a matter of course.

Exclude domains that hold no interest to you by adding them to the IGNOREDOMAINS list:

```
IGNOREDOMAINS = ('cgi.alexa.com', 'adserver1.backbeatmedia.com',
'ask.slashdot.org', 'freshmeat.net', 'readroom.ipl.org', 'amazon.com',
'ringsurf.com', 'blogger.com')
```

Google Neighborhood was written by Mark Pilgrim (*http://diveintomark.org/*).

#66 Running a Google Popularity Contest

Put two terms, spelling variations, animals, vegetables, or minerals head to head in a Google-based popularity contest.

Which is the most popular word? Which spelling is more commonly used? Who gets more mentions, Fred or Ethel Mertz? These and other equally critical questions are answered by Google Smackdown (*http://www.onfocus. com/googlesmack/down.asp*).

Why would you want to compare search counts? Sometimes finding out which terms appear more often can help you develop your queries better. Why use a particular word if it gets almost no results? Comparing misspellings can provide leads on hard-to-find terms or phrases. And sometimes it's just fun to run a popularity contest.

If you're just searching for keywords, Google Smackdown is very simple. Enter one word in each query box, a Google Web API developer's key [Chapter 1] if you have one, and click the "throw down!" button. Smackdown will return the winner and approximate count of each search.

If you're planning to use a special syntax, you'll have to be more careful. Unfortunately the link: syntax doesn't work. Interestingly, phonebook: does; do more people named Smith or Jones live in Boston, MA?

To use any special syntaxes, enclose the query in quotes: "intitle:windows".

The next tip is a little backwards. If you want to specify a phrase, do not use quotes; Smackdown, by default, searches for a phrase. If you want to search for the two words on one page but not necessarily as a phrase (jolly AND roger versus "jolly roger"), do use quotes. The reason the special syntaxes and phrases work this way is because the program automatically encloses phrases in quotes, and if you add quotes, you're sending a double quoted query to Google (""Google""). When Google runs into a double quote like that, it just strips out all the quotes.

> If you'd like to try a Google Smackdown without having to run it yourself, there's a live version available at: *http://www.onfocus.com/googlesmack/down.asp*.

The Code

Google Smackdown is written for ASP pages running under the Windows operating system and Microsoft Internet Information Server (IIS).

```
<%
'-------------------------------------------------------------
' Set the global variable strGoogleKey.
'-------------------------------------------------------------
Dim strGoogleKey
strGoogleKey = "you rkey goes here. "
'-------------------------------------------------------------
' The function GetResult( ) is the heart of Google Smackdown.
' It queries Google with a given word or phrase and returns
' the estimated total search results for that word or phrase.
```

```
' By running this function twice with the two words the user
' enters into the form, we have our Smackdown.
'------------------------------------------------------------
Function GetResult(term)
  '-----------------------------------------------------------
  ' Set the variable the contains the SOAP request. A SOAP
  ' software package will generate a similar request to this
  ' one behind the scenes, but the query for this application
  ' is very simple so it can be set "by hand."
  '-----------------------------------------------------------
  strRequest = "<?xml version='1.0' encoding='UTF-8'?>" & Chr(13) & Chr(10) &
Chr(13) & Chr(10)
  strRequest = strRequest & "<SOAP-ENV:Envelope xmlns:SOAP-ENV=""http://
schemas.xmlsoap.org/soap/envelope/"" xmlns:xsi=""http://www.w3.org/1999/
XMLSchema-instance"" xmlns:xsd=""http://www.w3.org/1999/XMLSchema"">" &
Chr(13) & Chr(10)
  strRequest = strRequest & " <SOAP-ENV:Body>" & Chr(13) & Chr(10)
  strRequest = strRequest & " <ns1:doGoogleSearch xmlns:ns1=""urn:
GoogleSearch"" SOAP-ENV:encodingStyle=""http://schemas.xmlsoap.org/soap/
encoding/"">" & Chr(13) & Chr(10)
  strRequest = strRequest & "  <key xsi:type=""xsd:string"">" & strGoogleKey
& "</key>" & Chr(13) & Chr(10)
  strRequest = strRequest & "  <q xsi:type=""xsd:string"">""" & term & """</
q>" & Chr(13) & Chr(10)
  strRequest = strRequest & "  <start xsi:type=""xsd:int"">0</start>" &
Chr(13) & Chr(10)
  strRequest = strRequest & "  <maxResults xsi:type=""xsd:int"">1</
maxResults>" & Chr(13) & Chr(10)
  strRequest = strRequest & "  <filter xsi:type=""xsd:boolean"">true</filter>
" & Chr(13) & Chr(10)
  strRequest = strRequest & "  <restrict xsi:type=""xsd:string""></restrict>"
& Chr(13) & Chr(10)
  strRequest = strRequest & "  <safeSearch xsi:type=""xsd:boolean"">false</
safeSearch>" & Chr(13) & Chr(10)
  strRequest = strRequest & "  <lr xsi:type=""xsd:string""></lr>" & Chr(13) &
Chr(10)
  strRequest = strRequest & "  <ie xsi:type=""xsd:string"">latin1</ie>" &
Chr(13) & Chr(10)
  strRequest = strRequest & "  <oe xsi:type=""xsd:string"">latin1</oe>" &
Chr(13) & Chr(10)
  strRequest = strRequest & " </ns1:doGoogleSearch>" & Chr(13) & Chr(10)
  strRequest = strRequest & " </SOAP-ENV:Body>" & Chr(13) & Chr(10)
  strRequest = strRequest & "</SOAP-ENV:Envelope>" & Chr(13) & Chr(10)
  '-----------------------------------------------------------
  ' The variable strRequest is now set to the SOAP request.
  ' Now it's sent to Google via HTTP using the Microsoft
  ' ServerXMLHTTP component.
  '
  ' Create the object...
  '-----------------------------------------------------------
  Set xmlhttp = Server.CreateObject("MSXML2.ServerXMLHTTP")
```

```
'--------------------------------------------------------------
' Set the variable strURL equal to the URL for Google Web
' Services.
'--------------------------------------------------------------
strURL = "http://api.google.com/search/beta2"


'--------------------------------------------------------------
' Set the object to open the specified URL as an HTTP POST.
'--------------------------------------------------------------
xmlhttp.Open "POST", strURL, false


'--------------------------------------------------------------
' Set the Content-Type header for the request equal to
' "text/xml" so the server knows we're sending XML.
'--------------------------------------------------------------
xmlhttp.setRequestHeader "Content-Type", "text/xml"


'--------------------------------------------------------------
' Send the XML request created earlier to Google via HTTP.
'--------------------------------------------------------------
xmlhttp.Send(strRequest)


'--------------------------------------------------------------
' Set the object AllItems equal to the XML that Google sends
' back.
'--------------------------------------------------------------
Set AllItems = xmlhttp.responseXML


'--------------------------------------------------------------
' If the parser hit an error--usually due to malformed XML,
' write the error reason to the user. And stop the script.
' Google doesn't send malformed XML, so this code shouldn't
' run.
'--------------------------------------------------------------
If AllItems.parseError.ErrorCode <> 0 Then
 response.write "Error: " & AllItems.parseError.reason
 response.end
End If


'--------------------------------------------------------------
' Release the ServerXMLHTTP object now that it's no longer
' needed--to free the memory space it was using.
'--------------------------------------------------------------
Set xmlhttp = Nothing


'--------------------------------------------------------------
' Look for <faultstring> element in the XML the google has
' returned. If it exists, Google is letting us know that
' something has gone wrong with the request.
'--------------------------------------------------------------
```

```
 Set oError = AllItems.selectNodes("//faultstring")
 If oError.length > 0 Then
  Set oErrorText = AllItems.selectSingleNode("//faultstring")
  GetResult = "Error: " & oErrorText.text
  Exit Function
 End If


 '-----------------------------------------------------------
 ' This is what we're after: the <estimatedTotalResultsCount>
 ' element in the XML that Google has returned.
 '-----------------------------------------------------------
 Set oTotal = AllItems.selectSingleNode("//estimatedTotalResultsCount")
 GetResult = oTotal.text
 Set oTotal = Nothing

End Function
'-----------------------------------------------------------
' Begin the HTML page. This portion of the page is the same
' for both the initial form and results.
'-----------------------------------------------------------
%>
<!DOCTYPE HTML PUBLIC "-//W3C//DTD HTML 4.0 Transitional//EN">
<html>
<head>
 <title>Google Smackdown</title>
 <meta http-equiv="Content-Type" content="text/html; charset=utf-8">
 <script language="JavaScript">
  // This client-side JavaScript function validates user input.
  // If the form fields are empty when the user clicks "submit"
  // this will stop the submit action, and prompt the user to
  // enter some information.
  function checkForm( ) {
   var f = document.frmGSmack
   if ((f.text1.value == '') || (f.text1.value == ' ')) {
    alert('Please enter the first word or phrase.')
    return false;
   }
   if ((f.text2.value == '') || (f.text2.value == ' ')) {
    alert('Please enter the second word or phrase.')
    return false;
   }
   return true;
  }
 </script>
</head>
<body>
<h1>Google Smackdown</h1>
This queries Google via its API and receives the estimated total results for
each word or phrase.
<%
```

```
'------------------------------------------------------------
' If the form request items "text1" and "text2" are not
' empty, then the form has been submitted to this page.
'
' It's time to call the GetResult() function and see which
' word or phrase wins the Smackdown.
'------------------------------------------------------------
If request("text1") <> "" AND request("text2") <> "" Then
  '------------------------------------------------------------
  ' Send the word from the first form field to GetResult(),
  ' and it will return the estimated total results.
  '------------------------------------------------------------
  intResult1 = GetResult(request("text1"))

  '------------------------------------------------------------
  ' Check to make sure the first result is an integer. If not,
  ' Google has returned an error message and the script will
  ' move on.
  '------------------------------------------------------------
  If isNumeric(intResult1) Then
   intResult2 = GetResult(request("text2"))
  End If

  '------------------------------------------------------------
  ' Check to make sure the second result is also an integer.
  ' If they're both numeric, the script can display the
  ' results.
  '------------------------------------------------------------
  If isNumeric(intResult1) AND isNumeric(intResult2) Then
   intResult1 = CDbl(intResult1)
   intResult2 = CDbl(intResult2)

   '------------------------------------------------------------
   ' Begin writing the results to the page...
   '------------------------------------------------------------
   response.write "<h2>The Results</h2>"
   response.write "And the undisputed champion is...<br>"
   response.write "<ol>"

   '------------------------------------------------------------
   ' Compare the two results to determine which should be
   ' displayed first.
   '------------------------------------------------------------
   If intResult1 > intResult2 Then
    response.write "<li>" & request("text1") & " (<a target=""_blank""
href=""http://www.google.com/search?hl=en&ie=UTF8&oe=UTF8&q=" & Server.
URLEncode("""" & request("text1") & """") & """>" &
FormatNumber(intResult1,0) & "</a>)<br>"
```

```
    response.write "<li>" & request("text2") & " (<a target=""_blank""
href=""http://www.google.com/search?hl=en&ie=UTF8&oe=UTF8&q=" & Server.
URLEncode(""""" & request("text2") & """"") & """>" &
FormatNumber(intResult2,0) & "</a>)<br>"
  Else
    response.write "<li>" & request("text2") & " (<a target=""_blank""
href=""http://www.google.com/search?hl=en&ie=UTF8&oe=UTF8&q=" & Server.
URLEncode(""""" & request("text2") & """"") & """>" &
FormatNumber(intResult2,0) & "</a>)<br>"
    response.write "<li>" & request("text1") & " (<a target=""_blank""
href=""http://www.google.com/search?hl=en&ie=UTF8&oe=UTF8&q=" & Server.
URLEncode(""""" & request("text1") & """"") & """>" &
FormatNumber(intResult1,0) & "</a>)<br>"
  End If
  '-----------------------------------------------------------
  ' Finish writing the results to the page and include a link
  ' to the page for another round.
  '-----------------------------------------------------------
  response.write "</ol>"
  response.write "<a href=""smackdown.asp"">Another Challenge?</a>"
  response.write "<br>"
Else
  '-----------------------------------------------------------
  ' One or both of the results are not numeric. We can assume
  ' this is because the developer's key has reached its
  ' 1,000 query limit for the day. Because the script has
  ' made it to this point, the SOAP response did not return
  ' an error. If it had, GetResult() would have stopped the
  ' script.
  '-----------------------------------------------------------
  intResult1 = Replace(intResult1,"key " & strGoogleKey,"key")
  intResult2 = Replace(intResult2,"key " & strGoogleKey,"key")


  '-----------------------------------------------------------
  ' Write out the error to the user...
  '-----------------------------------------------------------
  response.write "<h2>It Didn't Work, Error</h2>"
  '-----------------------------------------------------------
  ' If the results are the same, we don't need to write out
  ' both of them.
  '-----------------------------------------------------------
  If intResult1 = intResult2 Then
   response.write intResult1 & "<br><br>"
  Else
   response.write intResult1 & "<br><br>" & intResult2 & "<br><br>"
  End If
  '-----------------------------------------------------------
  ' A link to the script for another round.
  '-----------------------------------------------------------
  response.write "<a href=""smackdown.asp"">Another Challenge?</a>"
  response.write "<br>"
 End If
Else
```

```
'----------------------------------------------------------
' The form request items "text1" and "text2" are empty,
' which means the form has not been submitted to the page
' yet.
'----------------------------------------------------------
%>
<h2>The Arena</h2>
<div class="clsPost">The setting is the most impressive search engine ever
built: <a href="http://www.google.com/">Google</a>. As a test of its <a
href="http://www.google.com/apis">API</a>, two words or phrases will go
head-to-head in a terabyte tug-of-war. Which one appears in more pages
across the Web?
<h2>The Challengers</h2>
You choose the warring words...
<br><br>
<form name="frmGSmack" action="smackdown.asp" method="post" onSubmit="return
checkForm( );">
<table>
 <tr>
  <td align="right">word/phrase 1</td> <td><input type="text" name="text1">
</td>
 </tr>
 <tr>
  <td align="right">word/phrase 2</td> <td><input type="text" name="text2">
</td>
 </tr>
 <tr>
  <td> </td><td><input type="submit" value="throw down!"></td>
 </tr>
</table>
</form>
<%
End If
'----------------------------------------------------------
' This is the end of the If statement that checks to see
' if the form has been submitted. Both states of the page
' get the closing tags below.
'----------------------------------------------------------
%>
</body>
</html>
```

Running the Hack

The hack is run in exactly the same manner as the live version of Google Smackdown (*http://www.onfocus.com/googlesmack/down.asp*) running on Onfocus.com. Point your web browser at it and fill out the form. Figure 6-9 shows a sample Smackdown between negative feelings about Macintosh versus Windows.

Google Smackdown was written by Paul Bausch (*http://www.onfocus.com/*).

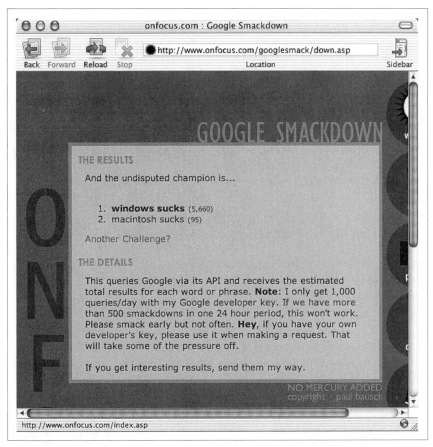

Figure 6-9. Macintosh/Windows Google Smackdown

HACK #67   Building a Google Box

Add a little box of Google results to any web page.

Most of the applications in this book stand by themselves or run via a web form. Google box is slightly different in that it creates a little output of URLs that you can take and integrate into a web page or other application.

What's a Google Box?

A "Google box" is a small HTML snippet that shows Google search results for whatever query you're searching for. You might wish to have on your web site a small box that shows pages similar to yours, or pages that link to yours, or just the results of a query.

Google Box

Google box can run from a server at a specified time, with results that you can then integrate into your web page. Or you might just want to keep an ongoing record of the top URLs that are generated for a query.

Google Boxes Everywhere

Google boxes as a concept—the idea of taking a shortened version of Google results an integrating them into a web page or some other place—are not new. In fact, they're on their way to becoming ubiquitous when it comes to weblog and content management software. Radio Userland and Movable Type both offer easy integration of Google boxes. You should note that you'll still need to get a developer's key to use these modifications, though you might not have to download the API developer's kit.

Radio Userland. Radio Userland makes "Google Glue" (*http://radio.userland. com/googleApi*) available for generating Google boxes quickly and easily. With Userland and Manila, it's as easy as integrating a single-line macro into your web page.

Movable Type. Josh Cooper has written a Movable Type hack (*http://www. 10500bc.org/code/mt_howto_googleapi.php*) that allows you to integrate Google results into your Movable Type weblog. This one is a little more complicated than the Radio Userland—you'll have to edit a couple of files— but once you've got the files edited, you can put result boxes anywhere on your Movable Type templates.

Other implementations. The Google box is an easy thing to implement and was one of the first examples of Google API usage to pop up last April. As such, it enjoys the position of "proto-application"—a lot of developers whip up a Google box just to see if they can. Do a Google search for "Google box" to see some other examples of Google boxes for different languages and applications. To get you started, Rael Dornfest has one at *http://www. oreillynet.com/cs/weblog/view/wlg/1283*.

What's in Your Google Box?

What goes in a Google box, anyway? Why would anybody want to integrate them into a web page?

It depends on the page. Putting a Google box that searches for your name onto a weblog provides a bit of egoboo and can give a little more information about you without seeming like bragging (yeah, right). If you've got a topic-specific page, set up a Google box that searches for the topic (the more specific, the better the results). And if you've got a general "news" type page, consider adding a Google box for the news topic. Google boxes can go pretty much anywhere, with Google updating its index often enough that the content of a Google box stays fresh.

The Code

```perl
#!/usr/local/bin/perl
# google_box.pl
# A classic Google box implementation
# Usage: perl google_box.pl <query> <# results>

# Your Google API developer's key
my $google_key='insert key here';

# Location of the GoogleSearch WSDL file
my $google_wdsl = "./GoogleSearch.wsdl";

use strict;

use SOAP::Lite;

# Bring in those command-line arguments
@ARGV == 2
  or die "Usage: perl googlebox.pl <query> <# results>\n";
my($query, $maxResults) = @ARGV;
$maxResults = 10 if ($maxResults < 1 or $maxResults > 10);

# Create a new SOAP::Lite instance, feeding it GoogleSearch.wsdl
my $google_search = SOAP::Lite->service("file:$google_wdsl");

# Query Google
my $results = $google_search ->
  doGoogleSearch(
    $google_key, $query, 0, $maxResults, "false", "",
    "false", "", "latin1", "latin1"
  );

# No results?
@{$results->{resultElements}} or die "no results";

print join "\n",
  map( {
    qq{<a href="$_->{URL}">} .
    ($_->{title} || $_->{URL}) .
    qq{</a> <br />}
  } @{$results->{resultElements}} );
```

Running the Hack

Google box takes two bits of information on the command line: the query you want to run and maximum number of results you'd prefer (up to ten). If you don't provide a number of results, Google box will default to ten.

```
% perl google_box.pl "query"
```

The Results

Here's a sample Google box for "camel book", referring to O'Reilly's popular *Programming Perl* title:

```
<a href="http://www.oreilly.com/catalog/pperl2/">oreilly.com --
Online Catalog:Programming Perl, 2nd Edition</a> <br />
<a href="http://www.oreilly.com/catalog/pperl3/">oreilly.com --
Online Catalog:Programming Perl, 3rd Edition</a> <br />
<a href="http://www.oreilly.com/catalog/pperl2/noframes.html">Programming
Perl, 2nd Edition</a> <br />
<a href="http://www.tuxedo.org/~esr/jargon/html/entry/Camel-Book.html">Camel
Book</a> <br />
<a href="http://www.cise.ufl.edu/perl/camel.html">The Camel
Book<a> <br />
```

Integrating a Google Box

When you incoporate a Google box into your web page, you'll have two considerations: refreshing the content of the box regularly and integrating the content into your web page. For refreshing the content of the box, you'll need to regularly run the program using something like cron under Unix or the Windows Scheduler.

For including the content on your web page, Server Side Includes (SSI) are always rather effective. SSI-including a Google box takes little more than something like:

```
<!-- #include virtual="./google_box.html" -->
```

For more information on using Server Side Includes, check out the NCSA SSI Tutorial (*http://hoohoo.ncsa.uiuc.edu/docs/tutorials/includes.html*), or search Google for Server Side Includes Tutorial.

HACK #68 Capturing a Moment in Time
Build a Google box for a particular moment in time.

Google boxes are a nice addition to your web pages, whether you run a weblog or a news site. But for many Google box searches, the search results won't change that often, especially for more common search words. The

Timely Google box—built upon the ordinary Google box [Hack #67] hack—captures a snapshot of newly indexed or reindexed material at a particular point in time.

Making the Google Box Timely

As you might remember, Google has a daterange: search syntax available. This version of Google box takes advantage of the daterange: [Hack #11] syntax, allowing you to specifying how many days back you want your query to run. If you don't provide a number, the default is 1, and there's no maximum. I wouldn't go back much further than a month or so. The fewer days back you go the more often the results in the Google box will change.

 You'll need the Julian::Day module to get this hack rolling (*http://search.cpan.org/search?query=time%3A%3Ajulianday*).

The Code

```
#!/usr/local/bin/perl
# timebox.pl
# A time-specific Google box
# Usage: perl timebox.pl <query> <# results> <# days back>

# Your Google API developer's key
my $google_key='insert key here';

# Location of the GoogleSearch WSDL file
my $google_wdsl = "./GoogleSearch.wsdl";

use strict;

use SOAP::Lite;
use Time::JulianDay;

# Bring in those command-line arguments
@ARGV == 3
    or die "Usage: perl timebox.pl <query> <# results> <# days back>\n";
my($query, $maxResults, $daysBack) = @ARGV;
$maxResults = 10 if ($maxResults < 1 or $maxResults > 10);
$daysBack = 1 if $daysBack <= 0;

# Figure out when yesterday was in Julian days
my $yesterday = int local_julian_day(time) - $daysBack;

# Create a new SOAP::Lite instance, feeding it GoogleSearch.wsdl
my $google_search = SOAP::Lite->service("file:$google_wdsl");

# Query Google
my $results = $google_search ->
```

```
doGoogleSearch(
  $google_key, "$query daterange:$yesterday-$yesterday", 0,
  $maxResults, "false", "",  "false", "", "latin1", "latin1"
);

# No results?
@{$results->{resultElements}} or die "no results";

print join "\n",
  map( {
    qq{<a href="$_->{URL}">} .
    ($_->{title} || $_->{URL}) .
    qq{</a> <br />}
  } @{$results->{resultElements}} );
```

Running the Hack

You'll have to provide three items of information on the command line: the query you want to run, maximum number of results you'd prefer (up to 10), and number of days back to travel.

```
% perl timebox.pl "query" <# of results> <# days back>
```

The Results

Here's a sample Google box for the top five "google hacks" results (this book included, hopefully) indexed yesterday:

```
% perl timebox.pl "google hacks" 5 1
<a href="http://isbn.nu/0596004478">Google Hacks</a> <br />
<a href="http://isbn.nu/0596004478/shipsort">Google Hacks</a> <br />
<a href="http://isbn.nu/0596004478/amazonca">Amazon.ca: Google Hacks</a> <br
/>
<a href="http://www.oreilly.de/catalog/googlehks/">Google Hacks</a> <br />
<a href="http://www.oreilly.de/catalog/googlehks/author.html">Google Hacks</
a> <br />
```

Hacking the Hack

Perhaps you'd like your Google box to reflect "this day in 1999." No problem for this slightly tweaked version of the Timely Google box (changes highlighted in bold):

```
#!/usr/local/bin/perl
# timebox_thisday.pl
# A Google box for this day in <year>
# Usage: perl timebox.pl <query> <# results> [year]

# Your Google API developer's key
my $google_key='insert key here';

# Location of the GoogleSearch WSDL file
my $google_wdsl = "./GoogleSearch.wsdl";
```

```perl
use strict;

use SOAP::Lite;
use Time::JulianDay;

my @now = localtime(time);

# Bring in those command-line arguments
@ARGV == 2
or die "Usage: perl timebox.pl <query> <# results> [year]\n";
 my($query, $maxResults, $year) = @ARGV;
$maxResults = 10 if ($maxResults < 1 or $maxResults > 10);
$year =~ /^\d{4}$/ or $year = 1999;

# Figure out when this day in the specified year is
my $then = int julian_day($year, $now[4], $now[3]);

# Create a new SOAP::Lite instance, feeding it GoogleSearch.wsdl
my $google_search = SOAP::Lite->service("file:$google_wdsl");

# Query Google
my $results = $google_search ->
  doGoogleSearch(
    $google_key, "$query daterange:$then-$then", 0,
    $maxResults, "false", "",  "false", "", "latin1", "latin1"
  );

# No results?
@{$results->{resultElements}} or die "no results";

print join "\n",
  "$query on this day in $year<p />",
  map( {
    qq{<a href="$_->{URL}">} .
    ($_->{title} || $_->{URL}) .
    qq{</a> <br />}
  } @{$results->{resultElements}} );
```

Running the Hacked Hack

The hacked version of Timely Google box runs just like the first version, except that you specify the maximum number of results and a year. Going back further than 1999 doesn't yield particularly useful results given that Google came online in 1998.

Let's take a peek at how Netscape was doing in 1999:

```
% perl timebox_thisday.pl "netscape" 5 1999
netscape on this day in 1999:<p />
<a href="http://www.showgate.com/aol.html">WINSOCK.DLL and NETSCAPE Info for
AOL Members</a> <br />
<a href="http://www.univie.ac.at/comment/99-3/993_23.orig.html">Comment 99/3
- Netscape Communicator</a> <br />
```

```
<a href="http://www.ac-nancy-metz.fr/services/docint/netscape.htm">NETSCAPE.
</a> <br />
<a href="http://www.ac-nancy-metz.fr/services/docint/Messeng1.htm">Le
Courrier électronique avec Netscape Messenger</a> <br />
<a href="http://www.airnews.net/anews_ns.htm">Setting up Netscape 2.0 for
Airnews Proxy News</a> <br />
```

HACK #69 Feeling Really Lucky

Take the domain in which the first result of a query appears, and do more
searching within that domain.

Does Google make you feel lucky [in "Google Basics" in Chapter 1]? How lucky?
Sometimes as lucky as the top result is, more results from the same domain
are just as much so.

This hack performs two Google queries. The domain of the top result of the
first search is saved. Then the second query is run, searching only the saved
domain for results.

Take, for example, Grace Hopper, famous both as a computer programmer
and as the person who coined the term "computer bug." If you were to run a
search result with "Grace Hopper" as the primary search and overlay a search
for COBOL on the domain of the first result returned, you'd find three pages
for the Grace Hopper Conference 2000:

```
Grace Hopper Conference 2000 - Biography
http://www.sdsc.edu/hopper/GHC_INFO/hopper.html
... The Murrays were a family with a long military
tradition;
Grace Hopper's ... language instructions led ultimately
to the
development of the business language COBOL ...
Note:
http://www.sdsc.edu/~woodka/intro.html
... publication, please contact me by email at:
woodka@sdsc.edu.
... and were important in its history, like Admiral
Grace Hopper,
the inventor of the COBOL ...
Grace Hopper
http://www.sdsc.edu/~woodka/hopper.html
... Hopper was a programmer on the world's first
large-scale
digital computer, Mark ... the first computer language
compiler,
and she worked on the development of COBOL ...
```

You could also do a primary search for a person ("Stan Laurel") and a sec-
ondary search for another person ("Oliver Hardy"). Or search for a person,
followed by their corporate affiliation.

Don't try doing a link: search with this hack. The link: special syntax doesn't work with any other special syntaxes, and
this hack relies upon inurl:.

The Code

```
#!/usr/local/bin/perl
# goolucky.cgi
# gleans the domain from the first (read: top) result returned, allows
# you to overlay another query, and returns the results, and so on...
# goolucky.cgi is called as a CGI with form input

# Your Google API developer's key
my $google_key='insert key here';

# Location of the GoogleSearch WSDL file
my $google_wdsl = "./GoogleSearch.wsdl";

use strict;

use SOAP::Lite;
use CGI qw/:standard/;

# Create a new SOAP instance
my $google_search = SOAP::Lite->service("file:$google_wdsl");

# If this is the second time around, glean the domain
my $query_domain = param('domain') ? "inurl:" . param('domain') : '';
my $results = $google_search ->
  doGoogleSearch(
    $google_key, param('query') . " $query_domain", 0, 10,
    "false", "", "false", "", "latin1", "latin1"
  );

# Set domain to the results of the previous query
param('domain', $results->{'resultElements'}->[0]->{'URL'});
param('domain', param('domain') =~ m#://(.*?)/#);

print
  header(),
  start_html("I'm Feeling VERY Lucky"),
  h1("I'm Feeling VERY Lucky"),
  start_form(),
  'Query: ', textfield(-name=>'query',
  -default=>'"Grace Hopper"'),
  '   ',
  'Domain: ', textfield(-name=>'domain'),
  '   ',
  submit(-name=>'submit', -value=>'Search'),
  p(),
  'Results:';
```

```
foreach (@{$results->{'resultElements'}}) {
  print p(
    b($_->{title}), br( ),
    a({href=>$_->{URL}}, $_->{URL}), br( ),
    i($_->{snippet})
  );
}

print
  end_form( ),
  end_html( );
```

Hacking the Hack

You can also run this hack so it only uses one query. For example, you do a search with Query A. The search grabs the domain from the first result. Then you run another search, again using Query A, but restricting your results to the domain that was grabbed in the first search. This is handy when you're trying to get information on one set of keywords, instead of trying to link two different concepts. Figure 6-10 illustrates the I'm Feeling Lucky search.

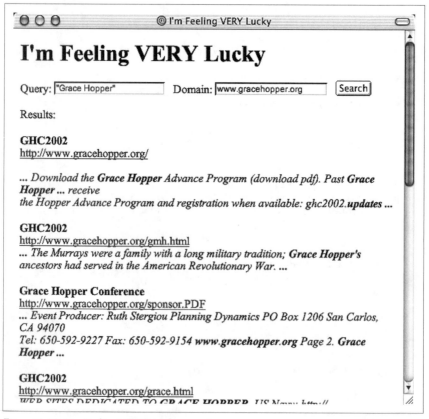

Figure 6-10. I'm Feeling VERY Lucky search

Gleaning Phonebook Stats

**HACK
#70**

The Google API doesn't return data from a search using the phonebook syntaxes, but that doesn't mean you can't have some fun with it.

The Google API doesn't return results for queries using the phonebook: [Hack #17] syntaxes. It does, however, provide a result count!

Because it doesn't actually get you any phone numbers, passing a phonebook query to the Google API has minimal value. Nevertheless, this little hack makes the most of it. Ever wonder how many people with a particular surname one might find in various U.S. cities—the 15 most populated, at least?

The Code

```perl
#!/usr/local/bin/perl
# kincount.cgi
# How many people share a surname in the 15 most populated
# US cities?
# kincount.cgi is called as a CGI with form input

# Your Google API developer's key
my $google_key='insert key here';

# Location of the GoogleSearch WSDL file

my $google_wdsl = "./GoogleSearch.wsdl";

# 15 most populated US cities
my @cities = ("New York NY", "Los Angeles CA", "Chicago IL",
"Houston TX", "Philadelphia PA", "Phoenix AZ", "San Diego CA",
"Dallas TX", "San Antonio TX", "Detroit MI", "San Jose CA",
"Indianapolis IN", "San Francisco CA", "Jacksonville FL",
"Columbus OH");

use strict;

use SOAP::Lite;
use CGI qw/:standard *table/;

print
   header(),
   start_html("KinCount"),
   h1("KinCount"),
   start_form(-method=>'GET'),
   'Surname: ', textfield(-name=>'query', -default=>'John Doe'),
   '   ',
   submit(-name=>'submit', -value=>'Search'),
   end_form(), p();

my $google_search  = SOAP::Lite->service("file:$google_wdsl");
```

```
    if (param('query')) {
      print
        start_table({-cellspacing=>'5'}),
        Tr([th({-align=>'left'}, ['City', 'Count'])]);

    foreach my $city (@cities) {
      my $cityquery = "rphonebook:" . param('query') . " $city";
      my $results = $google_search ->
        doGoogleSearch(
          $google_key, $cityquery, 0, 10, "false", "",  "false",
          "", "latin1", "latin1"
        );

      my $resultcount = "$results->{'estimatedTotalResultsCount'}";

      print Tr([ td([
        $city,
        $resultcount >= 600
        ? "Too many for an accurate count."
        : $resultcount
        ])
      ]);
    }

    print
      end_table(),
  }
```

Running the Hack

This hack runs as a CGI script; call it from your browser and fill in the form.

Results

Figure 6-11 the results of a phonebook search for Bush.

Notice that this script works equally well if fed a full name, "George Bush", as Figure 6-12 shows.

Hacking the Hack

Residential, business, or both. Notice that the script uses the rphonebook: syntax, guaranteeing only residential phonebook results. To restrict results to business listings, use bphonebook: instead, altering only one line (change in bold) in the code, like so:

```
    my $cityquery = "bphonebook:" . param('query') . " $city";
```

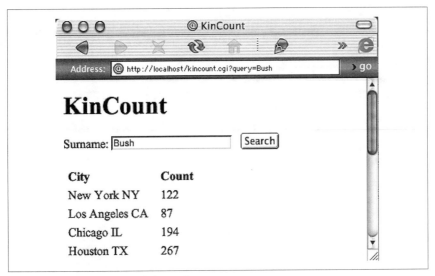

Figure 6-11. KinCount search for Bush

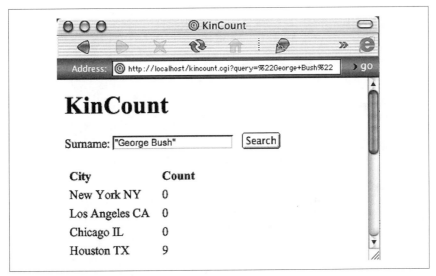

Figure 6-12. KinCount search for "George Bush"

A search for pizza provides a rundown of the number of pizza joints across U.S. cities. Searching for rphonebook:pizza, as one would expect, returns very few results. bphonebook:pizza behaves as expected.

The same holds true for replacing bphonebook: with phonebook:, thereby removing restriction by type of listing and returning all results, residential and business alike.

Of course you could always add a field to the form, allowing users to decide which type of survey they prefer. The following code (changes in bold) will do the trick nicely:

```perl
#!/usr/local/bin/perl
# kincount.cgi
# How many people share a surname in the 15 most populated
# US cities?
# kincount.cgi is called as a CGI with form input

# Your Google API developer's key
my $google_key='insert key here';

# Location of the GoogleSearch WSDL file
my $google_wdsl = "./GoogleSearch.wsdl";

# 15 most populated US cities
my @cities = ("New York NY", "Los Angeles CA", "Chicago IL",
"Houston TX", "Philadelphia PA", "Phoenix AZ", "San Diego CA",
"Dallas TX", "San Antonio TX", "Detroit MI", "San Jose CA",
"Indianapolis IN", "San Francisco CA", "Jacksonville FL",
"Columbus OH");

use strict;

use SOAP::Lite;
use CGI qw/:standard *table/;

print
  header(),
  start_html("KinCount"),
  h1("KinCount"),
  start_form(-method=>'GET'),
  'Query: ', textfield(-name=>'query', -default=>'John Doe'),
  '   ',
  popup_menu(
    -name=>'listing_type',
    -values=>['rphonebook:', 'bphonebook:', 'phonebook:'],
    -labels=&t;{ 'rphonebook:'=>'Residential',
      'bphonebook:'=>'Business', 'phonebook:'=>'All Listings' }
  ),
  '   ',
  submit(-name=>'submit', -value=>'Search'),
  end_form(), p();

my $google_search  = SOAP::Lite->service("file:$google_wdsl");

if (param('query')) {
  print
    start_table({-cellspacing=>'5'}),
    Tr([th({-align=>'left'}, ['City', 'Count'])]);
```

```
foreach my $city (@cities) {
  my $cityquery = param('listing_type') . param('query') . " $city";
  my $results = $google_search ->
    doGoogleSearch(
      $google_key, $cityquery, 0, 10, "false", "",  "false",
      "", "latin1", "latin1"
    );

  my $resultcount = "$results->{'estimatedTotalResultsCount'}";

  print Tr([ td([
    $city,
    $resultcount >= 600
    ? "Too many for an accurate count."
    : $resultcount
    ])
  ]);
}

print
  end_table(),
}
```

The results of a search for bphonebook:pizza using this altered form look something like Figure 6-13.

Figure 6-13. Results of bphonebook:pizza

And it doesn't just count the number of pizza joints, either! How about calculating a geek index based on the number of geek landmarks—business listings for: electronics stores, computer shops, Internet companies, cyber cafes, etc.

The cities. This script holds its list of cities in an array. Of course, you don't have to do it this way. You could create a form field that accepts user-entered city, state, or both. Just be sure to remind your users that the phonebook syntaxes require either the entire state name or the postal code abbreviation; either of these two will work:

```
bphonebook:pizza los angeles california
bphonebook:pizza los angeles ca
```

This will not:

```
bphonebook:pizza los angeles cali
```

The 600-Foot Ceiling

A phonebook syntax search via the Google Web API will consistently return a ceiling of 600 for any count higher than that; thus, the "Too many for an accurate count" error message. Without that error check, you'd find the 600s that kept showing up rather repetitive, not to mention useless.

Performing Proximity Searches
HACK #71
GAPS performs a proximity check between two words.

There are some times when it would be advantageous to search both forward and backward. For example, if you're doing genealogy research, you might find your uncle John Smith as both John Smith or Smith John. Similarly, some pages might include John's middle name—John Q Smith or Smith John Q.

> If all you're after is query permutations, the Permute hack [Hack #62] might do the trick.

You might also need to find concepts that exist near each other but aren't a phrase. For example, you might want to learn about keeping squirrels out of your bird feeder. Various attempts to create a phrase based on this idea might not work, but just searching for several words might not find specific enough results.

GAPS, created by Kevin Shay, allows you to run searches both forward and backward and within a certain number of spaces of each other. GAPS stands for "Google API Proximity Search," and that's exactly what this application is: a way to search for topics within a few words of each other without having to run several queries in a row. The program runs the queries and organizes the results automatically.

You enter two terms (there is an option to add more terms that will not be searched for proximity) and specify how far apart you want them (1, 2, or 3 words). You can specify that the words be found only in the order you request (wordA, wordB) or in either order (wordA, wordB, and wordB, wordA). You can specify how many results you want and in what order they appear (sorted by title, URL, ranking, and proximity).

Search results are formatted much like regular Google results, only they include a distance ranking beside each title. The distance ranking, between one and three, specifies how far apart the two query words were on the page. Figure 6-14 shows a GAPS search for google and hacks within two words of one another, order intact.

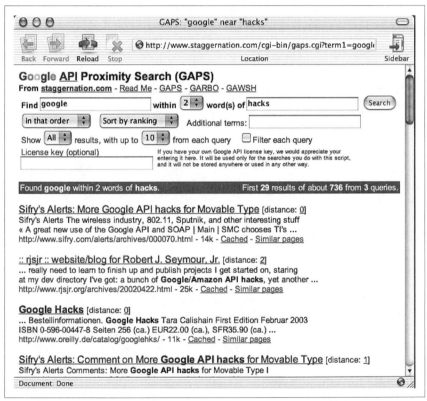

Figure 6-14. GAPS search for "google" and "hacks" within two words of one another

Click the distance rating link pass the generated query on to Google directly.

Making the Most of GAPS

GAPS works best when you have words on the same page that are ambiguously or not at all related to one another. For example, if you're looking for information on Google and search engine optimization, you might find that searching for the words Google and SEO don't find the results you want, while using GAPS to search for the words Google and SEO within three words of each other find material focused much more on search engine optimization for Google.

GAPS also works well when you're searching for information about two famous people who might often appear on the same page, though not necessarily in proximity to each other. For example, you might want information on Bill Clinton and Alan Greenspan, but might find that you're getting too many pages that happen to list the two of them. By searching for their names in proximity to each other, you'll get better results.

Finally, you might find GAPS useful in medical research. Many times your search results will include "index pages" that list several symptoms. However, including symptoms or other medical terms within a few words of each other can help you find more relevant results. Note that this technique will take some experimentation. Many pages about medical conditions contain long lists of symptoms and effects, and there's no reason that one symptom might be within a few words of another.

The Code

The GAPS source code is rather lengthy so we're not making it available here. You can, however, get it online at *http://www.staggernation.com/gaps/readme.html*.

Other Staggernation Scripts

If you like GAPS, you might want to try a couple of other scripts from Staggernation:

GAWSH (http://www.staggernation.com/gawsh/)
  Stands for Google API Web Search by Host. This program allows you to enter a query and get a list of domains that contain information on that query. Click on the triangle beside any domain name, and you'll get a list of pages in that domain that match your query. This program uses DHTML, which means it'll only work with Internet Explorer or Mozilla/Netscape.

GARBO (http://www.staggernation.com/garbo/)
  Stands for Google API Relation Browsing Outliner. Like GAWSH, this program uses DHTML so it'll only work with Mozilla and Internet Explorer. When you enter an URL, GARBO will do a search for either pages that link to the URL you specify or pages related to that URL.

Run a search and you'll get a list of URLs with triangles beside them. Click on a triangle, and you'll get a list of pages that either link to the URL you chose or are related to the URL you chose, depending on what you chose in the initial query.

Blending the Google and Amazon Web Services

A blending of the Google and Amazon web service APIs.

Google doesn't have a lock on the API concept. Other companies and sites, including online bookstore Amazon, have their own APIs. Mockerybird's Book Watch Plus (*http://mockerybird.com/bookwatch-plus/bookwatch-plus.cgi*) blends the Google and Amazon APIs with a feed of information from the Book Watch service (*http://onfocus.com/Book Watch/*) to create a list of books, referrals to them in Google, and a list of items that people who bought that book on Amazon also bought. Figure 6-15 illustrates this.

Figure 6-15. Book Watch Plus

How It Works

Book Watch Plus does several things to generate its page of information. First, it grabs a page of books most frequently mentioned on weblogs. That list is generated by another service run by Paul Bausch's Book Watch service.

Book Watch Plus wrangles the ISBNs (unique identifiers for books) and then places a couple of calls. The first is to the Amazon web service for detailed information on the book. Then Google is queried via the Google Web API for items related to the book. All this information is aggregated on a regular basis rather than on the fly for each visitor. Results are cached in XML and displayed in the form of a web page via the HTML::Template Perl module.

> You might think that with all this fetching and displaying of information, the hack would be a bit involved, and you'd be right. Running the hack requires two modules, a code snippet, and a template. They're all available at *http://mockerybird.com/bookwatch-plus/*.

The Modules

You'll need two modules for Book Watch Plus: AmazonAPI and GoogleAPI.

AmazonAPI. The AmazonAPI module is available at *http://mockerybird.com/bookwatch-plus/AmazonAPI.pm*. You'll have to get yourself a free Amazon Associates account (*http://amazon.com/webservices/*) before you can use it. Most of the module you can use as it stands, but you will have to make a small alteration to the beginning of the code:

```
# Your Amazon.com associates id and Web Services Dev Token.
# (learn more about these here: http://amazon.com/webservices/)
my $ASSOCIATE_ID = 'mockerybird';
my $AMAZON_DEV_TOKEN = 'a-token';
# The directory you'd like to store cached asins:
# (it defaults to the same directory as the script, but you'll
# probably want to change that.)
my $XML_DIR = "./";
```

You'll need to replace mockerybird with your own Amazon Associate ID, and a-token with your own Web Services Development Token.

If you want to have the cached book information stored in a different directory than where the script is located, you'll need to change the my $XML_DIR line to the directory of your choice.

For example, if your associate ID were tara, developer token googlehacks, and preferred cache directory /home/tara/google/bookwatchplus/cache, those lines should read:

```
# Your Amazon.com associates id and Web Services Dev Token.
# (learn more about these here: http://amazon.com/webservices/)
my $ASSOCIATE_ID = 'tara';
my $AMAZON_DEV_TOKEN = 'googlehacks';
# The directory you'd like to store cached asins:
```

```
# (it defaults to the same directory as the script, but you'll
# probably want to change that.)
my $XML_DIR = "/home/tara/google/bookwatchplus/cache";
```

(Note the changes highlighted in bold.)

GoogleAPI. The *GoogleAPI.pm* module is available at *http://mockerybird.com/ bookwatch-plus/GoogleAPI.pm*. You'll have to make a couple of changes to this module as well; the lines you're after are:

```
package GoogleAPI;
# The directory you'd like to store cached asins:
# (it defaults to the same directory as the script, but you'll
# probably want to change that.)
my $XML_DIR = "./"; # <-- PUT A DIRECTORY HERE TO STORE XML
# Get your Google API key here:
# http://www.google.com/apis/download.html
my $key = ""; # <-- PUT YOUR KEY HERE
```

Just like the AmazonAPI, you'll have an option to change the directory to which cached information is saved. If you want to change the directory (by default, the information is saved in the same directory where the script is installed) change the my $XML_DIR line. You'll also need to put your Google developer's key on the my $key = ""; line.

If your Google Web API developer's key were 12BuCK13mY5hOE/ 34KNOcK@ttH3DoOR and preferred cache directory /home/tara/google/ bookwatchplus/cache, those lines should read:

```
package GoogleAPI;
# The directory you'd like to store cached asins:
# (it defaults to the same directory as the script, but you'll
# probably want to change that.)
my $XML_DIR = "/home/tara/google/bookwatchplus/cache";
# <-- PUT A DIRECTORY HERE TO STORE XML
# Get your Google API key here:
# http://www.google.com/apis/download.html
my $key    = "12BuCK13mY5hOE/34KNOcK@ttH3DoOR";
# <-- PUT YOUR KEY HERE
```

(Note the changes highlighted in bold.)

The Template

There's a sample template available at *http://mockerybird.com/bookwatch-plus/bookwatch-plus.txt*.

The CGI Script

Finally, you'll need the CGI script itself; it's available at *http://mockerybird. com/bookwatch-plus/bookwatch-plus-cgi.txt*. You'll need to change several variables on the CGI script. They're listed at the beginning of the script and are as follows:

$default_book_rss_feed_url
>   The RSS feed you want as the default for the hack

$book_display_template
>   The default template with which you want to display the Book Watch items

$number_of_items_in_list
>   Number of items to display

$number_of_google_results
>   Number of results from Google (defaults to 5)

$number_of_amazon_similarities
>   Number of similar items listed at Amazon (defaults to 5)

$xml_cache_directory
>   Where to store the XML cache materials

$num_minutes_to_cache_rss_feeds
>   For how long your RSS feeds should be stored before being refreshed

In addition to these variables, you can alter the list of RSS feeds used by the site, from which the program gets its book information. If you don't have any RSS feeds in mind, leave the ones that are here alone and don't alter the $default_book_rss_feed_url above.

Running the Hack

Drop the CGI script (*bookwatch-plus.cgi*), the two modules (*AmazonAPI.pm* and *GoogleAPI.pm*), and the template file (*bookwatch-plus.txt*) into place. Invoke the CGI script from your browser and enjoy.

Bookwatch Plus application written by Erik Benson.

Getting Random Results (On Purpose)
#73
Surfing random pages can turn up some brilliant finds.

Why would any researcher worth her salt be interested in random pages? While surfing random pages isn't what one might call a focused search, you'd be surprised at some of the brilliant finds you'd never have come across otherwise. I've loved random page generators associated with search engines ever since discovering Random Yahoo! Link (*http://random.yahoo.com/bin/ryl*) and thought creating such a thing to work with the Google API might prove interesting, useful even.

The Code

What this code does is search for a random number between 0 and 99999 (yes, you can search for 0 with Google) in addition to a modifier pulled from the @modifiers array. To generate the random page, you don't, strictly speaking, need something from the modifer array. However, it helps make the page selection even more random.

With the combination of a number between 0 and 99999 and a modifier from the @modifiers array, Google will get a list of search results, and from that list you'll get a "random" page. You could go higher with the numbers if you wanted, but I wasn't sure that this hack would consistently find numbers higher than 99999. (Zip Codes are five digits, so I knew a five-digit search would find results more often than not.)

The Code

```perl
#!/usr/local/bin/perl
# goorandom.cgi
# Creates a random Google query and redirects the browser to
# the top/first result.
# goorandom.cgi is called as a CGI without any form input

# Your Google API developer's key
my $google_key='insert key here';

# Location of the GoogleSearch WSDL file
my $google_wdsl = "./GoogleSearch.wsdl";

use strict;

use SOAP::Lite;

# a list of search modifiers to be randomly chosen amongst for
# inclusion in the query
my @modifiers = ( "-site:com", "-site:edu", "-site:net",
                  "-site:org", "-site:uk", "-file:pdf", );

# picking a random number and modifier combination
my $random_number  = int( rand(99999) );
my $random_modifier = $modifiers[int( rand( scalar(@modifiers) ) )];

# Create a new SOAP object
my $google_search  = SOAP::Lite->service("file:$google_wdsl");

# Query Google
my $results = $google_search ->
  doGoogleSearch(
    $google_key, "$random_number $random_modifier",
    0, 1, "false", "",  "false", "", "latin1", "latin1"
  );
```

```
# redirect the browser to the URL of the top/first result
print "Location: $results->{resultElements}->[0]->{URL}\n\n";
```

Running the Hack

This hack runs as a CGI script; invoke it from your preferred web browser.

Hacking the Hack

There are a couple of ways to hack this hack.

Modifying the modifiers. You'll notice each modifier in the @modifier array is preceded by a negative ("exclude this"). You can, of course, add anything you wish, but it's highly recommended you keep to the negative theme; including something like "computers" in the list gives you a chance—a slight chance, but a chance nevertheless—of coming up with no search results at all. The hack randomly excludes domains; here are a few more possibilities:

```
-intitle:queryword
-inurl:www
-inurl:queryword
-internet
-yahoo
-intitle:the
```

If you want to, you could create modifiers that use OR (|) instead of negatives, and then slant them to a particular topic. For example, you could create an array with a medical slant that looks like this:

```
(medicine | treatment | therapy)
(cancer | chemotherapy | drug)
(symptoms | "side effects")
(medical | research | hospital)
(inurl:edu | inurl:gov )
```

Using the OR modifier does not guarantee finding a search result like using a negative does, so don't narrow your possible results by restricting your search to the page's title or URL.

Adding a touch more randomness. The hack, as it stands, always picks the first result. While its already highly unlikely you'll ever see the same random page twice, you can achieve a touch more randomness by choosing a random returned result. Take a gander at the actual search itself in the hack's code:

```
my $results = $google_search ->
   doGoogleSearch(
      $google_key, "$random_number $random_modifier",
      0, 1, "false", "",  "false", "", "latin1", "latin1"
   );
```

You see that 0 at the beginning of the fourth line? That's the offset: the number of the first result to return. Change that number to anything between 0 and 999, and you'll shift the results returned by that number—assuming, of course, that the number you choose is smaller than the number of results for the query at hand. For the sake of just about guaranteeing a result, it's probably best to stick to numbers between 0 and 10. How about randomizing the offset? Simply alter the code as follows (changes in bold):

```
...
# picking a random number, modifier, and offset combination
my $random_number   = int( rand(99999) );
my $random_modifier = $modifiers[int( rand( scalar(@modifiers) ) )];
my $random_offset = int( rand(10) );
...
my $results = $google_search ->
  doGoogleSearch(
    $google_key, "$random_number $random_modifier",
    $random_offset, 1, "false", "",  "false", "", "latin1", "latin1"
  );

...
```

Restricting Searches to Top-Level Results

Separate out search results by the depth at which they appear in a site.

Google's a mighty big haystack under which to find the needle you seek. And there's more, so much more; some experts believe that Google and its ilk index only a bare fraction of the pages available on the Web.

Because the Web's getting bigger all the time, researchers have to come up with lots of different tricks to narrow down search results. Tricks and—thanks to the Google API—tools. This hack separates out search results appearing at the top level of a domain from those beneath.

Why would you want to do this?

- Clear away clutter when searching for proper names. If you're searching for general information about a proper name, this is one way to clear out mentions in news stories, etc. For example, the name of a political leader like Tony Blair might be mentioned in a story without any substantive information about the man himself. But if you limited your results to only those pages on the top level of a domain, you would avoid most of those "mention hits."

- Find patterns in the association of highly ranked domains and certain keywords.

- Narrow search results to only those bits that sites deem important enough to have in their virtual foyers.
- Skip past subsites, the likes of home pages created by J. Random User on their service provider's web server.

The Code

```perl
#!/usr/local/bin/perl
# gootop.cgi
# Separates out top level and sub-level results
# gootop.cgi is called as a CGI with form input

# Your Google API developer's key
my $google_key='insert key here';

# Location of the GoogleSearch WSDL file
my $google_wdsl = "./GoogleSearch.wsdl";

# Number of times to loop, retrieving 10 results at a time
my $loops = 10;

use strict;

use SOAP::Lite;
use CGI qw/:standard *table/;

print
  header(),
  start_html("GooTop"),
  h1("GooTop"),
  start_form(-method=>'GET'),
  'Query: ', textfield(-name=>'query'),
  '   ',
  submit(-name=>'submit', -value=>'Search'),
  end_form(), p();

my $google_search  = SOAP::Lite->service("file:$google_wdsl");

if (param('query')) {
  my $list = { 'toplevel' => [], 'sublevel' => [] };

  for (my $offset = 0; $offset <= $loops*10; $offset += 10) {
    my $results = $google_search ->
      doGoogleSearch(
        $google_key, param('query'), $offset,
        10, "false", "",  "false", "", "latin1", "latin1"
      );

    foreach (@{$results->{'resultElements'}}) {
      push @{
        $list->{ $_->{URL} =~ m!://[^/]+/?$!
```

```
        ? 'toplevel' : 'sublevel' }
    },
    p(
        b($_->{title}||'no title'), br( ),
        a({href=>$_->{URL}}, $_->{URL}), br( ),
        i($_->{snippet}||'no snippet')
    );
    }
}

print
    h2('Top-Level Results'),
    join("\n", @{$list->{toplevel}}),
    h2('Sub-Level Results'),
    join("\n", @{$list->{sublevel}});
}

print end_html;
```

Gleaning a decent number of top-level domain results means throwing out quite a bit. It's for this reason that this script runs the specified query a number of times, as specified by my $loops = 10;, each loop picking up 10 results, some subset being top-level. To alter the number of loops per query, simply change the value of $loops. Realize that each invocation of the script burns through $loops number of queries, so be sparing and don't bump that number up to anything ridiculous—even 100 will eat through a daily alotment in just 10 invocations.

The heart of the script, and what differentiates it from your average Google API Perl script [Hack #50], lies in this snippet of code:

```
push @{
    $list->{ $_->{URL} =~ m!://[^/]+/?$!
    ? 'toplevel' : 'sublevel' }
}
```

What that jumble of characters is scanning for is :// (as in http://) followed by anything other than a / (slash), thereby sifting between top-level finds (e.g., *http://www.berkeley.edu/welcome.html*) and sublevel results (e.g., *http://www.berkeley.edu/students/john_doe/my_dog.html*). If you're Perl savvy, you may have noticed the trailing /?$; this allows for the eventuality that a top-level URL ends with a slash (e.g., *http://www.berkeley.edu/*), as is often true.

Running the Hack

This hack runs as a CGI script. Figure 6-16 shows the results of a search for non-gmo (Genetically Modified Organisms, that is).

Figure 6-16. GooTop search for non-gmo

Hacking the Hack

There are a couple of ways to hack this hack.

More depth. Perhaps your interests lie in just how deep results are within a site or sites. A minor adjustment or two to the code, and you have results grouped by depth:

```
    ...
    foreach (@{$results->{'resultElements'}}) {
      push @{ $list[scalar ( split(/\//, $_->{URL} . ' ') - 3 ) ] },
        p(
          b($_->{title}||'no title'), br( ),
          a({href=>$_->{URL}}, $_->{URL}), br( ),
          i($_->{snippet}||'no snippet')
        );
    }
  }

  for my $depth (1..$#list) {
    print h2("Depth: $level");
    ref $list[$depth] eq 'ARRAY' and print join "\n",@{$list[$depth]};
```

```
        }
    }

    print end_html;
```

Figure 6-17 shows that non-gmo search again using the depth hack.

Figure 6-17. non-gmo search using depth hack

Query tips. Along with the aforementioned code hacking, here are a few query tips to use with this hack:

- Consider feeding the script a date range [Hack #11] query to further narrow results.

- Keep your searches specific, but not too much so for fear of turning up no top-level results. Instead of cats, for example, use "burmese cats", but don't try "burmese breeders" feeding.

- Try the link: [in "The Special Syntaxes" in Chapter 1] syntax. This is a nice use of a syntax otherwise not allowed in combination [Hack #8] with any others.

- On occasion, intitle: works nicely with this hack. Try your query without special syntaxes first, though, and work your way up, making sure you're getting results after each change.

Searching for Special Characters

#75   Search for the tilde and other special characters in URLs.

Google can find lots of different things, but at this writing, it can't find special characters in its search results. That's a shame, because special characters can come in handy. The tilde (~), for example, denotes personal web pages.

This hack takes a query from a form, pulls results from Google, and filters the results for the presence of several different special characters in the URL, including the tilde.

Why would you want to do this? By altering this hack slightly (see "Hacking the Hack") you could restrict your searches to just pages with a tilde in the URL, an easy way to find personal pages. Maybe you're looking for dynamically generated pages with a question mark (?) in the URL; you can't find these using Google by itself, but you can thanks to this hack. And of course you can turn the hack inside out and not return results containing ~, ?, or other special characters. In fact, this code is more of a beginning than an end unto itself; you can tweak it in several different ways to do several different things.

The Code

```perl
#!/usr/local/bin/perl
# aunt_tilde.pl
# Finding special characters in Google result URLs

# Your Google API developer's key
my $google_key='insert key here';

# Number of times to loop, retrieving 10 results at a time
my $loops = 10;

# Location of the GoogleSearch WSDL file
my $google_wdsl = "./GoogleSearch.wsdl";

use strict;

use CGI qw/:standard/;
use SOAP::Lite;

print
  header( ),
  start_html("Aunt Tilde"),
  h1("Aunt Tilde"),
  start_form(-method=>'GET'),
  'Query: ', textfield(-name=>'query'),
```

```
        br( ),
        'Characters to find: ',
        checkbox_group(
          -name=>'characters',
          -values=>[qw/ ~ @ ? ! /],
          -defaults=>[qw/ ~ /]
        ),
        br( ),
        submit(-name=>'submit', -value=>'Search'),
        end_form( ), p( );

  if (param('query')) {

    # Create a regular expression to match preferred special characters
    my $special_regex = '[\\' . join('\\', param('characters')) . ']';

    my $google_search  = SOAP::Lite->service("file:$google_wdsl");

    for (my $offset = 0; $offset <= $loops*10; $offset += 10) {
      my $results = $google_search ->
        doGoogleSearch(
          $google_key, param('query'), $offset, 10, "false", "",  "false",
          "", "latin1", "latin1"
        );

      last unless @{$results->{resultElements}};

      foreach my $result (@{$results->{'resultElements'}}) {

        # Output only matched URLs, highlighting special characters in red
        my $url = $result->{URL};
        $url =~ s!($special_regex)!<font color="red">$1</font>!g and
          print
            p(
              b(a({href=>$result->{URL}},$result->{title}||'no title')), br( ),
              $url, br( ),
              i($result->{snippet}||'no snippet')
            );
      }
    }

    print end_html;
}
```

Hacking the Hack

There are two main ways you can change this hack.

Choosing special characters. You can easily alter the list of special characters you're interested in by changing one line in the script:

```
    -values=>[qw/ ~ @ ? ! /],
```

Simply add or remove special characters from the space-delimited list between the / (forward slash) characters. If, for example, you want to add & (ampersands) and z (why not?), while dropping ? (question marks), that line of code should look be:

```
-values=>[qw/ ~ @ ! & z /],
```

(Don't forget those spaces between characters in the list.)

Excluding special characters. You can just as easily decide to exclude URLs containing your special characters as include them. Simply change the =~ (read: does match) in this line:

```
$url  =~ s!($special_regex)!<font color="red">$1</font>!g and
```

to !~ (read: does *not* match), leaving:

```
$url  !~ s!($special_regex)!<font color="red">$1</font>!g and
```

Now, any result containing the specific characters will *not* show up.

HACK #76   Digging Deeper into Sites

Dig deeper into the hierarchies of web sites matching your search criteria.

One of Google's big strengths is that it can find your search term instantly and with great precision. But sometimes you're not interested so much in one definitive result as in lots of diverse results; maybe you even want some that are a bit more on the obscure side.

One method I've found rather useful is to ignore all results shallower than a particular level in a site's directory hierarchy. You avoid all the clutter of finds on home pages and go for subject matter otherwise often hidden away in the depths of a site's structure. While content comes and gos, ebbs and flows from a site's main focus, it tends to gather in more permanent locales, categorized and archived, like with like.

This script asks for a query along with a preferred depth, above which results are thrown out. Specify a depth of four and your results will come only from *http://example.com/a/b/c/d*, not */a*, */a/b/*, or */a/b/c*.

Because you're already limiting the kinds of results you see, it's best to use more common words for what you're looking for. Obscure query terms can often cause absolutely no results to turn up.

The default number of loops, retrieving 10 items apiece, is set to 50. This is to assure you glean some decent number of results, because many will be tossed. You can, of course, alter this number but bear in mind that you're using that number of your daily quota of 1,000 Google API queries per developer's key.

The Code

```perl
#!/usr/local/bin/perl
# deep_blue_g.cgi
# Limiting search results to a particular depth in a web
# site's hierarchy.
# deep_blue_g.cgi is called as a CGI with form input

# Your Google API developer's key
my $google_key='insert key here';

# Location of the GoogleSearch WSDL file
my $google_wdsl = "./GoogleSearch.wsdl";

# Number of times to loop, retrieving 10 results at a time
my $loops = 10;

use SOAP::Lite;
use CGI qw/:standard *table/;

print
  header( ),
  start_html("Fishing in the Deep Blue G"),
  h1("Fishing in the Deep Blue G"),
  start_form(-method=>'GET'),
  'Query: ', textfield(-name=>'query'),
  br( ),
  'Depth: ', textfield(-name=>'depth', -default=>4),
  br( ),
  submit(-name=>'submit', -value=>'Search'),
  end_form( ), p( );

# Make sure a query and numeric depth are provided
if (param('query') and param('depth') =~ /\d+/) {

  # Create a new SOAP object
  my $google_search  = SOAP::Lite->service("file:$google_wdsl");

  for (my $offset = 0; $offset <= $loops*10; $offset += 10) {
    my $results = $google_search ->
      doGoogleSearch(
```

```
            $google_key, param('query'), $offset, 10, "false", "",  "false",
            "", "latin1", "latin1"
    );

    last unless @{$results->{resultElements}};

    foreach my $result (@{$results->{'resultElements'}}) {

        # Determine depth
        my $url = $result->{URL};
        $url =~ s!^\w+://|/$!!g;

        # Output only those deep enough
        ( split(/\//, $url) - 1) >= param('depth') and
          print
            p(
              b(a({href=>$result->{URL}},$result->{title}||'no title')), br(),
              $result->{URL}, br(),
              i($result->{snippet}||'no snippet')
            );
    }
}

    print end_html;
}
```

Running the Hack

This hack runs as a CGI script. Point your browser at it, fill out query and
depth fields, and click the "Submit" button.

Figure 6-18 shows a query for "Jacques Cousteau", restricting results to a
depth of 6—that's six levels down from the site's home page. You'll notice
some pretty long URLs in there.

Hacking the Hack

Perhaps you're interested in just the opposite of what this hack provides:
you want only results from higher up in a site's hierarchy. Hacking this hack
is simple enough: swap in a < (less than) symbol instead of the > (great than)
in the following line:

```
            ( split(/\//, $url) - 1) <= param('depth') and
```

See Also

- Restricting Searches to Top-Level Results [Hack #74]

Figure 6-18. A search for "Jacques Cousteau", restricting results to six levels down

HACK #77 Summarizing Results by Domain

Getting an overview of the sorts of domains (educational, commercial, foreign, and so forth) found in the results of a Google query.

You want to know about a topic, so you do a search. But what do you have? A list of pages. You can't get a good idea of the types of pages these are without taking a close look at the list of sites.

This hack is an attempt to get a "snapshot" of the types of sites that result from a query. It does this by taking a "suffix census," a count of the different domains that appear in search results.

This is most ideal for running link: queries, providing a good idea of what kinds of domains (commercial, educational, military, foreign, etc.) are linking to a particular page.

You could also run it to see where technical terms, slang terms, and unusual words were turning up. Which pages mention a particular singer more often? Or a political figure? Does the word "democrat" come up more often on *.com* or *.edu* sites?

Of course this snapshot doesn't provide a complete inventory; but as overviews go, it's rather interesting.

The Code

```perl
#!/usr/local/bin/perl
# suffixcensus.cgi
# Generates a snapshot of the kinds of sites responding to a
# query.  The suffix is the .com, .net, or .uk part.
# suffixcensus.cgi is called as a CGI with form input

# Your Google API developer's key
my $google_key='insert key here';

# Location of the GoogleSearch WSDL file
my $google_wdsl = "./GoogleSearch.wsdl";

# Number of times to loop, retrieving 10 results at a time
my $loops = 10;

use SOAP::Lite;
use CGI qw/:standard *table/;

print
  header(),
  start_html("SuffixCensus"),
  h1("SuffixCensus"),
  start_form(-method=>'GET'),
  'Query: ', textfield(-name=>'query'),
  '   ',
  submit(-name=>'submit', -value=>'Search'),
  end_form(), p();

if (param('query')) {
  my $google_search  = SOAP::Lite->service("file:$google_wdsl");
  my %suffixes;

  for (my $offset = 0; $offset <= $loops*10; $offset += 10) {

    my $results = $google_search ->
      doGoogleSearch(
        $google_key, param('query'), $offset, 10, "false", "",  "false",
        "", "latin1", "latin1"
      );

    last unless @{$results->{resultElements}};

    map { $suffixes{ ($_->{URL} =~ m#://.+?\.(\w{2,4})/#)[0] }++ }
      @{$results->{resultElements}};
  }
```

```
print
  h2('Results: '), p( ),
  start_table({cellpadding => 5, cellspacing => 0, border => 1}),
  map( { Tr(td(uc $_),td($suffixes{$_})) } sort keys %suffixes ),
  end_table( );
}

print end_html( );
```

Running the Hack

This hack runs as a CGI script. Install it in your *cgi-bin* or appropriate directory, and point your browser at it.

The Results

Searching for the prevalence of "soda pop" by suffix finds, as one might expect, the most mention on *.com*s, as Figure 6-19 shows.

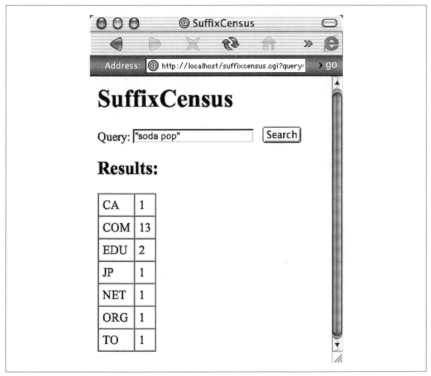

Figure 6-19. Prevalence of "soda pop" by suffix

Hacking the Hack

There are a couple of ways to hack this hack.

Going back for more. This script, by default, visits Google 10 times, grabbing the top 100 (or fewer, if there aren't as many) results. To increase or decrease the number of visits, simply change the value of the $loops variable at the top of the script. Bear in mind, however, that making $loops = 50 might net you 500 results, but you're also eating quickly into your daily alotment of 1,000 Google API queries.

Comma-separated. It's rather simple to adjust this script to run from the command line and return a comma-separated output suitable for Excel or your average database. Remove the starting HTML, form, and ending HTML output, and alter the code that prints out the results. In the end, you come to something like this (changes in bold):

```perl
#!/usr/local/bin/perl
# suffixcensus_csv.pl
# Generates a snapshot of the kinds of sites responding to a
# query.  The suffix is the .com, .net, or .uk part.
# usage: perl suffixcensus_csv.pl query="your query" > results.csv

# Your Google API developer's key
my $google_key='insert key';

# Location of the GoogleSearch WSDL file
my $google_wdsl = "./GoogleSearch.wsdl";

# Number of times to loop, retrieving 10 results at a time
my $loops = 1;

use SOAP::Lite;
use CGI qw/:standard/;

param('query')
  or die qq{usage: suffixcensus_csv.pl query="{query}" [> results.csv]\n};

print qq{"suffix","count"\n};

my $google_search  = SOAP::Lite->service("file:$google_wdsl");

my %suffixes;

for (my $offset = 0; $offset <= $loops*10; $offset += 10) {

  my $results = $google_search ->
    doGoogleSearch(
      $google_key, param('query'), $offset, 10, "false", "",  "false",
      "", "latin1", "latin1"
    );
```

```
    last unless @{$results->{resultElements}};

    map { $suffixes{ ($_->{URL} =~ m#://.+?\.(\w{2,4})/#)[0] }++ }
      @{$results->{resultElements}};
}
```

print map { qq{"$_", "$suffixes{$_}"\n} } sort keys %suffixes;

Invoke the script from the command line like so:

```
$ perl suffixcensus_csv.pl query="query" > results.csv
```

Searching for mentions of "colddrink," the South African version of "soda pop," sending the output straight to the screen rather than a *results.csv* file, looks like this:

```
$ perl suffixcensus_csv.pl query="colddrink"
"suffix","count"
"com", "12"
"info", "1"
"net", "1"
"za", "6"
```

Scraping Yahoo! Buzz for a Google Search

A proof of concept hack that scrapes the buzziest items from Yahoo! Buzz and submits them to a Google search.

No web site is an island. Billions of hyperlinks link to billions of documents. Sometimes, however, you want to take information from one site and apply it to another site.

Unless that site has a web service API like Google's, your best bet is scraping. Scraping is where you use an automated program to remove specific bits of information from a web page. Examples of the sorts of elements people scrape include: stock quotes, news headlines, prices, and so forth. You name it and someone's probably scraped it.

There's some controversy about scraping. Some sites don't mind it, while others can't stand it. If you decide to scrape a site, do it gently; take the minimum amount of information you need and, whatever you do, don't hog the scrapee's bandwidth.

So, what are we scraping?

Google has a query popularity page; it's called Google Zeitgeist (*http://www.google.com/press/zeitgeist.html*). Unfortunately, the Zeitgeist is only updated once a week and contains only a limited amount of scrapable data. That's where Yahoo! Buzz (*http://buzz.yahoo.com/*) comes in. The site is rich with constantly updated information. Its "Buzz Index" keeps tabs on what's hot in popular culture: celebs, games, movies, television shows, music, and more.

This hack grabs the buzziest of the buzz, top of the "Leaderboard," and searches Google for all it knows on the subject. And to keep things current, only pages indexed by Google within the past few days [Hack #11] are considered.

 This hack requires additional Perl modules: Time::JulianDay (*http://search.cpan.org/search?query=Time%3A%3AJulianDay*) and LWP::Simple (*http://search.cpan.org/ search?query=LWP%3A%3ASimple*). It won't run without them.

The Code

```perl
#!/usr/local/bin/perl
# buzzgle.pl
# Pull the top item from the Yahoo Buzz Index and query the last
# three day's worth of Google's index for it
# Usage: perl buzzgle.pl

# Your Google API developer's key
my $google_key='insert key here';

# Location of the GoogleSearch WSDL file
my $google_wdsl = "./GoogleSearch.wsdl";

# Number of days back to go in the Google index
my $days_back = 3;

use strict;

use SOAP::Lite;
use LWP::Simple;
use Time::JulianDay;

# Scrape the top item from the Yahoo Buzz Index

# Grab a copy of http://buzz.yahoo.com

my $buzz_content = get("http://buzz.yahoo.com/")
  or die "Couldn't grab the Yahoo Buzz: $!";

# Find the first item on the Buzz Index list
my($buzziest) =  $buzz_content =~ m!<TR BGCOLOR=white.+?1.+?<a href="http://
search.yahoo.com/search\?p=.+?&cs=bz">(.+?)!i;
die "Couldn't figure out the Yahoo! buzz\n" unless $buzziest;

# Figure out today's Julian date
my $today = int local_julian_day(time);

# Build the Google query
my $query = "\"$buzziest\" daterange:" . ($today - $days_back) . "-$today";
```

```
print
    "The buzziest item on Yahoo Buzz today is: $buzziest\n",
    "Querying Google for: $query\n",
    "Results:\n\n";

# Create a new SOAP::Lite instance, feeding it GoogleSearch.wsdl
my $google_search = SOAP::Lite->service("file:$google_wdsl");

# Query Google
my $results = $google_search ->
    doGoogleSearch(
        $google_key, $query, 0, 10, "false", "",  "false",
        "", "latin1", "latin1"
    );

# No results?
@{$results->{resultElements}} or die "No results";

# Loop through the results
foreach my $result (@{$results->{'resultElements'}}) {
 my $output =
   join "\n",
   $result->{title} || "no title",
   $result->{URL},
   $result->{snippet} || 'no snippet',
   "\n";
     $output =~ s!<.+?>!!g; # drop all HTML tags
     print $output;
}
```

Running the Hack

The script runs from the command line without need of arguments of any kind. Probably the best thing to do is to direct the output to a pager (a command-line application that allows you to page through long output, usually by hitting the spacebar), like so:

```
% perl buzzgle.pl | more
```

Or you can direct the output to a file for later perusal:

```
% perl buzzgle.pl > buzzgle.txt
```

As with all scraping applications, this code is fragile, subject to breakage if (read: when) HTML formatting of the Yahoo! Buzz page changes. If you find you have to adjust to match Yahoo!'s formatting, you'll have to alter the regular expression match as appropriate:

```
my($buzziest) = $buzz_content =~ m!<TR BGCOLOR=white.+?1.+?<a href="http
://search.yahoo.com/search\?p=.+?&cs=bz">(.+?)!i;
```

Regular expressions and general HTML scraping are beyond the scope of this book. For more information, I suggest you consult O'Reilly's *Perl and*

LWP (*http://www.oreilly.com/catalog/perllwp/*) or *Mastering Regular Expressions* (*http://www.oreilly.com/catalog/regex/*).

The Results

At the time of this writing—and probably for some time yet to come—musical sensation, Eminem, is all the rage.

```
% perl buzzgle.pl | less
The buzziest item on Yahoo Buzz today is: Eminem
Querying Google for: "Eminem" daterange:2452593-2452596
Results:
Eminem World
http://www.eminemworld.com/
Eminem World specializing in Eminem News and Information. With
Pictures, Discogr aphy, Lyrics ... your #1 Eminem Resource. Eminem
World, ...
Eminem
http://www.eminem.com/frameset.asp?PageName=eminem
no snippet
Eminem Planet - Your Ultimate Resource
http://www.eminem-planet.com/
Eminem Planet - A Great Resource about the Real Slim Shady. .:8 Mile .:News
.:Bi
ography ... More News. ::Order Eminem's book. Click Here to Check ...
...
```

Hacking the Hack

Here are some ideas for hacking the hack:

- The program as it stands returns 10 results. You could change that to one result and immediately open that result instead of returning a list. Bravo, you've just written I'm Feeling Popular!, as in Google's I'm Feeling Lucky!

- This version of the program searches the last three days of indexed pages. Because there's a slight lag in indexing news stories, I would index at least the last two days' worth of indexed pages, but you could extend it to seven days or even a month. Simply change my $days_back = 3;, altering the value of the $days_back variable.

- You could create a "Buzz Effect" hack by running the Yahoo! Buzz query with and without the date-range limitation. How do the results change between a full search and a search of the last few days?

- Yahoo!'s Buzz has several different sections. This one looks at the Buzz summary, but you could create other ones based on Yahoo!'s other buzz charts (television, *http://buzz.yahoo.com/television/*, for instance).

Measuring Google Mindshare

Measure the Google mindshare of a particular person within a query domain.

Based on an idea by author Steven Johnson (*http://www.stevenberlinjohnson/*),
this hack determines the Google mindshare of a person within a particular set
of Google queried keywords. What's Willy Wonka's Google mindshare of
"Willy"? What percentage of "weatherman" does Al Roker hold? Who has the
greater "The Beatles" Google mindshare, Ringo Starr or Paul McCartney?
More importantly, what Google mindshare of your industry does your company own?

Google mindshare is calculated as follows: determine the size of the result
set for a keyword or phrase. Determine the result set size for that query
along with a particular person. Divide the second by the first and multiply
by 100, yielding percent Google mindshare. For example: A query for Willy
yields about 1,590,000 results. "Willy Wonka" +Willy finds 66,700. We can
conclude—however unscientifically—that Willy Wonka holds roughly a 4%
(66,700 / 1,590,000 × 100) Google mindshare of Willy.

Sure it's a little silly, but there's probably a grain of truth in it somewhere.

The Code

```
#!/usr/local/bin/perl
# google_mindshare.cgi
# This implementation by Rael Dornfest
# http://www.raelity.org/lang/perl/google/googleshare/
# Based on an idea by Steven Johnson
# http://www.stevenberlinjohnson.com/movabletype/archives/000009.html

# Your Google API developer's key
my $google_key='insert key here';

# Location of the GoogleSearch WSDL file
my $google_wdsl = "./GoogleSearch.wsdl";

use SOAP::Lite;
use CGI qw/:standard *table/;

print
  header(),
  start_html("Googleshare Calculator"),
  h1("Googleshare Calculator"),
  start_form(-method=>'GET'),
  'Query: ', br(), textfield(-name=>'query'),
  p(),
  'Person: ',br(), textfield(-name=>'person'),
  p(),
```

```
      submit(-name=>'submit', -value=>'Calculate'),
      end_form(), p();

  if (param('query') and param('person')) {
    my $google_search  = SOAP::Lite->service("file:$google_wdsl");

    # Query Google for they keyword, keywords, or phrase
    my $results = $google_search ->
      doGoogleSearch(
        $google_key, '"'.param('query').'"', 0, 1, "false", "",  "false",
        "", "latin1", "latin1"
      );

    # Save the results for the Query
    my $query_count = $results->{estimatedTotalResultsCount};

    my $results = $google_search ->
      doGoogleSearch(
        $google_key, '+"'.param('query').'" +"'.param('person').'"', 0, 1,
        "false", "",  "false", "", "latin1", "latin1"
      );
    # Save the results for the Query AND Person
    my $query_person_count = $results->{estimatedTotalResultsCount};

    print
      p(
        b(sprintf "%s has a %.2f%% googleshare of %s",
          param('person'),
          ($query_person_count / $query_count * 100),
          '"'.param('query').'"'
        )
      )
  }

  print end_html();
```

Running the Hack

Visit the CGI script in your browser. Enter a query and a person. The name doesn't necessarily have to be a person's full name. It can be a company, location, just about any proper noun, or anything, actually. Click the "Calculate" button and enjoy. Figure 6-20 shows the Willy Wonka example.

Fun Hack Uses

You can't do too many practical things with this hack, but you can have a lot of fun with it. Playing "unlikely percentages" is fun; see if you can find a name/word combo that gets a higher percentage than other percentages you

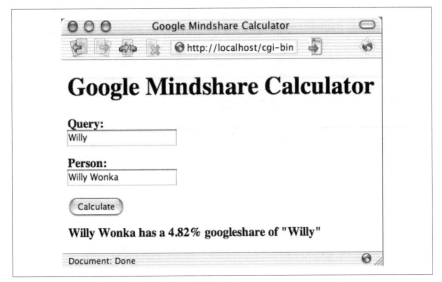

Figure 6-20. Google mindshare for Willy Wonka

would consider more likely. Here are the answers to the questions posted at the beginning of this hack, and more:

- Willy Wonka has a 4.82% Google mindshare of "Willy."
- Al Roker has a 1.45% Google mindshare of "weatherman."
- Ringo Starr has a 1.69% Google mindshare of "The Beatles."
- Paul McCartney has a 3.71% Google mindshare of "The Beatles."
- Red Hat has a 3.63% Google mindshare of "Linux."
- Microsoft has a 4.37% Google mindshare of "Linux."

HACK #80 Comparing Google Results with Those of Other Search Engines

Comparing Google search results with results from other search engines.

True Google fanatics might not like to think so, but there's really more than one search engine. Google's competitors include the likes of AltaVista, AlltheWeb, and Teoma.

Equally surprising to the average Google fanatic is the fact that Google doesn't index the entire Web. There are, at the time of this writing, over 2 billion web pages in the Google index, but that's just a fraction of the Web. You'd be amazed how much non-overlapping content there is in each search engine. Some queries that bring only a few results on one search engine bring plenty on another search engine.

This hack gives you a program that compares counts for Google and several other search engines, with an easy way to plug in new search engines that you want to include. This version of the hack searches different domains for the query, in addition to getting the full count for the query itself.

This hack requires the LWP::Simple (*http://search.cpan.org/ search?query=LWP%3A%3ASimple*) module to run.

The Code

```
#!/usr/local/bin/perl
# google_compare.cgi
# Compares Google results against those of other search engines

# Your Google API developer's key
my $google_key='insert key here';

# Location of the GoogleSearch WSDL file
my $google_wdsl = "./GoogleSearch.wsdl";

use strict;

use SOAP::Lite;
use LWP::Simple qw(get);
use CGI qw{:standard};

my $googleSearch = SOAP::Lite->service("file:$google_wdsl");

# setup our browser output.
print "Content-type: text/html\n\n";
print "<html><title>Google Compare Results</title><body>\n";

# ask and we shell receive.
my $query = param('query');
unless ($query) {
    print "<h1>No query defined.</h1></body></html>\n\n";
    exit; # If there's no query there's no program.
}

# spit out the original before we encode.
print "<h1>Your original query was '$query'.</h1>\n";

$query =~ s/\s/\+/g ;   #changing the spaces to + signs
$query =~ s/\"/%22/g;   #changing the quotes to %22

# Create some hashes of queries for various search engines.
# We have four types of queries ("plain", "com", "edu", and "org"),
# and three search engines ("Google", "AlltheWeb", and "Altavista".
# Each engine has a name, query, and regular expression used to
# scrape the results.
```

```perl
my $query_hash = {
   plain => {
      Google => { name => "Google", query => $query, },
      AlltheWeb => {
         name    => "AlltheWeb",
         regexp => "Displaying results <b>.*<\/b> of <b>(.*)<\/b>",
         query  => "http://www.alltheweb.com/search?cat=web&q=$query",
      },
      Altavista => {
         name    => "Altavista",
         regexp => "We found (.*) results",
         query => "http://www.altavista.com/sites/search/web?q=$query",
      }
   },
   com => {
      Google => { name => "Google", query => "$query site:com", },
      AlltheWeb => {
         name    => "AlltheWeb",
         regexp => "Displaying results <b>.*<\/b> of <b>(.*)<\/b>",
         query  => "http://www.alltheweb.com/
search?cat=web&q=$query+domain%3Acom",
      },
      Altavista => {
         name => "Altavista", regexp => "We found (.*) results",
         query => "http://www.altavista.com/sites/search/
web?q=$query+domain%3Acom",
      }
   },
   org => {
      Google => { name => "Google", query => "$query site:org", },
      AlltheWeb => {
         name    => "AlltheWeb",
         regexp => "Displaying results <b>.*<\/b> of <b>(.*)<\/b>",
         query  => "http://www.alltheweb.com/
search?cat=web&q=$query+domain%3Aorg",
      },
      Altavista => {
         name => "Altavista", regexp => "We found (.*) results",
         query => "http://www.altavista.com/sites/search/
web?q=$query+domain%3Aorg",
      }
   },
   net => {
      Google => { name => "Google", query => "$query site:net", },
      AlltheWeb => {
         name    => "AlltheWeb",
         regexp => "Displaying results <b>.*<\/b> of <b>(.*)<\/b>",
         query  => "http://www.alltheweb.com/
search?cat=web&q=$query+domain%3Anet",
      },
      Altavista => {
         name => "Altavista", regexp => "We found (.*) results",
         query => "http://www.altavista.com/sites/search/
web?q=$query+domain%3Anet",
```

```
            }
        }
    };

    # now, we loop through each of our query types,
    # under the assumption there's a matching
    # hash that contains our engines and string.
    foreach my $query_type (keys (%$query_hash)) {
        print "<h2>Results for a '$query_type' search:</h2>\n";

        # now, loop through each engine we have and get/print the results.
        foreach my $engine (values %{$query_hash->{$query_type}}) {
            my $results_count;

            # if this is Google, we use the API and not port 80.
            if ($engine->{name} eq "Google") {
                my $result = $googleSearch->doGoogleSearch(
                    $google_key, $engine->{query}, 0, 1,
                    "false", "", "false", "", "latin1", "latin1");
                $results_count = $result->{estimatedTotalResultsCount};
                # the google api doesn't format numbers with commas.
                my $rresults_count = reverse $results_count;
                $rresults_count =~ s/(\d\d\d)(?=\d)(?!\d*\.)/$1,/g;
                $results_count = scalar reverse $rresults_count;
            }

            # it's not google, so we GET like everyone else.
            elsif ($engine->{name} ne "Google") {
                my $data = get($engine->{query}) or print "ERROR: $!";
                $data =~ /$engine->{regexp}/; $results_count = $1 || 0;
            }

            # and print out the results.
            print "<strong>$engine->{name}</strong>: $results_count<br />\n";
        }
    }
```

Running the Hack

This hack runs as a CGI script, called from your web browser as: google_
compare.cgi?query=your query keywords.

Why?

You might be wondering why you would want to compare result counts
across search engines? It's a good idea to follow what different search
engines offer in terms of results. While you might find that a phrase on one
search engine provides only a few results, another might return results a-
plenty. It makes sense to spend your time and energy using the latter for the
research at hand.

—Tara Calishain and Morbus Iff

SafeSearch Certifying URLs

Feed URLs to Google's SafeSearch to determine whether or not they point at
questionable content.

Only three things in life are certain: death, taxes, and accidentally visiting a
once family-safe web site that now contains text and images that would
make a horse blush.

As you probably know if you've ever put up a web site, domain names are
registered for finite lengths of time. Sometimes registrations accidentally
expire; sometimes businesses fold and allow the registrations to expire.
Sometimes other companies take them over.

Other companies might just want the domain name, some companies want
the traffic that the defunct site generated, and in a few cases, the new owners of the domain name try to hold it "hostage," offering to sell it back to the
original owners for a great deal of money. (This doesn't work as well as it
used to because of the dearth of Internet companies that actually have a
great deal of money.)

When a site isn't what it once was, that's no big deal. When it's not what it
once was and is now rated X, that's a bigger deal. When it's not what it once
was, is now rated X, and is on the link list of a site you run, that's a really
big deal.

But how to keep up with all the links? You can go visit every link periodi-
cally and see if it's still okay, or you can wait for the hysterical emails from
site visitors, or you can just not worry about it. Or you can put the Google
API to work.

This program lets you give provide a list of URLs and check them in Google's SafeSearch Mode. If they appear in the SafeSearch mode, they're probably okay. If they don't appear, they're either not in Google's index or not
good enough to pass Google's filter. The program then checks the URLs
missing from a SafeSearch with a nonfiltered search. If they do not appear in
a nonfiltered search, they're labeled as unindexed. If they do appear in a
nonfiltered search, they're labeled as "suspect."

Danger Will Robinson

While Google's SafeSearch filter is good, it's not infallible. (I have yet to see
an automated filtering system that is infallible.) So if you run a list of URLs
through this hack and they all show up in a SafeSearch query, don't take
that as a guarantee that they're all completely inoffensive. Take it merely as
a pretty good indication that they are. If you want absolute assurance,
you're going to have to visit every link personally and often.

Here's a fun idea if you need an Internet-related research project. Take 500 or so domain names at random and run this program on the list once a week for several months, saving the results to a file each time. It'd be interesting to see how many domains/URLs end up being filtered out of SafeSearch over time.

The Code

```perl
#!/usr/local/bin/perl
# suspect.pl
# Feed URLs to a Google SafeSearch. If inurl: returns results, the
# URL probably isn't questionable content.  If inurl: returns no
# results, either it points at questionable content or isn't in
# the Google index at all.

# Your Google API developer's key
my $google_key = 'put your key here';

# Location of the GoogleSearch WSDL file
my $google_wdsl = "./GoogleSearch.wsdl";

use strict;

use SOAP::Lite;

$|++; # turn off buffering

my $google_search = SOAP::Lite->service("file:$google_wdsl");

# CSV header
print qq{"url","safe/suspect/unindexed","title"\n};

while (my $url = <>) {
  chomp $url;
  $url =~ s!^\w+?://!!;
  $url =~ s!^www\.!!;

  # SafeSearch
  my $results = $google_search ->
     doGoogleSearch(
       $google_key, "inurl:$url", 0, 10, "false", "",  "true",
       "", "latin1", "latin1"
    );

  print qq{"$url",};

  if (grep /$url/, map { $_->{URL} } @{$results->{resultElements}}) {
    print qq{"safe"\n};
  }
  else {
    # unSafeSearch
```

```
    my $results = $google_search ->
        doGoogleSearch(
        $google_key, "inurl:$url", 0, 10, "false", "",  "false",
        "", "latin1", "latin1"
      );

    # Unsafe or Unindexed?
    print (
      (scalar grep /$url/, map { $_->{URL} } @{$results->{resultElements}})
        ? qq{"suspect"\n}
        : qq{"unindexed"\n}
      );
  }
}
```

Running the Hack

To run the hack, you'll need a text file that contains the URLs you want to check, one line per URL. For example:

```
http://www.oreilly.com/catalog/essblogging/
http://www.xxxxxxxxxx.com/preview/home.htm
hipporhinostricow.com
```

The program runs from the command line. Enter the name of the script , a less-than sign, and the name of the text file that contains the URLs you want to check. The program will return results that look like this:

```
% perl suspect.pl < urls.txt
"url","safe/suspect/unindexed"
"oreilly.com/catalog/essblogging/","safe"
"xxxxxxxxxx.com/preview/home.htm","suspect"
"hipporhinostricow.com","unindexed"
```

The first item is the URL being checked. The second is it's probable safety rating as follows:

safe

  The URL appeared in a Google SafeSearch for the URL.

suspect

  The URL did not appear in a Google SafeSearch, but did in an unfiltered search.

unindexed

  The URL appeared in neither a SafeSearch nor unfiltered search.

You can redirect output from the script to a file for import into a spreadsheet or database:

```
% perl suspect.pl < urls.txt > urls.csv
```

Hacking the Hack

You can use this hack interactively, feeding it URLs one at a time. Invoke the script with perl suspect.pl, but don't feed it a text file of URLs to check. Enter a URL and hit the return key on your keyboard. The script will reply in the same manner as it did when fed multiple URLs. This is handy when you just need to spot-check a couple of URLs on the command line. When you're ready to quit, break out of the script using Ctrl-D under Unix or Ctrl-Break on a Windows command line.

Here's a transcript of an interactive session with *suspect.pl*:

```
% perl suspect.pl
"url","safe/suspect/unindexed","title"
http://www.oreilly.com/catalog/essblogging/
"oreilly.com/catalog/essblogging/","safe"
http://www.xxxxxxxxxx.com/preview/home.htm
"xxxxxxxxxx.com/preview/home.htm","suspect"
hipporhinostricow.com
"hipporhinostricow.com","unindexed"
^d
%
```

HACK #82   Syndicating Google Search Results

Converting Google results to RSS suitable for syndication or incorporation into your own web site.

RSS is an XML-based syndication format used by web sites to provide abstracts of their content for open-ended syndication. RSS-syndicated content is incorporated into web sites, aggregated by news services, and consumed by RSS news readers similar in form to the Usenet newsreaders of old.

This hack converts sets of Google search results to RSS format for syndication. The C# .NET source code and full instructions are available at *http://www.razorsoft.net/weblog/stories/2002/04/13/google2rss.html*.

Running the Hack

Google2RSS is a command-line utility. To run it, you'll need to have a Windows machine with the .NET Framework installed. If you want to compile it from source yourself, you'll need to have the .NET Framework SDK too. It accepts a multitude of command-line switches, all of which are documented on the Google2RSS site.

Here's a sample run of Google2RSS, a SafeSearch query Google API :

```
google2rss.exe -key "12BuCK13mY5hOE/34KNOcK@ttH3DoOR" -query "Google API" -
safesearch true -filter true -title "Tracking the Google API" -link http://
www.example.com/API -description "Tracking the Google API Mentions in
Google" -webMaster info@example.com -outfile "googleapi.rss"
```

This will produce an RSS document fit for consumption by any number of
RSS tools, applications, and services. Drop it into your web server's docu-
ment directory and announce its whereabouts so that others may use it.
Incorporate it into your own web page using any number of tools.

Searching Google Topics

A hack that runs a query against some of the available Google API specialty
topics.

Google doesn't talk about it much, but it does make specialty web searches
available. And I'm not just talking about searches limited to a certain
domain. I'm talking about searches that are devoted to a particular topic.
The Google API makes four of these searches available: The U.S. Government, Linux, BSD, and Macintosh.

In this hack, we'll look at a program that takes a query from a form and provides a count of that query in each specialty topic, as well as a count of
results for each topic. This program runs via a form.

Why Topic Search?

Why would you want to topic search? Because Google currently indexes
over 3 billion pages. If you try to do more than very specific searches you
might find yourself with far too many results. If you narrow your search
down by topic, you can get good results without having to exactly zero in on
your search.

You can also use it to do some decidedly unscientific research. Which topic
contains more iterations of the phrase "open source"? Which contains the
most pages from *.edu* (educational) domains? Which topic, Macintosh or
FreeBSD, has more on user interfaces? Which topic holds the most for
Monty Python fans?

The Code

```
#!/usr/local/bin/perl
# gootopic.cgi
# Queries across Google Topics (and All of Google), returning
# number of results and top result for each topic.
# gootopic.cgi is called as a CGI with form input
```

```perl
# Your Google API developer's key
my $google_key='insert key here';

# Location of the GoogleSearch WSDL file
my $google_wdsl = "./GoogleSearch.wsdl";

# Google Topics
my %topics = (
  ''        => 'All of Google',
  unclesam => 'U.S. Government',
  linux     => 'Linux',
  mac       => 'Macintosh',
  bsd       => 'FreeBSD'
);

use strict;

use SOAP::Lite;
use CGI qw/:standard *table/;

# Display the query form
print
  header(),
  start_html("GooTopic"),
  h1("GooTopic"),
  start_form(-method=>'GET'),
  'Query: ', textfield(-name=>'query'), '   ',
  submit(-name=>'submit', -value=>'Search'),
  end_form(), p();

my $google_search  = SOAP::Lite->service("file:$google_wdsl");

# Perform the queries, one for each topic area
if (param('query')) {
  print
    start_table({-cellpadding=>'10', -border=>'1'}),
    Tr([th({-align=>'left'}, ['Topic', 'Count', 'Top Result'])]);

  foreach my $topic (keys %topics) {

    my $results = $google_search ->
      doGoogleSearch(
        $google_key, param('query'), 0, 10, "false", $topic,  "false",
        "", "latin1", "latin1"
      );

    my $result_count = $results->{'estimatedTotalResultsCount'};

    my $top_result = 'no results';

    if ( $result_count ) {
      my $t = @{$results->{'resultElements'}}[0];
      $top_result =
```

```
            b($t->{title}||'no title') . br() .
            a({href=>$t->{URL}}, $t->{URL}) . br() .
            i($t->{snippet}||'no snippet');
    }

    # Output
    print Tr([ td([
      $topics{$topic},
      $result_count,
      $top_result
      ])
    ]);
  }

  print
    end_table(),
}

print end_html();
```

Running the Hack

The form code is built into the hack, so just call the hack with the URL of the CGI script. For example, if I was running the program on researchbuzz. com and it was called *gootopics.pl*, my URL might look like *http://www. researchbuzz.com/cgi-bin/gootopic.cgi*.

Provide a query and the script will search for your query in each special topic area, providing you with an overall ("All of Google") count, topic area count, and the top result for each. Figure 6-21 shows a sample run for "user interface" with Macintosh coming out on top.

Search Ideas

Trying to figure out how many pages each topic finds for particular top-level domains (e.g., *.com*, *.edu*, *.uk*) is rather interesting. You can query for inurl: *xx* site:*xx*, where *xx* is the top-level domain you're interested in. For example, inurl:va site:va searches for any of the Vatican's pages in the various topics; there aren't any. inurl:mil site:mil finds an overwhelming number of results in the U.S. Government special topic—no surprise there.

If you are in the mood for a party game, try to find the weirdest possible searches that appear in all the special topics. "Papa Smurf" is as good a query as any other. In fact, at this writing, that search has more results in the U.S. Government specialty search than in the others.

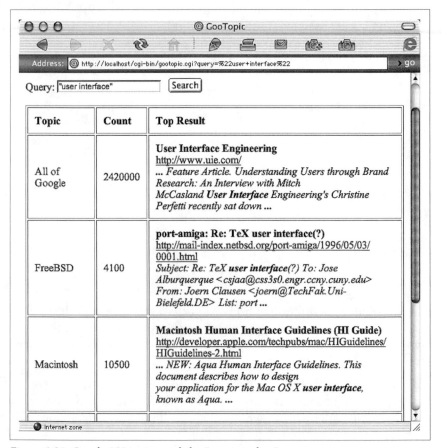

Figure 6-21. Google API topic search for "user interface"

HACK #84 Finding the Largest Page

We all know about Feeling Lucky with Google. But how about Feeling Large?

Google sorts your search result by PageRank. Certainly makes sense. Some-times, however, you may have a substantially different focus in mind and want things ordered in some other manner. Recency is one that comes to mind. Size is another.

In the same manner as Google's "I'm Feeling Lucky" button redirects you to the search result with the highest PageRank, this hack sends you directly to the largest (in Kilobytes).

This hack works rather nicely in combination with repetition [Hack #7].

The Code

```
#!/usr/local/bin/perl
# goolarge.cgi
# A take-off on "I'm feeling lucky", redirects the browser to the largest
# (size in K) document found in the first n results.  n is set by number
# of loops x 10 results per.
# goolarge.cgi is called as a CGI with form input

# Your Google API developer's key
my $google_key='insert key here';

# Location of the GoogleSearch WSDL file
my $google_wdsl = "./GoogleSearch.wsdl";

# Number of times to loop, retrieving 10 results at a time
my $loops = 10;

use strict;

use SOAP::Lite;
use CGI qw/:standard/;

# Display the query form
unless (param('query')) {
  print
    header(),
    start_html("GooLarge"),
    h1("GooLarge"),
    start_form(-method=>'GET'),
    'Query: ', textfield(-name=>'query'),
    '   ',
    submit(-name=>'submit', -value=>"I'm Feeling Large"),
    end_form(), p();
}

# Run the query
else {
  my $google_search  = SOAP::Lite->service("file:$google_wdsl");
  my($largest_size, $largest_url);

  for (my $offset = 0; $offset <= $loops*10; $offset += 10) {
```

```
    my $results = $google_search ->
        doGoogleSearch(
            $google_key, param('query'), $offset,
            10, "false", "",  "false", "", "latin1", "latin1"
        );

    @{$results->{'resultElements'}} or print p('No results'), last;

    # Keep track of the largest size and its associated URL
    foreach (@{$results->{'resultElements'}}) {
        substr($_->{cachedSize}, 0, -1) > $largest_size and
            ($largest_size, $largest_url) =
            (substr($_->{cachedSize}, 0, -1), $_->{URL});
    }
}

    # Redirect the browser to the largest result
    print redirect $largest_url;
}
```

Running the Hack

Call up the CGI script in your web browser. Enter a query and click the "I'm Feeling Large" button. You'll be transported directly to the largest page matching your query—within the first specified number of results, that is.

Usage Examples

Perhaps you're looking for bibliographic information for a famous person. You might find that a regular Google search doesn't net you with any more than a mention on a plethora of content-light web pages. Running the same query through this hack sometimes turns up pages with extensive bibliographies.

Maybe you're looking for information about a state. Try queries for the state name along with related information like motto, capitol, or state bird.

Hacking the Hack

This hack isn't so much hacked as tweaked. By changing the value assigned to the $loops variable in my $loops = 10;, you can alter the number of results the script checks before redirecting you to what it's found to be the largest. Remember, the maximum number of results is the number of loops multiplied by 10 results per loop. The default of 10 considers the top 100 results. A $loops value of 5 would consider only the top 50; 20, the top 200; and so forth.

Instant Messaging Google

#85 Accessing Google with AOL Instant Messenger.

If we're going to step out beyond the Google interface, why even bother to use the Web at all? The Google API makes it possible to access Google's information in many different ways. Googlematic makes it possible to query Google from the comfort of AOL Instant Messenger.

Here's how it works: send a message (a Google query) to the instant messenger buddy, "googlematic." Googlematic will message you back with the top result for your query. Reply with "More" and you'll get more results formatted as a numbered list. Figure 6-22 illustrates this.

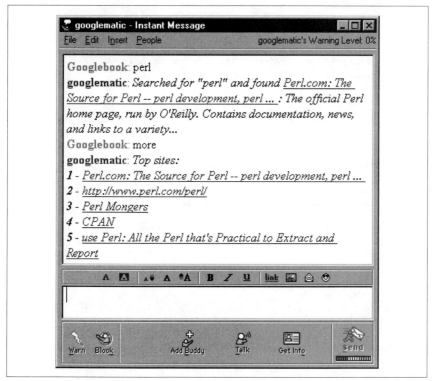

Figure 6-22. Query to googlematic through AOL Instant Messenger

Message with the number associated with a particular result for further details, as shown in Figure 6-23.

The Googlematic script, further instructions, and links to required modules may be found at *http://interconnected.org/googlematic/*.

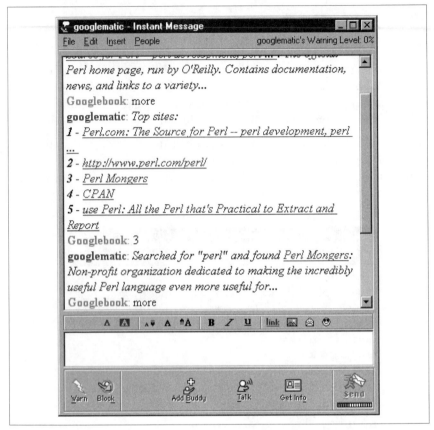

Figure 6-23. Requesting further detail for a googlematic result

The Code

```
#!/usr/bin/perl -w
# googlematic.pl
# Provides an AIM interface to Google, using the Google SOAP API
# and POE to manage all the activity.
#
# Usage
# ./googlematic.pl &
#
# Requirements
# - Googlematic::IM, Googlematic::Responder, Googlematic::Search,
#   which are all distributed with this script
# - CGI
# - HTML::Entities
# - Net::AOLIM
```

```
# - POE
# - SOAP::Lite
# - XML::Parser
#
# Essential configuration (below)
# - AIM username and password (used in Googlematic::IM)
# - Google API Developer Key (used in Googlematic::Search)
#
# Optional configuration (below)
# - Search request throttling (used in Googlematic::Search)
# - Limit of number of user sessions open (used in Googlematic::IM)
# - Time limit on a user session (used in Googlematic::Responder)
#
# (c) 2002 Matt Webb <matt@interconnected.org> All rights reserved

use strict;
use POE;

$| = 1;

use Googlematic::IM;
use Googlematic::Search;

# Configuration variables
$Googlematic::CONFIG = {
  aim_username => "xxxxxxx",
  aim_password => "xxxxxxx",
  google_key   => "your key goes here",
  searches_per_hour => "35", # the Google limit is 1000/day
  max_user_sessions => "5",
  user_session_timeout => "120" # in seconds
};

# There are two POE sessions:
# 1 - Googlematic::IM, known as 'im', takes care of the Instant Messager
#     connection and looks after user sessions (which are created as new
#     POE sessions, and known as Responders).
POE::Session->create(
  package_states => [
    Googlematic::IM => [
      '_start', 'login_aim', 'loop', 'spawner',
      'handler_aim', 'send', '_child', '_stop', 'proxy'
    ]
  ]
);

# 2 - Googlematic::Search, known as 'google', takes care the SOAP::Lite
#     object making the searches on Google. Requests to it are sent from the
#     individual Responders.
```

```
POE::Session->create(
  package_states => [
    Googlematic::Search => [
      '_start', 'loop', 'search', 'reset'
    ]
  ]
);

# Run the POE machine.
$poe_kernel->run( );

exit;
```

—*Tara Calishain and Matt Webb*

Google Pranks and Games
Hacks #86–92

The culture of the Internet has its own sense of humor—a Monty Python, Tom Lehrer, Terry Pratchett–esque sense of humor. It should come as no surprise, therefore, that Google and the Google API have been used for a variety of silly, weird, and just plain strange search applications.

Having fun with search engines isn't a new thing. See *http://www.cse.unsw.edu.au/~andrewm/misc/segames/* for a whole page of search engine games—including a search engine drinking game, believe it or not. Search engine users have also discovered that searching for certain phrases in Google can lead to interesting results. And earlier this year, the idea of "Google bombing"—groups linking to sites using pre-agreed upon descriptions to boost that site in Google's search results—became so prevalent that rumor has it that Google took steps to prevent the practice affecting the listings in its index.

If you've got a sense of humor but no sense of programming, don't worry; you can pull some decent pranks and have a little fun without writing a line of code. Of course, if you're using the Google API, you've the programming power to add punch and complexity to your pranks and pratfalls.

Let's have a little fun!

The No-Result Search (Prank)

Want to prank your friends using Google? These techniques that will make sure your search has no results.

Ah, pranking with a search engine. Nothing quite so much fun as befuddling your friends with some utterly weird search results. One fun and easy thing to do is make a search result that one would think is wildly popular and set it up so it has no results.

There are a couple ways you can set up the prank. The first way is to hack the URL. The second is to create a search that will never have a result.

Hacking the URL

To hack a URL so a query has no results, just add the following code to the end of a URL:

```
&num=-1
```

Even if a `num` modifer already exists in the URL, adding another to the end overrides the first value. The &num=-1 switch informs Google that you want −1 results. Because it's not possible to return −1 results, Google will provide the next best thing: none.

Hacking the Search

Maybe you won't have a chance to hack the URL, and you'll need to hack the search instead. You can do that by creating a search with the special search codes that can't have any results.

One easy way to create a no-result query is to add any two `site:` syntaxes to it:

```
site:org site:com
```

Google operates with a default `AND`; a single page in Google's index can't be simultaneously found from both the *.org* and *.com* domains.

Or you can search for a site you know doesn't exist:

```
site:microsoft
```

While `site:microsoft.com` is a valid search for the site syntax, `microsoft` by itself (without the *.com* suffix) isn't. So a query like `windows site:microsoft` would get you zero results.

You can also fool Google by specifying that something must be included and not included at the sime time. This works best with really long queries so that the query visible from the query box looks normal. Try this one:

```
microsoft windows programming developer source -windows
```

The only problem is that Google echoes the search terms on its result pages, so if someone's paying attention, none of these tricks will work. A word to the wise: try only on your less observant friends.

Finally, if the person you're pranking doesn't know much about the Google date-range search syntax, you can also fake a search with a bogus date range. Use a five-digit number for the code so it looks semi-authentic, but it still won't give you any search results.

```
microsoft daterange:99991-99992
```

Delivering the Prank

There are three ways to deliver the prank to the prankee. The first way is in person. If you're working on a computer with them, slip in a couple of these searches, and then point confused to the Google search page that shows no results for Perl.

The second way is to send a search query to the prankee. The best way to do this is to use a special syntax that doesn't really work, like site:microsoft.

And the third way is to send an URL to the prankee. Google search URLs tend to be long, so you might want to use one of the URL-shortening services [Hack #38] before you send the URL to your prankee. And if you do shorten the URL, use the opportunity to put a couple of the more elaborate special syntax hacks in it, like site:com site:org, or a fake date-range search.

HACK #87 Google Whacking

With over 2 billion pages in its index, is it possible to get only one result for a search?

With an index of over 2 billion pages, Google attracts lots of interest from searchers. New methods of searching are tested, new ways of classifying information are explored, new games are invented.

New games are invented? Well, yes, actually. This *is* the Internet, after all.

The term "Google whacking" was coined by Gary Stock. The idea is to find a two-word query that has only one result. The two words may not be enclosed in quotes (that's too easy), and the words must be found in Google's own dictionary (no proper names, made-up words, etc). If the one result comes from a word list, such as a glossary or dictionary, the whack is disqualified.

If you manage a Google whack—and its harder than it sounds—be sure to list your find on the official Whack Stack (*http://www.googlewhack.com/*). Perusing the most recent 2,000 whacks is highly recommended if your brain is stuck and you need a little inspiration in your research. Examples include "endoscopy cudgels," "nebbish orthodontia," and "peccable oink."

Are you stuck for a Google whack query? This hack should help. It takes a random word from each of two "word of the day" sites and queries Google in hopes of a Google whack (or as experienced players would say, "To see if they make a whack").

```
#!/usr/local/bin/perl
# google_whack.pl
# An automated Google whacker.
# Usage: perl google_whack.pl
```

```perl
# Your Google API developer's key
my $google_key='insert key here';

# Location of the GoogleSearch WSDL file
my $google_wdsl = "./GoogleSearch.wsdl";

use strict;

# Use the SOAP::Lite and LWP::Simple Perl modules
use SOAP::Lite;
use LWP::Simple;

# Generate some random numbers to be used as dates for choosing
# random word one.
srand();
my $year  = int( rand(2) ) + 2000;
my $month = int( rand(12) ) + 1;
$month < 10 and $month = "0$month";
my $day = int( rand(28) ) +1;
$day < 10 and $day = "0$day";

# Pulling our first random word from Dictionary.com
my $whackone =
  get("http://www.dictionary.com/wordoftheday/archive/$year/$month/$day.
html")
  or die "Couldn't get whack word 1: $!";
($whackone) =
  ($whackone =~ /<TITLE>Dictionary.com\/Word of the Day: (.*)<\/TITLE>/i);

# Generate a new year between 1997 and 2000 for choosing
# random word two
srand();
$year  = int( rand(5) ) + 1997;

# Pulling our second random word from the now defunct Maven's
# Word of the Day (thank goodness for archives)
my $whacktwo =
  get("http://www.randomhouse.com/wotd/index.pperl?date=$year$month$day")
  or die "Couldn't get whack word 2:: $!";
($whacktwo) = ($whacktwo =~ !m<h2><B>(.*)</b></h2>!i);

# Build our query out of the two random words
my $query = "$whackone $whacktwo";

# Create a new SOAP::Lite instance, feeding it GoogleSearch.wsdl
my $google_search = SOAP::Lite->service("file:$google_wdsl");

# Query Google
my $results = $google_search ->
    doGoogleSearch(
      $google_key, $query, 0, 10, "false", "",  "false",
      "", "latin1", "latin1"
    );
```

```
# A single result means a possible Google whack
if ($results->{'estimatedTotalResultsCount'} == 1) {
  my $result = $results->{'resultElements'}->[0];
  print
    join "\n",
      "Probable Google whack for $query",
      "Title: " . $result->{title}||'no title',
      "URL: $result->{URL}",
      "Snippet: " . $result->{snippet}||'no title',
      "\n";
}

# Anything else is Google jack
else {
  print "Google jack for $query, with " .
    $results->{'estimatedTotalResultsCount'}  . " results\n";
}
```

Running the Hack

Simply call the script on the command line with no arguments at all.

The Results

Here's a sample Google whack session. Told you it was hard!

```
% perl google_whack.pl Google jack for wan palooka, with 48 results
% perl google_whack.pl Google jack for hebetude Maisie, with 0 results
% perl google_whack.pl Google jack for lexicography doldrums,
  with 90 results
% perl google_whack.pl Google jack for foundling hokey,
  with 12 results
% perl google_whack.pl Google jack for cataract pettifogger,
  with 6 results
...
```

HACK
#88 GooPoetry

Google's got the soul of a poet, or at least knows how to toss a good word
salad.

Perhaps you didn't realize it, but with a little help from a hack, Google can
churn out poetry that will bring a tear to your eye. Okay, perhaps not. But
Google sure can mix a mean word salad.

This hack takes a query and uses random words from the titles returned by
the query to spit out a poem of random length. The user can specify a poetry
"flavor," adding words to the array to be used. The flavors in this version of
the hack include: hippie, beatnik, and Swedish Chef. Here's a paean to the
O'Reilly Camel Book, flavored by Shakespeare:

```
-- 3rd alas! to the
O'Reilly thee |
2nd Camel Book
Catalog: | hither Book Welcome oreilly.com Edition --
2000 Programming The
-- Dictionary] Book sirrah alas!
-- Perl 2000 2nd
2000 node: Camel Dictionary] Better node: Jargon oreilly.com
thee thee -- oreilly.com Programming 2nd oreilly.com
```

The Code

```perl
#!/usr/local/bin/perl
# goopoetry.cgi
# Generates a mean word salad.
# goopoetry.cgi is called as a CGI with form input

# Your Google API developer's key
my $google_key='insert key here';

# Location of the GoogleSearch WSDL file
my $google_wdsl = "./GoogleSearch.wsdl";

# Number of lines per poem
my $numlines = 10;

# Number of words per line
my $numwords = 6;

use strict;

use SOAP::Lite;
use CGI qw/:standard/;

my $flavors = {
  'Hippie' => ['wow', 'groovy man!', 'far out!', 'Right on!',
    'funky', 'outta sight', 'Like,','peace out!',
    'munchies'],
  'Beatnik' => ['daddy-o', 'long gone', 'hepcat', 'jazzy',
    'cool', 'hip','cool','jazzman','zoot'],
  'Shakespeare' => ['thee', 'hark!', 'forsooth,', 'alas!', 'sirrah',
    'hither', 'hence'],
  'Swedish Chef' => ['bork bork bork!', 'hmdordeborkbork', 'BORK!',
    'hrm de hr', 'bork?', 'hur chikee chikee'],
  'Default' => ['...', '!', '(?)', '---']
};

print
  header(),
  start_html("GooPoetry"),
  h1("GooPoetry"),
  start_form(-method=>'GET'),
```

```
     'Query: ', textfield(-name=>'query'),
     br(),
     'Flavor: ', popup_menu(
        -name=>'flavor', -values=>[keys %$flavors], -default=>'Default'
     ),
     br(),
     submit(-name=>'submit', -value=>'Toss that Word Salad'),
     end_form(), p();

  if (param('flavor')) {
     my $google_search = SOAP::Lite->service("file:$google_wdsl");

     # Create an array for the random words
     my @words;
     # Mix in the flavored words
     push @words, @{$flavors->{param('flavor')}};

     # Query Google
     my $results = $google_search ->
        doGoogleSearch(
          $google_key, param('query'), 0, 10, "false", "", "false",
          "", "latin1", "latin1"
        );

     # Glean and clean title words from results
     foreach my $result (@{$results->{'resultElements'}}) {
        $result->{title} =~ s!\n!!g; # drop spurious newlines
        $result->{title} =~ s!!!g; # drop all HTML tags
        push @words, split /\s+/, $result->{title};
     }

     for (my $l = 0; $l <= $numlines; $l++) {
        # Randomly decide the number of words in this sentence
        for (my $w = 0; $w <= int(rand($numwords))+3; $w++) {
          print lc $words[rand(scalar @words)] . ' ';
        }
        print "";
     }
  }
}
```

Running the Hack

Point your browser at the CGI script, fill out the form, and click the "Toss that Word Salad" button. Figure 7-1 shows an example.

Hacking the Hack

You may have noticed that this code does not have an error message, if the query submitted does not get any results. That's on purpose; because there is always a "flavor" array pushed into the "words" array, even a query that gets no results will create a poem. For example, if you searched for an query

---

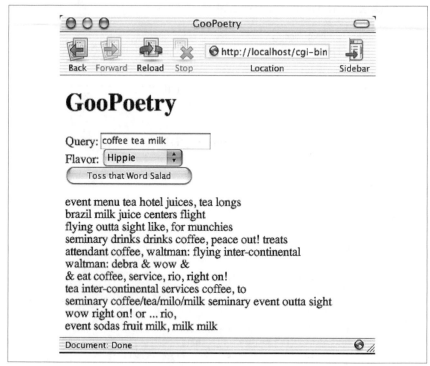

Figure 7-1. Google-generated poetry

that got no results, and were using the "beatnik" flavor, you'd get a poem with lines like this:

```
cool jazzy
long gone jazzman long gone hepcat zoot
cool zoot zoot jazzman hepcat jazzman zoot long gone
```

As you can see, it's just words from the beatnik flavor repeated over and over, as there's nothing else in the @words array.

You can add flavors to your heart's content. Simply add another entry in the $flavors data structure. Say, for instance, you wanted to add a "Confused" flavor; you'd add the following bolded line just after the opening my $flavors = {:

```
my $flavors = {
  'Confused' => ['huh?', 'duh', 'what?', 'say again?',
    'do what now?', 'wubba?'],
  'Hippie' => ['wow', 'groovy man!', 'far out!', 'Right on!',
    'funky', 'outta sight', 'Like,','peace out!',
    'munchies'],
  'Beatnik' => ['daddy-o', 'long gone', 'hepcat', 'jazzy',
    'cool', 'hip','cool','jazzman','zoot'],
```

```
'Shakespeare' => ['thee', 'hark!', 'forsooth,', 'alas!', 'sirrah',
  'hither', 'hence'],
'Swedish Chef' => ['bork bork bork!', 'hmdordeborkbork', 'BORK!',
  'hrm de hr', 'bork?', 'hur chikee chikee'],
'Default' => ['...', '!', '(?)', '---']
};
```

That's all there is to it. You've successfully added a new flavor to the hack.

You can also change the number of lines and maximum words per line of the generated poem by changing the values of $numlines and $numwords, respectively. I did find, however, that the defaults are pretty optimal for creating interesting "poetry"; less than 10 lines and there wasn't much flavor, more than 10 and it repeated itself far too often.

Creating Google Art

#89

Save a Usenet news post for later searching and viewing as a work of art.

Google's a poet, a chef, an oracle, not to mention a great artist. Who knew? With a little help from you, Google can be the next Picasso.

Okay, Whistler.

Okay, Billy from Mrs. Miller's third grade class.

When you search for something on Google Groups, the words for which you searched are highlighted in glorious primary colors within any posts you peruse. The main Google web search does this as well but only on the cached version of a web page. Some people far more artistically inclined with far more time on their hands than I ran with this idea, manipulating the highlights to create works of art. For example, there's a portrait of Lincoln at *http://groups.google.com/groups?q=aa+ae+ao+ea+ee+eo+oa+oe&selm=3e0d404c.* *0207241043.539ae9f7%40posting.google.com* and Bart Simpson at *http://groups.google.com/groups?q=aa+ae+ao+ea+ee+eo&selm=3e0d404c.* *0207261202.a0246c1%40posting.google.com.*

But it's not simply a matter of pushing a picture into Google Groups. What's involved is creating a text-based image on a grid, populating each square with a two-letter code signifying a color from the Google syntax highlighting palette. You need to post that "image" to a Usenet newsgroup, wait until it shows up in Google Groups, and then search for it using some fancy URL footwork.

At least that's how it was done...

Making Your Own Art

Creating your own Google Groups art is as simple as drawing a picture, thanks to the Google Art Creator (*http://www.kryogenix.org/code/browser/aqgoogle/*).

If you've ever used even the most primitive of computer drawing applications (e.g., MacPaint on Macintosh or Paint on Windows), you'll find the tool a snap. Click on the color you want to use, then click on the square you want to paint. Use white to erase any errors you make. My masterpiece is shown in Figure 7-2.

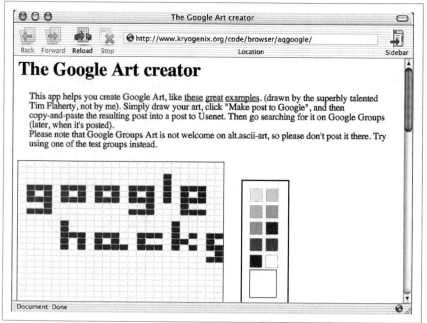

Figure 7-2. Art made using Google Art Creator

Once you've put the finishing touches on your masterpiece, name it by putting some keywords into the provided query box and click the "Make post to Google" button. You're not actually posting anything, mind you; instead, the tool will generate a post that you can copy and paste to Google, as shown in Figure 7-3.

Posting is the one bit of the process you still have to do manually. Fire up your favorite Usenet newsreader or make use of Google Groups' posting functionality. Whatever you do, don't post to just any group; use one of the test groups. There's a huge hierarchy under alt.test to choose from.

Wait.

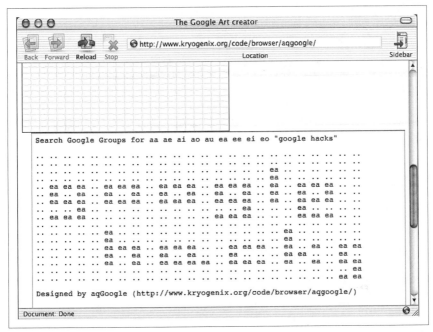

Figure 7-3. Art post generated by Google

Notice that the Google Art Creator not only provides the post itself, but also what to search for in Google Groups. In my case, that's aa ae ai ao au ea ee ei eo "google hacks". If all goes to plan, with a little patience and perseverance, my artwork should be on show in Google Groups within a day or so.

HACK #90 Google Bounce

You can get random results from Google with a database of words and random numbers. Why not try a Google Bounce?

The Google Bounce accepts a query word from the user and does a search. It pulls a random title word from one of the search results and searches for that word. It does this a random number of times. In the end, it'll list the top 10 results for the final query. There's a filter to try to make sure that common Google "stop words" (e.g., the, is, a) are removed from the query.

The Code

```
#!/usr/local/bin/perl
# Version 1.3, 7/29/2002
# googlebounce.cgi
# Bounce around from a user-specified query to a random set
# of results.
```

```
# googlebounce.cgi is called as a CGI with form input

use vars qw/$google_key $google_wsdl $max_bounces $current_bounce/;

# Your Google API developer's key
$google_key='insert key here';

# Location of the GoogleSearch WSDL file
$google_wdsl = "./GoogleSearch.wsdl";

use SOAP::Lite;

use LWP::Simple qw/get/;
use CGI qw/:standard/;

print
  header(),
  start_html("GoogleBounce"),
  h1("GoogleBounce"),
  start_form(-method=>'GET'),
  'Query: ', textfield(-name=>'query'),
  '   ',
  submit(-name=>'submit', -value=>'Search'),
  end_form(), p();

print "\n"x4;

if (param('query')) {
  $|++; # turn off buffering

  print h3("Progress Report...");

  # Choose a random number of bounces
  $max_bounces = int(rand(5))+2;

  # Set the counter to bounce number 1
  $current_bounce = 1;
  bounce(param('query'));
}

sub bounce {
  my($query) = @_;
  my $new_query;

  # Filter query for stopwords
  my $stopwords_regex = join '|', qw/the and -- - 1 www com of is a/;

  #$query =~ s/$stopwords_regex//gi;

  # Choose a random number of results
  my $max_results = int(rand(9))+2;

  my $google_search  = SOAP::Lite->service("file:$google_wdsl");
```

```
my $results = $google_search ->
  doGoogleSearch(
    $google_key, $query, 0, $max_results,
    "false", "",  "false", "", "latin1", "latin1"
  );

# Progress Report
print
  join br( )."\n",
    "<p>Bounce $current_bounce of $max_bounces",
    "Searching for:$query",
    "Asking for $max_results results",
    "Got " . scalar @{$results->{resultElements}}  . " results</p>";

my $new_query;
for (my $ii = $#{$results->{resultElements}}; $ii >= 0; $ii--) {
  $new_query = $results->{resultElements}->[$ii]->{title};
  $new_query  =~ s!<.+?>!!g; # drop all HTML tags
  $new_query =~ /\w/ and last;
}

# If there's a new query and  we're not overbounced, bounce again
++$current_bounce <= $max_bounces and
  $new_query =~ /\w/ and
    $new_result = bounce($new_query) and
      return $new_result;

# Otherwise, print out the top 10 for the final query
print h3("Final Results...");

my $google_search = SOAP::Lite->service("file:$google_wdsl");

my $results = $google_search ->
  doGoogleSearch(
    $google_key, $query, 0, 10,
    "false", "",  "false", "", "latin1", "latin1"
  );

@{$results->{'resultElements'}} or print "None";

foreach (@{$results->{'resultElements'}}) {
  print p(
    b($_->{title}||'no title'), br( ),
    a({href=>$_->{URL}}, $_->{URL}), br( ),
    i($_->{snippet}||'no snippet')
  );
}

print end_html( );
exit;
}
```

Figure 7-4 shows the results.

GoogleBounce

Query: [perl]   [Search]

Progress Report...

Bounce 1 of 6
Searching for perl
Asking for 6 results
Got 6 results

Bounce 2 of 6
Searching for perl.com: What's New in Perlland? [Jul. 25, 1999]
Asking for 5 results
Got 5 results

Bounce 3 of 6
Searching for Search Results for Portable Home Bars
Asking for 4 results
Got 4 results

Bounce 4 of 6
Searching for Compare Products and Stores - Ratings and Prices for Luxury Home ...
Asking for 10 results
Got 10 results

Figure 7-4. Google Bounce results for perl

See Also

* Getting Random Results (On Purpose) **[Hack #73]**

Google Mirror
#91   If you want a different perspective on Google, check out the Google Mirror.

In the Internet sense, a "mirror" is a site that copies the content of another site. But there's a Google mirror that is a mirror in the traditional sense; it is the image of Google, backward.

Antoni Chan's Google Mirror (*http://www.alltooflat.com/geeky/elgoog/*), shown in Figure 7-5, copies Google's main page with everything mirror-imaged, including the graphic. It's a working search engine, too—you'll need to enter your search backward too ;-). If you want to find "fred," for example, you need to search for `derf`. Search results are mirrored as well, naturally.

In fact, just about every page you can visit on the regular Google site is mirrored here. You can read mirrored copies of Google's press releases, jobs available (Figure 7-6), even backward copies of the official logos.

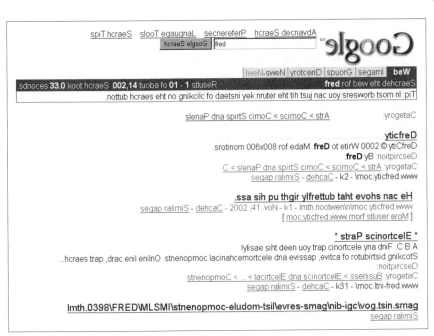

Figure 7-5. Antoni Chan's Google Mirror

Figure 7-6. Google's job page viewed through Google Mirror

The only thing I couldn't do with the Google Mirror site was set the language options to something besides English. It looks as if the Google Mirror interface can't accept the cookies Google requires to set language preferences. I figured that if reading English backwards was fun, reading "Bork Bork Bork!" (the Swedish Chef interface) would have been a howl!

HACK #92   Finding Recipes

Let the Google API transform those random ingredients in your fridge into a wonderful dinner.

Google can help you find news, catalogs, discussions, web pages, and so much more—and it can also help you figure out what to have for dinner tonight!

This hack uses the Google API to help you transform those random ingredients in your fridge into a wonderful dinner. Well, you do have to do some of the work. But it all starts with this hack.

Using the Hack

This hack comes with a built-in form that calls the query and the recipe type, so there's no need to set up a separate form.

```perl
#!/usr/local/bin/perl
# goocook.cgi
# Finding recipes with google
# goocook.cgi is called as a CGI with form input

# Your Google API developer's key
my $google_key='insert key here';

# Location of the GoogleSearch WSDL file
my $google_wdsl = "./GoogleSearch.wsdl";

use SOAP::Lite;
use CGI qw/:standard/;

my %recipe_types = (
  "General"             => "site:allrecipes.com | site:cooking.com | site:
epicurious.com | site:recipesource.com",
  "Vegetarian/Vegan"    => "site:fatfree.com | inurl:veganmania | inurl:
vegetarianrecipe | inurl:veggiefiles",
  "Wordwide Cuisine" => "site:Britannia.org | inurl:thegutsygourmet |
inurl:simpleinternet | inurl:soupsong"
);

print
  header(),
```

```
    start_html("GooCook"),
    h1("GooCook"),
    start_form(-method=>'GET'),
    'Ingredients: ', textfield(-name=>'ingredients'),
    br(),
    'Recipe Type: ', popup_menu(-name=>'recipe_type',
      -values=>[keys %recipe_types], -default=>'General'),
    br(),
    submit(-name=>'submit', -value=>"Get Cookin'!"),
    submit(-name=>'reset', -value=>"Start Over"),
    end_form(), p();

  if (param('ingredients')) {
    my $google_search  = SOAP::Lite->service("file:$google_wdsl");
    my $results = $google_search ->
      doGoogleSearch(
        $google_key,
        param('ingredients') . " " . $recipe_types{param('recipe_type')},
        0, 10, "false", "",  "false", "", "latin1", "latin1"
      );

    @{$results->{'resultElements'}} or print "None";
    foreach (@{$results->{'resultElements'}}) {
      print p(
        b($_->{title}||'no title'), br(),
        a({href=>$_->{URL}}, $_->{URL}), br(),
        i($_->{snippet}||'no snippet')
      );
    }
  }

  print end_html();
```

Hacking the Hack

Of course the most obvious way to hack this hack is to add new recipe options to it. That involves first finding new recipe sites, and then adding them to the hack.

Finding New Recipe Domains

Adding new recipe sites entails finding the domains you want to search. Use the cooking section of Google's Directory to find recipes; start with recipe collections at *http://directory.google.com/Top/Home/Cooking/Recipe_Collections/*.

From here, find what you want and build it into a query supplement like the one in the form, surrounded by parens with each item separated by a |. Remember, using the site: syntax means you'll be searching for an entire domain. So if you find a great recipe site at *http://www.geocities.com/ reallygreat/food/recipes/*, don't use the site: syntax to search it, use the inurl: search instead (inurl:geocities.com/reallygreat/food/recipes). Just remember that an addition like this counts heavily against your ten-word query limit.

Let's take an example. The Cookbook section of the Google directory has a Seafood section with several sites. Let's pull five examples out of that and make it a query supplement. Here's what one could look like:

```
(site:simplyseafood.com | site:baycooking.com | site:coastangler.com | site:
welovefish.com | site:sea-ex.com)
```

Next, test the query supplement in Google by adding a query term to it and running it as a search, for example:

```
salmon (site:simplyseafood.com | site:baycooking.com | site:coastangler.com
| site:welovefish.com | site:sea-ex.com)
```

Run a few different queries with a few different query words (salmon, scallops, whatever) and make sure that you're getting a decent number of results. Once you're confident that you're getting a good selection of recipes, you'll need to add this new option to the hack. You'll need to add it to this part of the code:

```
my %recipe_types = (
    "General"              => "site:allrecipes.com | site:cooking.com | site:
epicurious.com | site:recipesource.com",
    "Vegetarian/Vegan"  => "site:fatfree.com | inurl:veganmania | inurl:
vegetarianrecipe | inurl:veggiefiles",
    "Wordwide Cuisine" => "site:Britannia.org | inurl:thegutsygourmet |
inurl:simpleinternet | inurl:soupsong"
);
```

Simply add the name you want to call the option, =>, and the search string. Make sure you add it before closed parantheses and the semicolon.

```
my %recipe_types = (
    "General"              => "site:allrecipes.com | site:cooking.com | site:
epicurious.com | site:recipesource.com",
    "Vegetarian/Vegan"  => "site:fatfree.com | inurl:veganmania | inurl:
vegetarianrecipe | inurl:veggiefiles",
    "Wordwide Cuisine" => "site:Britannia.org | inurl:thegutsygourmet |
inurl:simpleinternet | inurl:soupsong"

    "Seafood" => "site:simplyseafood.com | site:baycooking.com | site:
coastangler.com | site:welovefish.com | site:sea-ex.com"

);
```

You can add as many search sets as you want to the hack. You may want to add Chinese Cooking, Desserts, Soups, Salads, or any number of other options.

—*Tara Calishain and Judy Hourihan*

## CHAPTER EIGHT

The Webmaster Side of Google

Hacks #93–100

You might be wondering why there's a Google for webmasters section in this book. After all, you're learning how to make the most out of Google, not how to be a webmaster, right?

Even if you're not the owner of a commercial web site, and even if you're not looking for as much search engine traffic as possible, it's critical that you understand how Google treats search engines, if you want to get any Google traffic at all.

Google's Preeminence

When the Web was younger, the search engine field was all but wide open. There were lots of major search engines, including: AltaVista, Excite, Hot-Bot, and Webcrawler. This proliferation of search engines had both its advantages and disadvantages. One disadvantage was that you had to make sure you had submitted to several different places. One advantage was that you had several inflows of search engine spawned trafffic.

As the number of search engines dwindle, Google's index (and influence) is growing. You don't have to worry so much about submitting to different places, but you have to be aware of Google at all times.

Google's Importance to Webmasters

But isn't Google just a search engine web site like any other? Actually, its reach is far greater than that. Google partners with other sites to use the Google index results, including the likes of heavyweight properties AOL and Yahoo!. Not to mention the multitude of sites out there making use of the Google API. So when you think about potential visitors from Google's search results, you have to think beyond traditional search site borders.

It's becoming ever more important what Google thinks of your site. That means you're going to be sure that your site abides by the Google rules or risk not being picked up. If you're very concerned about search engine traffic, you're going to have to make sure that your site is optimized for luring in Google's spiders and being indexed in an effective manner. And if you're concerned that Google should *not* index some parts of your site, you need to understand the ins and outs of configuring your *robots.txt* file to reflect your preferences.

The Mysterious PageRank

You'll hear a lot of people talk about Google's PageRank, bragging about attaining the misty heights of rank seven or eight, talking in hushed tones of sites that have achived nine or ten. PageRanks range from 0 (sites that haven't been ranked or have been penalized) to 10 (reserved only for the most popular sites like Yahoo! and Google itself). The only place where you can actually see what PageRank a given URL has is from the Google Toolbar [Hack #24], though you can get some idea of popularity from the Google Directory. Listings in the Google Directory contain a green bar next to them that allow you to give a good idea of the listing's popularity without having an exact number.

Google has never provided the entire formula for their PageRank, so all you'll find in this book is conjecture. And it wouldn't surprise me to learn that it's changing all the time; as millions of people try myriad things to make sure their pages rank better, Google has to take these efforts into account and (sometimes) reacted against them.

Why is PageRank so important? Because Google uses that as one aspect of determining how a given URL will rank among millions of possible search results, but that's only one aspect. The other aspects are determined via Google's ranking algorithm.

The Equally Mysterious Algorithm

If you thought Google was close-mouthed about how it determine's PageRank, it's an absolute oyster when it comes to the ranking algorithm, the way that Google determines the order of search results. The articles in this book can give you some ideas, but again it's conjecture and again it's constantly changing. Your best bet is to create a content-rich web site and update it often. Google appreciates good content.

Of course, getting listed in Google's index is not the only way to tell visitors about your site. You also have the option to advertise on Google.

Google's Ad Programs

If the picture that arises when you think of Internet advertising involves people in Armani suits pitchforking huge mounds of money into bank vaults, think again. Huge ad budgets are so 1999. Google's AdWords programs allow even small advertisers to do keyword-based advertising on Google's search results (or even on the keyword results of Google's partner sites, if they wish). In this section, Andrew Goodman chimes in to gives some tips on how to make the most of your Google Adwords program, and we provide a scraper that'll help you save AdWords on results pages if you're doing a little research.

Keeping Up with Google's Changes

With Google having such a leading position in the search engine world, and so many webmasters looking to Google for traffic, you might guess that there's a lot of discussion about Google in various places around the Web. And you'd be right! My favorite place for Google news and gossip is Webmaster World. It's not often that you can put the words "civilized" and "online forums" right next to each other, but I'm doing it now. Discourse on this site is friendly, informative, and generally flame free. I have learned a lot from this site.

In a Word: Relax

One of the things I've learned is that a lot of people spend a lot of time worrying about how Google works, and further, they worry about how they can get the highest possible ranking.

I can appreciate their worry, because search engine traffic means a lot to an online business. But for the rest of us, we should just relax. As long as we concentrate on good content that's good for visitors (and not just spiders), Google's ranking algorithms will appreciate our sites.

HACK
#93

A Webmaster's Introduction to Google
Steps to take for optimal Google indexing of your site.

The cornerstone of any good search engine is highly relevant results. Google's unprecedented success has been due to its uncanny ability to match quality information with a user's search terms. The core of Google's search results are based upon a patented algorithm called PageRank.

There is an entire industry focused on getting sites listed near the top of search engines. Google has proven to be the toughest search engine for a site to do well on. Even so, it isn't all that difficult for a new web site to get listed and begin receiving some traffic from Google.

It can be a daunting task to learn the ins and outs of getting your site listed with any search engine. There is a vast array of information about search engines on the Web, and not all of it is useful or proper. This discussion of getting your site into the Google database focuses on long term techniques for successfully promoting your site through Google. It will stay well away from some of the common misconceptions and problems that a new site owner faces.

Search Engine Basics

When you type in a search term at a search engine, it looks up potential matches in its database. It then presents the best web page matches first. How those web pages get into the database, and consequently, how you can get yours in there too, is a three step process:

1. A search engine visits a site with an automated program called a spider (sometimes they're also called robots). A spider is just a program similar to a web browser that downloads your site's pages. It doesn't actually display the page anywhere, it just downloads the page data.

2. After the spider has acquired the page, the search engine passes the page to a program called an indexer. An indexer is another robotic program that extracts most of the visible portions of the page. The indexer also analyzes the page for keywords, the title, links, and other important information contained in the code.

3. The search engine adds your site to its database and makes it available to searchers. The greatest difference between search engines is in this final step where rankings or results positions under a particular keyword are determined.

Submitting Your Site to Google

For the site owner, the first step is to get your pages listed in the database. There are two ways to get added. The first is direct submission of your site's URL to Google via its add URL or Submission page. To counter programmed robots, search engines routinely move submission pages around on their sites. You can currently find Google's submission page linked from their Help pages or Webmaster Info pages (*http://www.google.com/addurl.html*).

Just visit the add URL page and enter the main index page for your site into the Google submission page form, and press submit. Google's spider (called

GoogleBot) will visit your page usually within four weeks. The spider will traverse all pages on your site and add them to its index. Within eight weeks, you should be able to find your site listed in Google.

The second way to get your site listed in Google is to let Google find you. It does this based upon links that may be pointing to your site. Once Google-Bot finds a link to your site from a page it already has in its index, it will visit your site.

Google has been updating its database on a monthly basis for three years. It sends its spider out in crawler mode once a month too. Crawler mode is a special mode for a spider when it traverses or *crawls* the entire Web. As it runs into links to pages, it then indexes those pages in a never ending attempt to download all the pages it can. Once your pages are listed in Google, they are revisited and updated on a monthly basis. If you frequently update your content, Google may index your search terms more often.

Once you are indexed and listed in Google, the next natural question for a site owner is, "How can I rank better under my applicable search terms?"

The Search Engine Optimization Template

This is my general recipe for the ubiquitous Google. It is generic enough that it works well everywhere. It's as close as I have come to a "one-size-fits-all" SEO—that's Search Engine Optimization—template.

Use your targeted keyword phrase:

- In META keywords. It's not necessary for Google, but a good habit. Keep your META keywords short (128 characters max, or 10).
- In META description. Keep keyword close to the left but in a full sentence.
- In the title at the far left but possibly not as the first word.
- In the top portion of the page in first sentence of first full bodied paragraph (plain text: no bold, no italic, no style).
- In an H3 or larger heading.
- In bold—second paragraph if possible and anywhere but the first usage on page.
- In italic—anywhere but the first usage.
- In subscript/superscript.
- In URL (directory name, filename, or domain name). Do not duplicate the keyword in the URL.
- In an image filename used on the page.

- In ALT tag of that previous image mentioned.
- In the title attribute of that image.
- In link text to another site.
- In an internal link's text.
- In title attribute of all links targeted in and out of page.
- In the filename of your external CSS (Cascading Style Sheet) or Java-Script file.
- In an inbound link on site (preferably from your home page).
- In an inbound link from off site (if possible).
- In a link to a site that has a PageRank of 8 or better.

Other search engine optimization things to consider include:

- Use "last modified" headers if you can.
- Validate that HTML. Some feel Google's parser has become stricter at parsing instead of milder. It will miss an entire page because of a few simple errors—we have tested this in depth.
- Use an HTML template throughout your site. Google can spot the template and parse it off. (Of course, this also means they are pretty good a spotting duplicate content.)
- Keep the page as *.html* or *.htm* extension. Any dynamic extension is a risk.
- Keep the HTML below 20K. 5–15K is the ideal range.
- Keep the ratio of text to HTML very high. Text should outweigh HTML by significant amounts.
- Double check your page in Netscape, Opera, and IE. Use Lynx if you have it.
- Use only raw HREFs for links. Keep JavaScript far, far away from links. The simpler the link code the better.
- The traffic comes when you figure out that 1 referral a day to 10 pages is better than 10 referrals a day to 1 page.
- Don't assume that keywords in your site's navigation template will be worth anything at all. Google looks for full sentences and paragraphs. Keywords just laying around orphaned on the page are not worth as much as when used in a sentence.

—Brett Tabke

Generating Google AdWords

You've written the copy and you've planned the budget. Now, what keywords are you going to use for your ad?

You've read about it and you've thought about it and you're ready to buy one of Google's AdWords. You've even got your copy together and you feel pretty confident about it. You've only got one problem now: figuring out your keywords, the search words that will trigger your AdWord to appear.

You're probably buying into the AdWords program on a budget, and you definitely want to make every penny count. Choosing the right keywords means that your ad will have a higher clickthrough. Thankfully, the Google AdWords program allows you to do a lot of tweaking, so if your first choices don't work, experiment, test, and test some more!

Choosing AdWords

So where do you get the search keywords for your ad? There are four places that might help you find them:

Log files

> Examine your site's log files. How are people finding your site now? What words are they using? What search engines are they using? Are the words they're using too general to be used for AdWords? If you look at your log files, you can get an idea of how people who are interested in your content are finding your site. (If they weren't interested in your content, why would they visit?)

Examine your own site

> If you have an internal search engine, check its logs. What are people searching for once they get to your site? Are there any common misspellings that you could use as an AdWord? Are there any common phrases you could use?

Brainstorm

> What do people think of when they look at your site? What keywords do you want them to think of? Brainstorm about the product that's most closely associated with your site. What words come up?

> Imagine someone goes to a store and asks about your products. How are they going to ask? What words would they use? Consider all the different ways someone could look for or ask about your product or service, and then consider if there's a set of words or a phrase that pops up over and over again.

Glossaries

If you've brainstormed until wax dribbles out your ears but you're no closer to coming up with words relevant to your site or product, visit some online glossaries to jog your brain. The Glossarist (*http://www.glossarist.com*) links to hundreds of glossaries on hundreds of different subjects. Check and see if they have a glossary relevant to your product or service, and see if you can pull some words from there.

Exploring Your Competitors' AdWords

Once you've got a reasonable list of potential keywords for your ad, take them and run them in the Google search engine. Google rotates advertisements based on the spending cap for each campaign, so even after running a search three or four times you may see different advertisements each time. Use the AdWords scraper to save these ads to a file and review them later.

If you find a potential keyword that apparently contains no advertisements, make a note. When you're ready to buy an AdWord, you'll have to check its frequency; it might not be searched often enough to be a lucrative keyword for you. But if it is, you'll found a potential advertising spot with no other ads competing for searchers' attention.

See Also

- Scraping Google AdWords [Hack #45]
- Getting the Most out of AdWords [Hack #99]

HACK #95 Inside the PageRank Algorithm

Delving into the inner-workings of Google PageRank algorithm and how it affects results.

What Is PageRank?

PageRank is the algorithm used by the Google search engine, originally formulated by Sergey Brin and Larry Page in their paper "The Anatomy of a Large-Scale Hypertextual Web Search Engine."

It is based on the premise, prevalent in the world of academia, that the importance of a research paper can be judged by the number of citations the paper has from other research papers. Brin and Page have simply transferred this premise to its web equivalent: the importance of a web page can be judged by the number of hyperlinks pointing to it from other web pages.

So What Is the Algorithm?

It may look daunting to nonmathematicians, but the PageRank algorithm is in fact elegantly simple and is calculated as follows:

$$PR(A) = (1-d) + d\left(\frac{PR(T1)}{C(T1)} + \dots + \frac{PR(Tn)}{C(Tn)}\right)$$

where:

- PR(A) is the PageRank of a page A.
- PR(T1) is the PageRank of a page T1.
- C(T1) is the number of outgoing links from the page T1.
- d is a damping factor in the range $0 < d < 1$, usually set to 0.85.

The PageRank of a web page is therefore calculated as a sum of the Page-Ranks of all pages linking to it (its incoming links), divided by the number of links on each of those pages (its outgoing links).

And What Does This Mean?

From a search engine marketer's point of view, this means there are two ways in which PageRank can affect the position of your page on Google:

- The number of incoming links. Obviously the more of these, the better. But there is another thing the algorithm tells us: no incoming link can have a negative effect on the PageRank of the page it points at. At worst, it can simply have no effect at all.
- The number of outgoing links on the page that points to your page. The fewer of these, the better. This is interesting: it means given two pages of equal PageRank linking to you, one with 5 outgoing links and the other with 10, you will get twice the increase in PageRank from the page with only 5 outgoing links.

At this point, we take a step back and ask ourselves just how important PageRank is to the position of your page in the Google search results.

The next thing we can observe about the PageRank algorithm is that it has nothing whatsoever to do with relevance to the search terms queried. It is simply one single (admittedly important) part of the entire Google relevance ranking algorithm.

Perhaps a good way to look at PageRank is as a multiplying factor, applied to the Google search results after all its other computations have been completed. The Google algorithm first calculates the relevance of pages in its index to the search terms, and then multiplies this relevance by the Page-Rank to produce a final list. The higher your PageRank, therefore, the higher up the results you will be, but there are still many other factors related to the positioning of words on the page that must be considered first.

So What's the Use of the PageRank Calculator?

If no incoming link has a negative effect, surely I should just get as many as possible, regardless of the number of outgoing links on its page?

Well, not entirely. The PageRank algorithm is very cleverly balanced. Just like the conservation of energy in physics with every reaction, PageRank is also conserved with every calculation. For instance, if a page with a starting PageRank of 4 has two outgoing links on it, we know that the amount of PageRank it passes on is divided equally between all its outgoing links. In this case, 4 / 2 = 2 units of PageRank is passed on to each of 2 separate pages, and 2 + 2 = 4—so the total PageRank is preserved!

> There are scenarios where you may find that total PageRank is not conserved after a calculation. PageRank itself is supposed to represent a probability distribution, with the individual PageRank of a page representing the likelihood of a "random surfer" chancing upon it.

On a much larger scale, supposing Google's index contains a billion pages, each with a PageRank of 1, the total PageRank across all pages is equal to a billion. Moreover, each time we recalculate PageRank, no matter what changes in PageRank may occur between individual pages, the total Page-Rank across all 1 billion pages will still add up to a billion.

First, this means that although we may not be able to change the total Page-Rank across all pages, by strategic linking of pages within our site, we can affect the distribution of PageRank between pages. For instance, we may want most of our visitors to come into the site through our home page. We would therefore want our home page to have a higher PageRank relative to other pages within the site. We should also recall that all the PageRank of a page is passed on and divided equally between each outgoing link on a page. We would therefore want to keep as much combined PageRank as possible within our own site without passing it on to external sites and losing its benefit. This means we would want any page with lots of external links (i.e., links to other people's web sites) to have a lower PageRank relative to other pages within the site to minimize the amount of PageRank that is "leaked" to external sites. Bear in mind also our earlier statement, that PageRank is simply a multiplying factor applied once Google's other calculations regarding relevance have already been calculated. We would therefore want our more keyword-rich pages to also have a higher relative PageRank.

Second, if we assume that every new page in Google's index begins its life with a PageRank of 1, there is a way we can increase the combined Page-Rank of pages within our site—by increasing the number of pages! A site with 10 pages will start life with a combined PageRank of 10, which is then redistributed through its hyperlinks. A site with 12 pages will therefore start with a combined PageRank of 12. We can thus improve the PageRank of our site as a whole by creating new content (i.e., more pages), and then control the distribution of that combined PageRank through strategic interlinking between the pages.

And this is the purpose of the PageRank Calculator—to create a model of the site on a small scale including the links between pages, and see what effect the model has on the distribution of PageRank.

How Does the PageRank Calculator Work?

To get a better idea of the realities of PageRank, visit the PageRank Calculator (*http://www.markhorrell.com/seo/pagerank.asp*).

It's very simple really. Start by typing in the number of interlinking pages you wish to analyze and hit Submit. I have confined this number to just 20 pages to ease server resources. Even so, this should give a reasonable indication of how strategic linking can affect the PageRank distribution.

Next, for ease of reference once the calculation has been performed, provide a label for each page (e.g., Home Page, Links Page, Contact Us Page, etc.) and again hit Submit.

Finally, use the list boxes to select which pages each page links to. You can use Ctrl and Shift to highlight multiple selections.

You can also use this screen to change the initial PageRanks of each page. For instance, if one of your pages is supposed to represent Yahoo!, you may wish to raise its initial PageRank to, say, 3. However, in actual fact, starting PageRank is irrelevant to its final computed value. In other words, even if one page were to start with a PageRank of 100, after many iterations of the equation (see below), the final computed PageRank will converge to the same value as it would had it started with: a PageRank of only 1!

You can play around with the damping factor d, which defaults to 0.85 as this is the value quoted in Brin and Page's research paper.

—*Mark Horrell*

26 Steps to 15K a Day
HACK #96
Solid content thoughtfully prepared can make more impact than a decade's worth of fiddling with META tags and building the perfect title page.

Too often, getting visitors from search engines is boiled down to a succession of tweaks that may or may not work. But as Brett Tabke shows in this section, solid content thoughtfully put together can make more impact than a decade's worth of fiddling with META tags and building the perfect title page.

From A to Z, following these 26 steps will build you a successful site, bringing in plenty of visitors from Google.

A. Prep Work

Prepare work and begin building content. Long before the domain name is settled on, start putting together notes to build at least a 100 page site. That's just for openers. That's 100 pages of "real content," as opposed to link pages, resource pages, about, copyright—necessary but not content-rich pages.

Can't think of 100 pages' worth of content? Consider articles about your business or industry, Q&A pages, or back issues of an online newsletter.

B. Choose a Brandable Domain Name

Choose a domain name that's easily brandable. You want Google.com and not Mykeyword.com.

Keyword domains are out; branding and name recognition are in. Big time in. The value of keywords in a domain name have never been less to search engines. Learn the lesson of Goto.com becoming Overture.com and why they did it. It's one of the powerful gut check calls I've ever seen on the Internet. That took resolve and nerve to blow away several years of branding. (That's a whole 'nuther article, but learn the lesson as it applies to all of us).

C. Site Design

The simpler your site design, the better. As a rule of thumb: text content should outweigh the HTML content. The pages should validate and be usable in everything from Lynx to leading browsers. In other words, keep it close to HTML 3.2 if you can. Spiders are not to the point they really like eating HTML 4.0 and the mess that it can bring. Stay away from heavy Flash, Java, or JavaScript.

Go external with scripting languages if you must have them, though there's little reason to have them that I can see. They will rarely help a site and stand to hurt it greatly due to many factors most people don't appreciate (the search engines' distaste for JavaScript is just one of them). Arrange the site in a logical manner with directory names hitting the top keywords you wish to emphasize. You can also go the other route and just throw everything in the top level of the directory (this is rather controversial, but it's been producing good long term results across many engines). Don't clutter and don't spam your site with frivolous links like "best viewed" or other things like counters. Keep it clean and professional to the best of your ability.

Learn the lesson of Google itself: simple is retro cool. Simple is what surfers want.

Speed isn't everything, it's almost the only thing. Your site should respond almost instantly to a request. If your site has three to four seconds' delay until "something happens" in the browser, you are in long term trouble. That three to four seconds response time may vary in sites destined to be viewed in other countries than your native one. The site should respond locally within three to four seconds (maximum) to any request. Longer than that, and you'll lose 10% of your audience for each additional second. That 10% could be the difference between success and not.

D. Page Size

The smaller the page size, the better. Keep it under 15K, including images, if you can. The smaller the better. Keep it under 12K if you can. The smaller the better. Keep it under 10K if you can—I trust you are getting the idea here. Over 5K and under 10K. It's tough to do, but it's worth the effort. Remember, 80% of your surfers will be at 56K or even less.

E. Content

Build one page of content (between 200–500 words) per day and put it online.

If you aren't sure what you need for content, start with the Overture keyword suggestor (*http://inventory.overture.com/d/searchinventory/suggestion/*) and find the core set of keywords for your topic area. Those are your subject starters.

F. Keyword Density and Keyword Positioning

This is simple, old fashioned, SEO (Search Engine Optimization) from the ground up.

Use the keyword once in title, once in description tag, once in a heading, once in the URL, once in bold, once in italic, once high on the page, and make sure the density is between 5 and 20% (don't fret about it). Use good sentences and spellcheck them! Spellchecking is becoming important as search engines are moving to autocorrection during searches. There is no longer a reason to look like you can't spell.

G. Outbound Links

From every page, link to one or two high ranking sites under the keyword you're trying to emphasize. Use your keyword in the link text (this is ultra important for the future).

H. Cross-Links

Cross links are links *within* the same site.

Link to on-topic quality content across your site. If a page is about food, make sure it links to the apples and veggies page. With Google, on-topic cross-linking is very important for sharing your PageRank value across your site. You do not want an "all star" page that outperforms the rest of your site. You want 50 pages that produce one referral each a day; you don't want one page that produces 50 referrals a day. If you do find one page that drastically outproduces the rest of the site with Google, you need to offload some of that PageRank value to other pages by cross-linking heavily. It's the old share-the-wealth thing.

I. Put It Online

Don't go with virtual hosting; go with a standalone IP address.

Make sure the site is "crawlable" by a spider. All pages should be linked to more than one other page on your site, and not more than two levels deep from the top directory. Link the topic vertically as much as possible back to the top directory. A menu that is present on every page should link to your site's main "topic index" pages (the doorways and logical navigation system down into real content). Don't put it online before you have a quality site to put online. It's worse to put a "nothing" site online than no site at all. You want it fleshed out from the start.

Go for a listing in the ODP (the Open Directory Project, *http://dmoz.org/add. html*). Getting accepted to the Open Directory project will probably get your pages listed in the Google Directory.

J. Submit

Submit your main URL to: Google, FAST, AltaVista, WiseNut, Teoma, DirectHit, and Hotbot. Now comes the hard part: forget about submissions for the next six months. That's right, submit and forget.

K. Logging and Tracking

Get a quality logger/tracker that can do justice to inbound referrals based on log files. Don't use a graphic counter; you need a program that's going to provide much more information than that. If your host doesn't support referrers, back up and get a new host. You can't run a modern site without full referrals available 24/7/365 in real time.

L. Spiderings

Watch for spiders from search engines—one reason you need a good logger and tracker! Make sure those that are crawling the full site can do so easily. If not, double-check your linking system to make sure the spider found its way throughout the site. Don't fret if it takes two spiderings to get your whole site done by Google or FAST. Other search engines are pot luck; with them, it's doubtful that you will be added at all if you haven't been added within 6 months.

M. Topic Directories

Almost every keyword sector has an authority hub on its topic. Find it (Google Directory can be very helpful here, because you can view sites based on how popular they are) and submit within the guidelines.

N. Links

Look around your keyword section in the Google Directory; this is best done *after* getting an Open Directory Project listing—or two. Find sites that have link pages or freely exchange links. Simply request a swap. Put a page of on-topic, in-context links up on your site as a collection spot. Don't worry if you can't get people to swap links—move on. Try to swap links with one fresh site a day. A simple personal email is enough. Stay low key about it and don't worry if site Z won't link to you. Eventually they will.

O. Content

Add one page of quality content per day. Timely, topical articles are always the best. Try to stay away from too much weblogging personal materials and look more for "article" topics that a general audience will like. Hone your writing skills and read up on the right style of "web speak" that tends to work with the fast and furious web crowd: lots of text breaks—short sentences—lots of dashes—something that reads quickly.

Most web users don't actually read, they scan. This is why it is so important to keep key pages to a minimum. If people see a huge overblown page, a portion of them will hit the back button before trying to decipher it. They've got better things to do than waste 15 seconds (a stretch) at understanding your whizbang menu system. Because some big support site can run Flash-heavy pages is no indication that you can. You don't have the pull factor they do.

Use headers and bold standout text liberally on your pages as logical separators. I call them scanner stoppers where the eye will logically come to rest on the page.

P. Gimmicks

Stay far away from any "fades of the day" or anything that appears spammy, unethical, or tricky. Plant yourself firmly on the high ground in the middle of the road.

Q. Linkbacks

When *you* receive requests for links, check sites out before linking back to them. Check them through Google for their PageRank value. Look for directory listings. Don't link back to junk just because they asked. Make sure it is a site similar to yours and on topic. Linking to "bad neighborhoods," as Google calls them, can actually cost you PageRank points.

R. Rounding Out Your Offerings

Use options such as "email a friend," forums, and mailing lists to round out your site's offerings. Hit the top forums in your market and read, read, read until your eyes hurt. Stay away from "affiliate fades" that insert content onto your site like banners and pop-up windows.

S. Beware of Flyer and Brochure Syndrome

If you have an economical site or online version of bricks and mortar, be careful not to turn your site into a brochure. These don't work at all. Think about what people want. They aren't coming to your site to view "your content," they are coming to your site looking for "their content." Talk as little about your products and yourself as possible in articles (sounds counterintuitive, doesn't it?)

T. Keep Building One Page of Content Per Day

Head back to the Overture suggestion tool to get ideas for fresh pages.

U. Study Those Logs

After a month or two you will start to see a few referrals from places you've gotten listed. Look for the keywords people are using. See any bizarre combinations? Why are people using those to find your site? If there is something you have overlooked, then build a page around that topic. Engineer your site to feed the search engine what it wants. If your site is about oranges, but your referrals are all about orange citrus fruit, then you can get busy building articles around citrus and fruit instead of the generic oranges. The search engines will tell you exactly what they want to be fed; listen closely! There is gold in referral logs, it's just a matter of panning for it.

V. Timely Topics

Nothing breeds success like success. Stay abreast of developments in your topic of interest. If big site Z is coming out with product A at the end of the year, build a page and have it ready in October so that search engines get it by December.

W. Friends and Family

Networking is critical to the success of a site. This is where all that time you spend in forums will pay off. Here's the catch-22 about forums: lurking is almost useless. The value of a forum is in the interaction with your fellow colleagues and cohorts. You learn long term by the interaction, not by just reading. Networking will pay off in linkbacks, tips, email exchanges, and will generally put you "in the loop" of your keyword sector.

X. Notes, Notes, Notes

If you build one page per day, you will find that brainstorm-like inspiration will hit you in the head at some magic point. Whether it is in the shower (dry off first), driving down the road (please pull over), or just parked at your desk, write it down! Ten minutes of work later, you will have forgotten all about that great idea you just had. Write it down and get detailed about what you are thinking. When the inspirational juices are no longer flowing, come back to those content ideas. It sounds simple, but it's a lifesaver when the ideas stop coming.

Y. Submission Check at Six Months

Walk back through your submissions and see if you got listed in all the search engines you submitted to after six months. If not, resubmit and forget again. Try those freebie directories again, too.

Z. Keep Building Those Pages of Quality Content!

Starting to see a theme here? Google loves content, lots of quality content. The content you generate should be based around a variety of keywords. At the end of a year's time, you should have around 400 pages of content. That will get you good placement under a wide range of keywords, generate reciprocal links, and overall position your site to stand on its own two feet.

Do those 26 things, and I guarantee you that in one year's time you will call your site a success. It will be drawing between 500 and 2,000 referrals a day from search engines. If you build a good site and achieve an average of 4 to 5 pageviews per visitors, you should be in the 10–15K page views per day range in one year's time. What you do with that traffic is up to you!

—*Brett Tabke*

HACK #97   Being a Good Search Engine Citizen

Five don'ts and one do for getting your site indexed by Google.

A high ranking in Google can mean a great deal of traffic. Because of that, there are lots of people spending lots of time trying to figure out the infallible way to get a high ranking from Google. Add this. Remove that. Get a link from this. Don't post a link to that.

Submitting your site to Google to be indexed is simple enough. Google's got a site submission form (*http://www.google.com/addurl.html*), though they say if your site has at least a few inbound links (other sites that link to you), they should find you that way. In fact, Google encourages URL submitters to get listed on The Open Directory Project (DMOZ, *http://www.dmoz.org/*) or Yahoo! (*http://www.yahoo.com/*).

Nobody knows the holy grail secret of high page rank without effort. Google uses a variety of elements, including page popularity, to determine page rank. Page rank is one of the factors determining how high up a page appears in search results. But there are several things you should not be doing combined with one big thing you absolutely should.

Does breaking one of these rules mean that you're automatically going to be thrown out of Google's index? No; there are over 2 billion pages in Google's index at this writing, and it's unlikely that they'll find out about your rule-breaking immediately. But there's a good chance they'll find out eventually. Is it worth it having your site removed from the most popular search engine on the Internet?

Thou shalt not:

Cloak. "Cloaking" is when your web site is set up such that search engine spiders get different pages from those human surfers get. How does the web site know which are the spiders and which are the humans? By identifying the spider's User Agent or IP—the latter being the more reliable method.

An IP (Internet Protocol) address is the computer address from which a spider comes from. Everything that connects to the Internet has an IP address. Sometimes the IP address is always the same, as with web sites. Sometimes the IP address changes—that's called a dynamic address. (If you use a dial-up modem, chances are good that every time you log on to the Internet your IP address is different. That's a dynamic IP address.)

A "User Agent" is a way a program that surfs the Web identifies itself. Internet browsers like Mozilla use User Agents, as do search engine spiders. There are literally dozens of different kinds of User Agents; see the Web Robots Database (*http://www.robotstxt.org/wc/active.html*) for an extensive list.

Advocates of cloaking claim that cloaking is useful to absolutely optimize content for spiders. Anticloaking critics claim that cloaking is an easy way to misrepresent site content—feeding a spider a page that's designed to get the site hits for pudding cups when actually it's all about baseball bats. You can get more details about cloaking and different perspectives on it at *http://pandecta.com/search_engines/cloaking.html*, *http://www.apromotionguide.com/cloaking.html*, and *http://www.webopedia.com/TERM/C/cloaking.html*.

Hide text. Text is hidden by putting words or links in a web page that are the same color as the page's background—putting white words on a white background, for example. This is also called "fontmatching." Why would you do this? Because a search engine spider could read the words you've hidden on the page while a human visitor couldn't. Again, doing this and getting caught could get you banned from Google's index, so don't.

That goes for other page content tricks too, like title stacking (putting multiple copies of a title tag on one page), putting keywords in comment tags, keyword stuffing (putting multiple copies of keywords in very small font on page), putting keywords not relevant to your site in your META tags, and so on. Google doesn't provide an exhaustive list of these types of tricks on their site, but any attempt to circumvent or fool their ranking system is likely to be frowned upon. Their attitude is more like: "You can do anything you want to with your pages, and we can do anything we want to with our index—like exclude your pages."

Use doorway pages. Sometimes doorway pages are called "gateway pages." These are pages that are aimed very specifically at one topic, which don't have a lot of their own original content, and which lead to the main page of a site (thus the name doorway pages).

For example, say you have a page devoted to cooking. You create doorway pages for several genres of cooking—French cooking, Chinese cooking, vegetarian cooking, etc. The pages contain terms and META tags relevant to each genre, but most of the text is a copy of all the other doorway pages, and all it does is point to your main site.

This is illegal in Google and annoying to the Google-user; don't do it. You can learn more about doorway pages at *http://searchenginewatch. com/webmasters/bridge.html* or *http://www.searchengineguide.com/ whalen/2002/0530_jw1.html.*

Check your link rank with automated queries. Using automated queries (except for the sanctioned Google API) is against Google's Terms of Service anyway. Using an automated query to check your PageRank every 12 seconds is triple bad; it's not what the search engine was built for and Google probably considers it a waste of their time and resources.

Link to "bad neighborhoods". Bad neighborhoods are those sites that exist only to propagate links. Because link popularity is one aspect of how Google determines PageRank, some sites have set up "link farms"—sites that exist only for the purpose of building site popularity with bunches of links. The links are not topical, like a specialty subject index, and they're not well-reviewed, like Yahoo!; they're just a pile of links. Another example of a "bad neighborhood" is a general FFA page. FFA stands for "free for all"; it's a page where anyone can add their link. Linking to pages like that is grounds for a penalty from Google.

Now, what happens if a page like that links to *you?* Will Google penalize you page? No. Google accepts that you have no control over who links to your site.

Thou shalt:

Create great content. All the HTML contortions in the world will do you little good if you've got lousy, old, or limited content. If you create great content and promote it without playing search engine games, you'll get noticed and you'll get links. Remember Sturgeon's Law ("Ninety percent of everything is crud.") Why not make your web site an exception?

What Happens if You Reform?

Maybe you've got a site that's not exactly the work of a good search engine citizen. Maybe you've got 500 doorway pages, 10 title tags per page, and enough hidden text to make an O'Reilly Pocket Guide. But maybe now you want to reform. You want to have a clean lovely site and leave the doorway pages to *Better Homes and Gardens.* Are you doomed? Will Google ban your site for the rest of its life?

No. The first thing you need to do is clean up your site—remove all traces of rule breaking. Next, send a note about your site changes and the URL to *help@google.com.* Note that Google really doesn't have the resources to answer every email about why they did or didn't index a site—otherwise, they'd be answering emails all day—and there's no guarantee that they will reindex your kinder, gentler site. But they will look at your message.

What Happens if You Spot Google Abusers in the Index?

What if some other site that you come across in your Google searching is abusing Google's spider and pagerank mechanism? You have two options. You can send an email to *spamreport@google.com* or fill out the form at *http://www.google.com/contact/spamreport.html.* (I'd fill out the form; it reports the abuse in a standard format that Google's used to seeing.)

HACK #98 Cleaning Up for a Google Visit

Before you submit your site to Google, make sure you've cleaned it up to make the most of your indexing.

You clean up your house when you have important guests over, right? Google's crawler is one of the most important guests you site will ever have if you want visitors. A high Google ranking can lead to incredible numbers of referrals, both from Google's main site and those site that have search powered by Google.

To make the most of your listing, step back and look at your site. By making some adjustments, you can make your site both more Google-friendly and more visitor-friendly.

If you must use a splash page, have a text link from it.   If I had a dollar for every time I went to the front page of a site and saw no way to navigate besides a Flash movie, I'd be able to nap for a living. Google doesn't index Flash files, so unless you have some kind of text link on your splash page (a "Skip This Movie" link, for example, that leads into the heart of your site) you're not giving Google's crawler anything to work with. You're also making it difficult for surfers who don't have Flash or are visually impaired.

Make sure your internal links work.   Sounds like a no-brainer, doesn't it? Make sure your internal page links work so the Google crawler can get to all your site's pages. You'll also make sure your visitors can navigate.

Check your title tags.   There are few things sadder than getting a page of search results and finding "Insert Your Title Here" as the title for some of them. Not quite as bad is getting results for the same domain and seeing the *exact same* title tag over and over and over and over.

Look. Google makes it possible to search just the title tags in its index. Further, the title tags are very easy to read on Google's search results and are an easy way for a surfer to quickly get an idea of what a page is all about. If you're not making the most of your title tag you're missing out on a lot of attention on your site.

The perfect title tag, to me, says something specific about the page it heads, and is readable to both spiders and surfers. That means you don't stuff it with as many keywords as you can. Make it a readable sentence, or—and I've found this useful for some pages—make it a question.

Check your META tags.   Google sometimes relies on META tags for a site description when there's a lot of navigation code that wouldn't make sense to a human searcher. I'm not crazy about META tags, but I'd make sure that at least the front page of my web site had a description and keyword META tag set, especially if your site relies heavily on code-based navigation (like from JavaScript).

Check your ALT tags.   Do you use a lot of graphics on your pages? Do you have ALT tags for them so that visually impaired surfers and the Google spider can figure out what those graphics are? If you have a splash page with nothing but graphics on it, do you have ALT tags on all those graphics so a Google spider can get some idea of what your page is all about? ALT tags are perhaps the most neglected aspect of a web site. Make sure yours are set up.

By the way, just because ALT tags are a good idea, don't go crazy. You don't have to explain in your ALT tags that a list bullet is a list bullet. You can just mark it with a *.

Check your frames. If you use frames, you might be missing out on some indexing. Google recommends you read Danny Sullivan's article, "Search Engines and Frames," at *http://www.searchenginewatch.com/ webmasters/frames.html*. Be sure that Google can either handle your frame setup or that you've created an alternative way for Google to visit, such as using the NOFRAMES tag.

Consider your dynamic pages. Google says they "limit the number of amount of dynamic pages" they index. Are you using dynamic pages? Do you have to?

Consider how often you update your content. There is some evidence that Google indexes popular pages with frequently updated content more often. How often do you update the content on your front page?

Make sure you have a robots.txt file if you need one. If you want Google to index your site in a particular way, make sure you've got a *robots.txt* file for the Google spider to refer to. You can learn more about *robots.txt* in general at *http://www.robotstxt.org/wc/norobots.html*.

If you don't want Google to cache your pages, you can add a line to every page that you don't want cached. Add this line to the <HEAD> section of your page:

```
<META NAME="ROBOTS" CONTENT="NOARCHIVE">
```

This will tell all robots that archive content, including engines like Daypop and Gigablast, not to cache your page. If you want to exclude just the Google spider from caching your page, you'd use this line:

```
<META NAME="GOOGLEBOT" CONTENT="NOARCHIVE">
```

Getting the Most out of AdWords

Guest commentary by Andrew Goodman of Traffick on how to write great AdWords.

AdWords (*https://adwords.google.com/select/?hl=en*) is just about the sort of advertising program you might expect to roll out of the big brains at Google. The designers of the advertising system have innovated thoroughly to provide precise targeting at low cost with less work—it really is a good deal. The flipside is that it takes a fair bit of savvy to get a campaign to the point where it stops failing and starts working.

For larger advertisers, AdWords Select is a no-brainer. Within a couple of weeks, a larger advertiser will have enough data to decide whether to significantly expand their ad program on AdWords Select or perhaps to upgrade to a premium sponsor account.

I'm going to assume you have a basic familiarity with how cost-per-click advertising works. AdWords Select ads currently appear next to search results on Google.com (and some international versions of the search engine) and near search results on AOL and a few other major search destinations. There are a great many quirks and foibles to this form of advertising. My focus here will be on some techniques that can turn a mediocre, nonperforming campaign into one that actually makes money for the advertiser while conforming to Google's rules and guidelines.

One thing I should make crystal clear is that advertising with Google bears no relationship to having your web site's pages indexed in Google's search engine. The search engine remains totally independent of the advertising program. Ad results never appear within search results.

I'm going to offer four key tips for maximizing AdWords Select campaign performance, but before I do, I'll start with four basic assumptions:

- High CTRs (click-through rates) save you money, so that should be one of your main goals as an AdWords Select advertiser. Google has set up the keyword bidding system to reward high-CTR advertisers. Why? It's simple. If two ads are each shown 100 times, the ad that is clicked on eight times generates revenue for Google twice as often as the ad that is clicked on four times over the same stretch of 100 search queries served. So if your CTR is 4% and your competitor's is only 2%, Google factors this into your bid. Your bid is calculated as if it were "worth" twice as much as your competitor's bid.

- Very low CTRs are bad. Google disables keywords that fall below a minimum CTR threshold ("0.5% normalized to ad position," which is to say, 0.5% for position 1, and a more forgiving threshold for ads as they fall further down the page). Entire campaigns will be gradually disabled if they fall below 0.5% CTR on the whole.

- Editorial disapprovals are a fact of life in this venue. Your ad copy or keyword selections may violate Google's editorial guidelines from time to time. Again, it's very difficult to run a successful campaign when large parts of it are disabled. You need to treat this as a normal part of the process rather than giving up or getting flustered.

- The AdWords Select system is set up like an advertising laboratory; that is to say, it makes experimenting with keyword variations and small variations in ad copy a snap. No guru can prejudge for you what will be your "magical ad copy secrets," and it would be irresponsible to do so, because Google offers such detailed real-time reporting that can tell you very quickly what does and does not catch people's attention.

Now onto four tips to get those CTRs up and to keep your campaign from straying out of bounds.

Matching Can Make a Dramatic Difference

You'll likely want to organize your campaign's keywords and phrases into several distinct "ad groups" (made easy by Google's interface). This will help you more closely match keywords to the actual words that appear in the title of your ad. Writing slightly different ads to closely correspond to the words in each group of keywords you've put together is a great way to improve your clickthrough rates. You'd think that an ad title (say, "Deluxe Topsoil in Bulk") would match equally well to a range of keywords that mean essentially the same thing. That is, you'd think this ad title would create about the same CTR with the phrase "bulk topsoil" as it would with a similar phrase ("fancy dirt wholesaler"). Not so. Exact matches tend to get significantly higher CTRs. Being diligent about matching your keywords reasonably closely to your ad titles will help you outperform your less diligent competition.

If you have several specific product lines, you should consider better matching different groups of key phrases to an ad written expressly for each product line. If your clients like your store because you offer certain specialized wine varieties, for example, have an ad group with "ice wine" and related keywords in it, with "ice wine" in the ad title. Don't expect the same generic ad to cover all your varieties. Someone searching for an "ice wine" expert will be thrilled to find a retailer who specializes in this area. They probably won't click on or buy from a retailer who just talks about wine in general. Search engine users are passionate about something, and their queries are highly granular. Take advantage of this passion and granularity.

The other benefit of getting more granular and matching keywords to ad copy is that you don't pay for clicks from unqualified buyers, so your sales conversion rate is likely to be much higher.

Copywriting Tweaks Generally Involve Improving Clarity and Directness

By and large, I don't run across major copywriting secrets. Psychological tricks to entice more people to click, after all, may wind up attracting unqualified buyers. But there are times when the text of an ad falls outside the zone of "what works reasonably well." In such cases, excessively low CTRs kill any chance your web site might have had to close the sale.

Consider using the Goldilocks method to diagnose poor-performing ads. Many ads lean too far to the "too cold" side of the equation. Overly technical jargon may be unintelligible and uninteresting even to specialists, especially given that this is still an emotional medium and that people are looking at search results first and glancing at ad results as a second thought.

The following example is "too cold":

```
Faster DWMGT Apps
Build GMUI modules 3X more secure than KLT. V. 2.0 rated as
"best pligtonferg" by WRSS Mag.
```

No one clicks. Campaign limps along. Web site remains world's best kept secret.

So then a "hotshot" (the owner's nephew) grabs the reins and tries to put some juice into this thing. Unfortunately, this new creative genius has been awake for the better part of a week, attending raves, placing second in a snowboarding competition, and tending to his various piercings. His agency work for a major Fortune 500 client's television spots once received rave reviews. Of course, those were rave reviews from industry pundits and his best friends, because the actual ROI on the big client's TV "branding" campaign was untrackable.

The hotshot's copy reads:

```
Reemar's App Kicks!
Reemar ProblemSolver 2.0 is the real slim shady. Don't trust
your Corporate security to the drones at BigCorp.
```

Unfortunately, in a non-visual medium with only a few words to work with, the true genius of this ad is never fully appreciated. Viewers don't click and may be offended by the ad and annoyed with Google.

The simple solution is something unglamorous but clear, such as:

```
Easy & Powerful Firewall
Reemar ProblemSolver 2.0 outperforms BigCorp
Exacerbator 3 to 1 in industry tests.
```

You can't say it all in a short ad. This gets enough specific (and true) info out there to be of interest to the target audience. Once they click, there will be more than enough info on your web site. In short, your ads should be clear. How's that for a major copywriting revelation?

The nice thing is, if you're bent on finding out for yourself, you can test the performance of all three styles quickly and cheaply, so you don't have to spend all week agonizing about this.

Be Inquisitive and Proactive with Editorial Policies (But Don't Whine)

Editorial oversight is a big task for Google AdWords staff—a task that often gets them in hot water with advertisers, who don't like to be reined in. For the most part, the rules are in the long term best interest of this advertising medium, because they're aimed at maintaining consumer confidence in the quality of what appears on the page when that consumer types something into a search engine. Human error, however, may mean that your campaign is being treated unfairly because of a misunderstanding. Or maybe a rule is ambiguous and you just don't understand it.

Reply to the editorial disapproval messages (they generally come from *adwords-support@google.com*). Ask questions until you are satisfied that the rule makes sense as it applies to your business. The more Google knows about your business, in turn, the more they can work with you to help you improve your results, so don't hesitate to give a bit of brief background in your notes to them. The main thing is, don't let your campaign just sit there disabled because you're confused or angry about being "disapproved." Make needed changes, make the appropriate polite inquiries, and move on.

Avoid the Trap of "Insider Thinking" and Pursue the Advantage of Granular Thinking

Using lists of specialized keywords will likely help you to reach interested consumers at a lower cost per click and convert more sales, than using more general industry keywords. Running your ad on keywords from specialized vocabularies is a sound strategy.

A less successful strategy, though, is to get lost in your own highly specialized social stratum when considering how to pitch your company. Remember that this medium revolves around consumer search engine behavior. You won't win new customers by generating a list of different ways of stating terminology that only management, competitors, or partners might actually use, unless your ad campaign is just being run for vanity's sake.

Break things down into granular pieces and use industry jargon where it might attract a target consumer, but when you find yourself listing phrases that only your competitors might know or buzzwords that came up at the last interminable management meeting, stop! You've started down the path of insider thinking! By doing so, you may have forgotten about the customer and about the role market research must play in this type of campaign.

It sounds simple to say it, but in your AdWords Select keyword selection, you aren't describing your business. You're trying to use phrases that consumers would use when trying to describe a problem they're having, a specific item they're searching for, or a topic that they're interested in. Mission statements from above versus what customers and prospects actually type into search engines. Big difference. (At this point, if you haven't yet done so, you'd better go back and read over *The Cluetrain Manifesto* to get yourself right out of this top-down mode of thinking.)

One way to find out about what consumers are looking for is to use Wordtracker (*http://www.wordtracker.com*) or other keyword research tools (such as the one that Google offers as part of the AdWords Select interface, a keyword research tool Google promises it's working on). However, these tools are not in themselves enough for every business; because more businesses are using these "keyphrase search frequency reports," the frequently searched terms eventually become picked over by competing advertisers—just what you want to avoid if you're trying to sneak along with good response rates at a low cost per click.

You'll need to brainstorm as well. In the future, there will be more sophisticated software-driven market research available in this area. Search technology companies like Ask Jeeves Enterprise Solutions are already collecting data about the hundreds of thousands of customer questions typed into the search boxes on major corporate sites, for example. This kind of market research is under used by the vast majority of companies today.

There are currently many low-cost opportunities for pay-per-click advertisers. As more and larger advertisers enter the space, prices will rise, but with a bit of creativity, granular thinking, and diligent testing, the smaller advertiser will always have a fighting chance on AdWords Select. Good luck!

See Also

- Scraping Google AdWords [Hack #45]

—Andrew Goodman

Removing Your Materials from Google

How to remove your content from Google's various web properties.

Some people are more than thrilled to have Google's properties index their sites. Other folks don't want the Google bot anywhere near them. If you fall into the latter category and the bot's already done its worst, there are several things you can do to remove your materials from Google's index. Each of Google's properties—Web Search, Google Images, and Google Groups—has its own set of methodologies.

Google's Web Search

Here are several tips to avoid being listed.

Making sure your pages never get there to begin with. While you can take steps to remove your content from the Google index after the fact, it's always much easier to make sure the content is never found and indexed in the first place.

Google's crawler obeys the "robot exclusion protocol," a set of instructions you put on your web site that tells the crawler how to behave when it comes to your content. You can implement these instructions in two ways: via a META tag that you put on each page (handy when you want to restrict access to only certain pages or certain types of content) or via a *robots.txt* file that you insert in your root directory (handy when you want to block some spiders completely or want to restrict access to kinds or directories of content). You can get more information about the robots exclusion protocol and how to implement it at *http://www.robotstxt.org/*.

Removing your pages after they're indexed. There are several things you can have removed from Google's results.

> These instructions are for keeping your site out of Google's index only. For information on keeping your site out of all major search engines, you'll have to work with the robots exclusion protocol.

Removing the whole site
Use the robots exclusion protocol, probably with *robots.txt*.

Removing individual pages
Use the following META tag in the HEAD section of each page you want to remove:

```
<META NAME="GOOGLEBOT" CONTENT="NOINDEX, NOFOLLOW">
```

Removing snippets

A "snippet" is the little excerpt of a page that Google displays on its search result. To remove snippets, use the following META tag in the HEAD section of each page for which you want to prevent snippets:

```
<META NAME="GOOGLEBOT" CONTENT="NOSNIPPET">
```

Removing cached pages

To keep Google from keeping cached versions of your pages in their index, use the following META tag in the HEAD section of each page for which you want to prevent caching:

```
<META NAME="GOOGLEBOT" CONTENT="NOARCHIVE">
```

Removing that content now. Once you implement these changes, Google will remove or limit your content according to your META tags and *robots.txt* file the next time your web site is crawled, usually within a few weeks. But if you want your materials removed right away, you can use the automatic remover at *http://services.google.com:8882/urlconsole/controller*. You'll have to sign in with an account (all an account requires is an email address and a password). Using the remover, you can request either that Google crawl your newly created *robots.txt* file, or you can enter the URL of a page that contains exclusionary META tags.

> Make sure you have your exclusion tags all set up before you use this service. Going to all the trouble of getting Google to pay attention to a *robots.txt* file or exclusion rules that you've not yet set up will simply be a waste of your time.

Reporting pages with inappropriate content. You may like your content fine, but you might find that even if you have filtering activated you're getting search results with explicit content. Or you might find a site with a misleading title tag and content completely unrelated to your search.

You have two options for reporting these sites to Google. And bear in mind that there's no guarantee that Google will remove the sites from the index, but they will investigate them. At the bottom of each page of search results, you'll see "Help Us Improve" link; follow it to a form for reporting inappropriate sites. You can also send the URL of explicit sites that show up on a SafeSearch but probably shouldn't to *safesearch@google.com*. If you have more general complaints about a search result, you can send an email to *search-quality@google.com*.

Google Images

Google Images' database of materials is separate from that of the main search index. To remove items from Google Images, you should use *robots.txt* to specify that the Google bot Image crawler should stay away from your site. Add these lines to your *robots.txt* file:

```
User-agent: Googlebot-Image
Disallow: /
```

You can use the automatic remover mentioned in the web search section to have Google remove the images from its index database quickly.

There may be cases where someone has put images on their server for which you own copyright. In other words, you don't have access to their server to add a *robots.txt* file, but you need to stop Google's indexing of your content there. In this case, you need to contact Google directly. Google has instructions for situations just like this at *http://www.google.com/remove.html*; look at Option 2, "If you do not have any access to the server that hosts your image."

Removing Material from Google Groups

Like the Google Web Index, you have the option to both prevent material from being archived on Google and to remove it after the fact.

Preventing your material from being archived. To prevent your material from being archived on Google, add the following line to the headers of your Usenet posts:

```
X-No-Archive: yes
```

If you do not have the options to edit the headers of your post, make that line the first line in your post itself.

Removing materials after the fact. If you want materials removed after the fact, you have a couple of options:

- If the materials you want removed were posted under an address to which you still have access, you may use the automatic removal tool mentioned earlier in this hack.

- If the materials you want removed were posted under an address to which you no longer have access, you'll need to send an email to *groups-support@google.com* with the following information:

— Your full name and contact information, including a verifiable email address.

— The complete Google Groups URL or message ID for each message you want removed.

— A statement that says "I swear under penalty of civil or criminal laws that I am the person who posted each of the foregoing messages or am authorized to request removal by the person who posted those messages."

— Your electronic signature.

Removing Your Listing from Google Phonebook

You may not wish to have your contact information made available via the phonebook searches on Google. You'll have to follow one of two procedures, depending on whether the listing you want removed is for a business or for a residential number.

If you want to remove a business phone number, you'll need to send a request on your business letterhead to:

Google PhoneBook Removal
2400 Bayshore Parkway
Mountain View, CA 94043

You'll also have to include a phone number where Google can reach you to verify your request.

If you want to remove a residential phone number, it's much simpler. You'll need to fill out a form at *http://www.google.com/help/pbremoval.html*. The form asks for your name, city and state, phone number, email address, and reason for removal, a multiple choice: incorrect number, privacy issue, or "other."

Index

We'd like to hear your suggestions for improving our indexes. Send email to *index@oreilly.com*.

Boolean basics, 3
bphonebook: syntax, 25, 43
Brin, Sergey (Google), 294
BSD Unix search, 75

C

C# and .NET and Google Web
  API, 166–169
C# Visual Studio .NET web site, 166
cache, blocking Google from
  caching, 309
/cache switch (Quick Search
  Toolbar), 67
cache: syntax, 6
Cape Clear (see CapeMail, search results
  via)
CapeMail, search results via, 102
CapeScience, x
CapeSpeller spellchecker, 178
case sensitivity, 4
catalog search, 75, 87
catalogs (see Google Catalogs)
category list, 13
certifying URLS using
  SafeSearch, 255–258
Chan, Antoni, x, 282
Ciampi, Tanya Harvey, x, 49
click-through-rate (CTR), 310
client-side application, date range
  search, 174–178
cloaking web sites, 305
company information, through stock
  symbol, 48
comparing Google results with other
  search engines, 251–254
content creation, date of, 36
cookies turned off and preferences, 11
copyright disclaimers, 53
Crimson XML parser web site, 161
cross links, 300

D

date range
  custom search form, 111
  Julian dates, 6
  queries, 174
  searching, 34–37
    with a client-side
    application, 174–178

Timely Google box application, 211
  tracking results over time, 183–187
daterange: syntax, 6, 34
  Gregorian dates, 37
  Julian dates, 35, 37
  use in Perl, 37
dates
  content creation, 36
  formats, 36
  Gregorian (see Gregorian dates)
  Julian (see Julian dates)
  searching, 32
    in Google Groups, 79
Dave's Quick Search Toolbar (see Quick
  Search Toolbar)
Daypop, source of Google Web API
  applications, 174
developer's key, 134
  using, 135
dictionary, 42
Dictionary of Slang web site, 16
Dictionary.com, 42
directories, 54–56
directory search, 76–78
/directory switch (Quick Search
  Toolbar), 66
distance ranking, 223
DMOZ (see Open Directory Project)
.doc files, searching for, 7
doGetCachedPage method, 94, 97
doGoogleSearch method, 94, 96
doGoogleSpellingSuggestion
  method, 94, 97
domain names, brandable, 298
doorway pages
  explained, 306
  not recommended, 306
Dooyoo bookmarklets, 71
Drayton, Peter, x
dynamic pages, 309

E

editorial disapproval messages, 313
email, Google search results by, 102
Excel filetype, 73
experimental features, in Google
  Toolbar, 63

F

FaganFinder customized search
    form, 33
family-friendly (see SafeSearch
    application)
FAST News Search web site, 86
filetype: syntax, 7
filetype variable, 31
filetypes
    Microsoft Excel, 73
    Microsoft PowerPoint, 73
    Microsoft Word, 73
    mixing example, 32
    PDF, 73
    Postscript, 73
    Rich Text Format (RTF), 73
filtering (see SafeSearch application)
Flegg, Andrew, xi, 103
Fool.com web site, 46
forums, 303
frames, 309
Froogle, 88
    adding a merchant, 89
    Advanced Froogle Search form, 88
    no Google Web API, 89
    syntaxes, 89
full-text search, 3

G

games and pranks, 269–286
gaming, using Google Groups, 81
GAPIS (Google Web API Searching In an
    Application), 68
GAPS proximity application, 222–225
    web site, 224
gateway pages, not recommended, 306
geek index, 221
Geeklog weblog web site, 60
glossaries (see slang; vocabularies)
Glossarist web site, 17
Gnews2RSS, violating terms of
    services, 110
Goldilocks method, for ad
    performance, 312
Goodman, Andrew, xi, 314
Google
    applications, non-API, 108–132
    history, xix

Microsoft Word dictionaries
    and, 178
    play on googol, xvii
Google AdWords (see AdWords
    program)
Google Answers, 74
Google Art Creator web site, 278
Google Art game, 277
Google Bounce game, 279–282
Google Box application, 207–210
Google Catalogs, 75, 87
    Advanced Catalog Search form, 87
    no Google Web API, 88
    scraping, 128–130
Google Compare application, 251–254
Google Directory, 13, 76–78
    no Google Web API, 78
    Open Directory Project, 14
    PageRank, 76
    recipes, 285
    source of Google Web API
        applications, 174
    syntaxes, 77
Google Froogle (see Froogle)
Google Glossary, 57
Google Groups, 13, 78–82
    Advanced Groups Search form, 79
    browsing, 79
    date searching, 79
    no Google Web API, 82
    reducing URL size, 103–105
    removing posts, 317
    scraping, 121–124
    use for gaming, 81
    use for news commentary, 81
    use for tech support, 81
Google Images, 13, 82–84
    Advanced Image Search form, 83
        domain, 83
        filetype, 83
        filtering, 83
        image color, 83
        image size, 83
    no Google Web API, 84
    syntaxes, 84
Google Jump bookmarklet, 71
Google Keyboard Shortcuts, 90
Google Labs, 57, 75, 89
    no Google Web API, 91
Google Mindshare application, 249
Google Mirror prank web site, 282

referral logs, 303
/related switch (Quick Search
        Toolbar), 67
related: syntax, 7
removing
    inappropriate content from
        Google, 316
    items from Google Images, 317
    listing from Google Phonebook, 318
    material from Google, 315–318
    posts from Google Groups, 317
    web pages from Google, 315
repetition
    examples, 23
    guidelines, 25
    of keywords, 22
Representational State Transfer (REST),
        defined, 93
ResearchBuzz.com, 28
resources, WebmasterWorld web
        site, 289
results, search
    by email, 102
    extending limits, 144–146
    Google Box application, 207–210
    in XML, 93–102
    interpreting, 13
    scraping, 26, 115–117
    slideshow, 91
    Timely Google Box
        application, 210–214
    tracking results counts over
        time, 183–187
    visual display
        (TouchGraph), 187–191
    when building your own
        applications, 140
reverse phonebook lookup, 45
Rich Text Format (RTF) filetype, 73
robots, 290
    robots.txt file, 309
    robots.txt web site, 309
robots exclusion protocol web site, 315
Rocketinfo news web site, 86
rphonebook: syntax, 25, 43
RSS application, 258

S

safe results filter, 30
SafeSearch application, 255–258
    filter, 10, 30
    when building your own
        applications, 140
scraping
    advantages, 109
    AdWords program, 117–121
    automated, 109
    controversy, 245
    defined, 108
    Google Catalogs, 128–130
    Google Groups results, 121–124
    Google News, 125–128
    Google Phonebook, 130–132
    limitations, 109
    search results, 26, 115–117
    versus Google Web API, 108
    Yahoo! Buzz application, 245–248
scraping application, 245–248
search engine basics, 290
search engine games, 269
search engine optimization
        (SEO), 287–318
    template, 291
Search Engines and Frames web
        site, 309
search forms
    advanced, 8–9
        date, 9
        file format, 8
        filtering, 8
        language, 8
        query word input, 8
    building custom date range
        form, 111
    creating your own, 33
    customized FaganFinder search, 33
    date searching, 32
    hacking, 31–33
    hidden variables, 31
    setting number of results, 32
    variables
        filetype, 31
        site search, 32
search results (see results, search)

Colophon

Our look is the result of reader comments, our own experimentation, and feedback from distribution channels. Distinctive covers complement our distinctive approach to technical topics, breathing personality and life into potentially dry subjects.

The tool on the cover of *Google Hacks* is a pair of locking pliers. Locking pliers are very versatile tools. They can be used for turning, twisting, cutting wire, tightening screws and bolts, and clamping. Locking pliers are specially designed to put pressure on a bolt or nut in such a way that the user can approach the nut or bolt from any angle. A simple squeeze can put up to a ton of pressure between the pliers' jaws, enabling them to lock onto even odd-shaped pieces. Locking pliers include a guarded release, which prevents accidental release or pinching, and a trigger, which unlocks the pliers.

Linley Dolby was the production editor and copyeditor for *Google Hacks*. Sarah Sherman was the proofreader. Emily Quill and Claire Cloutier provided quality control. Reg Aubry wrote the index.

Edie Freedman designed the cover of this book. The cover image is an original photograph by Edie Freedman. Emma Colby produced the cover layout with QuarkXPress 4.1 using Adobe's Helvetica Neue and ITC Garamond fonts.

David Futato designed the interior layout. This book was converted by Mike Sierra to FrameMaker 5.5.6 with a format conversion tool created by Erik Ray, Jason McIntosh, Neil Walls, and Mike Sierra that uses Perl and XML technologies. The text font is Linotype Birka; the heading font is Adobe Helvetica Neue Condensed; and the code font is LucasFont's TheSans Mono Condensed. The illustrations that appear in the book were produced by Robert Romano and Jessamyn Read using Macromedia FreeHand 9 and Adobe Photoshop 6. This colophon was written by Linley Dolby.